Class Attitudes in

This book explains a long-standing puzzle in American politics: why so many Americans support downwardly redistributive social welfare programs, when such support seems to fly in the face of standard conceptions of the American public as antigovernment, individualistic, and racially prejudiced. Bringing class attitudes into the investigation, Spencer Piston demonstrates through rigorous empirical analysis that sympathy for the poor and resentment of the rich explain American support for downwardly redistributive programs – not only those that benefit the middle class, but also those that explicitly target the poor. The book captures an important and neglected component of citizen attitudes toward a host of major public policies and candidate evaluations. It also explains why government does so little to combat economic inequality; in key instances, political elites downplay class considerations, deactivating sympathy for the poor and resentment of the rich.

Spencer Piston is Assistant Professor of Political Science at Boston University. He studies the influence of attitudes toward racial and class groups on public opinion and political behavior.

Class Attitudes in America

*Sympathy for the Poor, Resentment of the Rich,
and Political Implications*

SPENCER PISTON

Boston University

CAMBRIDGE
UNIVERSITY PRESS

CAMBRIDGE
UNIVERSITY PRESS

University Printing House, Cambridge CB2 8BS, United Kingdom

One Liberty Plaza, 20th Floor, New York, NY 10006, USA

477 Williamstown Road, Port Melbourne, VIC 3207, Australia

314–321, 3rd Floor, Plot 3, Splendor Forum, Jasola District Centre,
New Delhi – 110025, India

79 Anson Road, #06–04/06, Singapore 079906

Cambridge University Press is part of the University of Cambridge.

It furthers the University's mission by disseminating knowledge in the pursuit of
education, learning, and research at the highest international levels of excellence.

www.cambridge.org
Information on this title: www.cambridge.org/9781108426985
DOI: 10.1017/9781108676038

First published 2018

Printed in the United States of America by Sheridan Books, Inc.

A catalogue record for this publication is available from the British Library.

Library of Congress Cataloging-in-Publication Data
NAMES: Piston, Spencer, 1979– author.
TITLE: Class attitudes in America : sympathy for the poor, resentment of the rich, and
political implications / Spencer Piston, Boston University.
DESCRIPTION: Cambridge, United Kingdom ; New York, NY : Cambridge University
Press, 2018. | Includes bibliographical references.
IDENTIFIERS: LCCN 2017048766| ISBN 9781108426985 (hardback) | ISBN
9781108447126 (paperback)
SUBJECTS: LCSH: Income distribution – Government policy – United States. | Welfare
state – United States. | Social classes – United States.
CLASSIFICATION: LCC HC110.15 P57 2018 | DDC 305.50973–dc23
LC record available at https://lccn.loc.gov/2017048766

ISBN 978-1-108-42698-5 Hardback
ISBN 978-1-108-44712-6 Paperback

To Rob Piston and Jane Piston, who taught me
how to live and how to love

Contents

Figures

Tables

Acknowledgments

In a way, this book began when I was a community organizer for the Greater Lansing Association for Development and Empowerment (GLADE) in Lansing, Michigan. On a daily basis I worked with people who gladly paid the substantial costs of political action in order to build a more just world. They were willing to do so much in part because they saw the distribution of wealth in this country as profoundly unfair. In many cases their deepest sympathies were for the poor, and their greatest resentments were of the rich. Imagine my surprise when I began graduate school and was informed by social scientists that Americans do not care about class! Much of the evidence in this book can be viewed as corroboration of what the members of GLADE showed me long ago.

My greatest thanks go to the co-chairs of my dissertation committee: Vince Hutchings and Skip Lupia. Before I had even thought about what my dissertation might be about, I started a research paper on a separate topic and each of them met with me weekly (and sometimes more) over the winter semester of 2009. For the rest of my life I will be grateful to their contributions to that paper, to this book, and most of all to my development as a scholar. I would be remiss if I did not also mention the downside to having the two of them for advisors; because their mentorship was so exemplary, for years I was denied the opportunity to join in the graduate student ritual of complaining about faculty, which kept me from fully bonding with my peers.

Perhaps the most precious resource in graduate school is faculty time. It is only from faculty that graduate students can learn the art and science of conducting research, and there is no substitute for hours upon hours in their company, figuring out how they think. By this measure, Vince's generosity ranks above all other faculty I have known (or heard of). I have taken up a greater portion of his time than I ever expected I would, and every hour has been well spent. Vince also provided funding for much of my time in graduate school, allowing me time to conduct much of the research presented in this book. Finally, Vince's attention to detail, his professionalism, and above all his skepticism set an example that I hope to follow for the rest of my career. More than anything, I hope that as a professor I can be as kind and as generous to graduate students as he has been to me.

I first met Skip in his formal modeling course in 2008, and I was immediately impressed by the values that guide him as a researcher and a teacher: transparency, logic, rigor, and above all the production of knowledge of use to an audience. It has taken years to internalize these goals, but I have done so, and I am glad. Skip also has the ability, upon listening to a description of a research project, to select what is best about it and discard the rest. What he calls "just repeating back to you what you told me" has always in fact been a key contribution to my scholarship. Skip also invited me on many occasions to participate in the research process when I was a graduate student. Learning how he approaches the thorny problems associated with taking a research project from start to finish informed the process I went through that resulted in this book.

During my early stages in graduate school, I did not think I would have the chance to work with Don Kinder, as he was either chair of the department or on sabbatical while I was taking courses. Yet he took a chance on me, showing great patience in discussing my initial ramblings (that fortunately never made it into this book). It is no stretch to say that his scholarship has influenced my own more than anyone else's has. I believe that every publication of mine cites him more than it does any other author – this book included. His research is of course widely lauded, and deservedly so; yet I wonder whether his talents as a mentor likewise receive the recognition they deserve. Don is especially gifted at detecting not only what is wrong with a project but also what could be right about it; at numerous presentations I have seen him give a single constructive comment that, if followed, would make a good project great.

Rob Mickey may be the most well-read person I know, and because of knowing him I am much more well-read than I thought I would ever be; for that by itself I am grateful. His perspective on politics is mind-boggling. It is refreshing and more than a little intimidating to discuss politics with someone who thinks as historically and globally as he does. I fear that from his vantage point this book appears thin and shallow; yet it is both thicker and deeper than it would have been without him. I caution graduate students that Rob appears to remember not only every piece of scholarship he has read, and every class for which he assigned it, but also everyone who didn't read it. Given his intellect, it is surprising that he doesn't value his own comments more: he is the only person I've ever known who told me *not* to write down something he was saying. He did so because it was something that had just come to mind and seemed to him to be a trivial observation. But I believe many of his top-of-the-head considerations to be more profound than many political scientists' entire research agendas.

A number of additional people made key contributions to this project. Mary Corcoran gamely joined the dissertation committee at a late date and I am grateful for her suggestions: they proved particularly helpful as the dissertation evolved into a book. Ted Brader, John Jackson, and Chuck Shipan each played an important role in my development at the early stages of graduate school and beyond. Yanna Krupnikov and Adam Seth Levine provided valuable mentorship and friendship throughout the course of this project (and many others). Davin Phoenix taught me, and continues to teach me, that scholarship should benefit people's lives – and not only the scholar's.

Portions of this research have benefited from comments from participants at the 2012 Annual Meeting of the American Political Science Association, especially Philip Paolino; the 2011, 2012, and 2013 Annual Meetings of the Midwest Political Science Association, especially Chris Ellis, Nathan Kelly, Gary Segura, Taeku Lee, and Cara Wong; the 2012 Annual Meeting of the International Society of Political Psychology, especially Erin Paige Hennes; the University of Michigan's Center for Political Studies Workshop, especially Graeme Boushey, Nancy Burns, Jowei Chen, William Roberts Clark, W. Abraham Gong, David Magleby, C. Daniel Myers, Paul Poast, Gary Uzonyi, and Nicholas A. Valentino; and participants in a graduate course taught by Ted Brader: Matias A. Bargsted, Katie Brown, Allison Dale-Riddle, Nathan P. Kalmoe, Kristyn L. Karl, Ashley Jardina, Yioryos Nardis, and Timothy J. Ryan. Also at the University of Michigan, Logan S. Casey, Daniel Mintz, Joshua Shipper, Christopher Skovron, and William Zimmerman provided helpful comments.

I also presented the research described in this book at a number of institutions, including Northwestern University, the University of Maryland, the University of Washington, the University of North Carolina, Washington University in St. Louis, Grinnell College,

Villanova University, St. Olaf College, State University of New York at Geneseo, and Soka University of America. I received many helpful suggestions from members of these higher education communities, especially Antoine Banks, Tony Chen, Pam Conover, Jamie Druckman, Megan Francis, Jim Gibson, Frances Lee, Ben Page, Chris Parker, Jon Rogowski, Stella Rouse, Betsy Sinclair, Mark Smith, and Steve Smith.

After I obtained my doctoral degree from the University of Michigan, I moved to Syracuse University, and my colleagues there provided helpful advice as I worked to turn this dissertation into a book. A book workshop run by Peggy Herman, Audie Klotz, and Sue Wadley, with the generous support of the Moynihan Institute, came at the perfect time, infusing me with new energy as I reframed the project and collected additional survey data. Matt Cleary, Chris Faricy, Shana Gadarian, Brandon Metroka, and Danielle Thomsen were exceptionally helpful in reviewing critical portions of the manuscript and discussing what makes a book different from an article (and a dissertation). I was proud to be a part of the warm, constructive community created by these colleagues and friends. It was a hard place to leave, and I still miss it there.

That said, my new colleagues at Boston University could not have been more welcoming. They also provided fantastic suggestions as the book manuscript entered its final stages. I am especially grateful for comments from Taylor Boas, Dino Christenson, Katie Einstein, John Gerring, Doug Kriner, Cathie Jo Martin, David Mayers, Max Palmer, and Gina Sapiro. I cannot say enough about how happy I am to be part of the political science department at Boston University.

While I was preparing the manuscript for submission for review, Larry Bartels and Marty Gilens both challenged me to think about the book project in new ways. This slowed the process down a bit, but it was well worth the delay to incorporate their insights. Jenn Chudy, Ashley Jardina, and Nathan Kalmoe read the entire manuscript, and they each helped me with both large-scale organizational issues and important details. The participants of my undergraduate course on public opinion in the spring semester of 2017 also provided valuable comments as an important supplement to the formal review process. These participants were Lara Adekeye, Christopher Alexander, Kyle Bechet, Jacquie Carcamo, Matt Clark, Alex Coleman, Oriana Durand, Sophia Eppolito, Mark Haddad, Courtney Hagle, Saraann Kurkul, Alexa Lamanna, Daniel Lattarulo, Tara Martin-Chen, Gianpaulo Pons, Elise Renner, Curtis Stoychoff, and Sylvester Toldsted.

After the review process was complete, no single person, with the possible exception of the author, contributed to the final version of book more than Logan Strother. I tend to either get lost in the details or gloss over them; he somehow manages to look at both the forest and the trees at the same time. During the time he provided research assistance with this book, Logan's own scholarly career went through a number of changes, including finishing his dissertation and moving to Princeton University to begin a postdoctoral fellowship. In the midst of the upheaval, his attention to this research project never flagged. Logan is a fantastic scholar, and it has been my pleasure to work with him. This book is much better for his contributions to it.

Sara Doskow at Cambridge University Press has been the editor every author wishes to have. Her thoughtful comments were especially helpful in making the book clear and accessible to a broad audience. She made the transition from book manuscript to book seamless, expertly shepherding the manuscript through the review process – I am happy to say that the comments I received from the anonymous reviewers were among the most helpful I received on the project. Sara is particularly attuned to the unique challenges faced by authors who are junior faculty members on the tenure clock. I often recommend her to my colleagues, and I will continue to do so.

Survey research costs money and takes time. This book would not have been possible without financial support from a wide range of sources. The American National Election Studies, funded by the National Science Foundation, administered questions I proposed (after review through the Online Commons Process) on the 2013 ANES Recontact Study, a re-interview of respondents to the 2012 ANES Time Series. The National Science Foundation also subsidized a module I purchased (sharing costs with Shana Gadarian, Chris Faricy, and the Campbell Institute at Syracuse University) as part of the Cooperative Congressional Election Studies (Award #1430505). While I was still at the University of Michigan, each of the following financial awards supported the collection and/or analysis of data presented in this book: the Clark & Robin Chandler Award, the William Zimmerman Award, the Rackham Centennial Fellowship Award, the Gerald R. Ford Research Grant, the Rackham Research Grant for PhD Candidates, the Rackham Research Grant for PhD Pre-Candidates, the Department of Political Science Thesis Grant, and the Undergraduate Research Opportunity Program. Each of the following financial awards at Syracuse University also supported the research project reported here: the Appleby-Mosher Award, the Maxwell

Summer Project Assistantship Program, and the Campbell Institute Research Grant.

I also thank Hakeem Jefferson, Rachel MacMaster, Zac Hardwick, Tara Lanigan, Laura Meyer, and Troy Schott for their exemplary research assistance.

Finally, for love and support above and beyond the world of political science, I thank my friends Benjamin Maixner, Brian Quirk, and Nadav Tanners, and my family: my parents Rob Piston and Jane Piston, my brother Drew Piston, my sister Eliza Piston, my daughter Maya Bergom, and my wife and beloved partner in life, Inger Bergom.

Introduction: Reigning Myths about Class Attitudes

News articles often claim that Americans do not think about class very much,[1] and that when Americans do think about class their thinking tends to disparage the poor[2] and praise the rich.[3] Many news articles also claim that in America most people do not want government to help the poor. They would rather their elected representatives give a tax break to a millionaire than spend government money on somebody who actually needs it.[4]

These claims are examples of *reigning myths* about public attitudes about class. Like many myths, each of these claims contains a grain of truth. An enterprising reporter can uncover an underpaid trucker who says he thinks millionaires are taxed too much, because when he becomes rich someday he doesn't want to fork it all over to Uncle Sam. Another journalist, with enough effort, can find somebody who complains about poor people leeching off the government instead of working for a living.[5] This kind of story makes for good copy, and it has become a story that many have come to believe. But good copy, however often it is repeated, is not the same thing as truth. To say that Americans resent the poor,[6] or to say that they sympathize with the rich,[7] is to focus on the exception at the expense of the rule. On balance, the reigning myths distort our understanding of class attitudes and their role in American politics.

One of the reasons these myths about class attitudes have endured is that surprisingly few people have actually examined them rigorously. I analyze the beliefs of thousands of ordinary people, expressed in a series of national surveys, in order to paint a more accurate picture of the American public than is possible through the isolated anecdotes found in many newspaper articles.[8]

My findings lead to a very different account of the role of class attitudes in American politics than the one that newspaper readers typically encounter. I argue that many people do think about class, not just in their social lives but also when thinking about politics. They do so by considering and evaluating social class groups, and this book focuses on attitudes toward two such groups: poor people and rich people.[9] Of course, not all people mean the exact same thing when they use the terms "poor" and "rich." Any two given individuals might disagree about whether their neighbor is rich, just as they might disagree about Barack Obama's race[10] or Chelsea Manning's gender.[11] Despite the fuzzy boundaries of these categories, however, social groups are meaningful – even central – to public thinking about politics. Class is no exception.

Attitudes toward class groups make up two defining divisions in American public opinion. The first division lies in how one views the poor. Most Americans fall on the sympathetic side of this line. They tend to believe poor people have less than they deserve and report feelings of compassion for them. Other Americans, fewer in number, reject this sympathetic outlook toward poor people. If an analyst learns the extent to which a given person views the poor sympathetically, that analyst then becomes better able to predict which policies that person will support and how that person will vote.

Another key cleavage in the American public has to do with their views of the rich. Most Americans believe that the rich have more than they deserve; many also report feeling anger and resentment toward them. A smaller group of Americans actually believe that rich people get a raw deal – that they have less than they deserve. Those who resent the rich have very different political preferences from those who do not.

While sympathy for the poor and resentment of the rich are powerful forces that often shape political preferences, their power is variable: greater in some instances than in others. I argue that the importance of these attitudes toward class groups to public opinion hinges on two factors. The first of these is whether or not the public is provided with clear cues about whether a given policy or political candidate helps or hurts the poor or the rich. In extreme cases, when the relationship between a policy or candidate and these class groups is completely unknown, sympathy for the poor and resentment of the rich are irrelevant to public opinion. The second factor is the extent to which political elites frame issues in ways that draw attention to class considerations – or deflect attention away from these considerations. For example, I show that even though the federal estate tax on inheritances only affects the richest Americans, framing the policy as a "death tax" downplays class considerations, attenuating the impact of resentment of the rich on opinion about the policy. Sympathy for the poor and resentment of the rich, then, are powerful forces, but their influence on political preferences is neither inevitable nor totalizing. I speak to the importance of these attitudes toward class groups even as I also qualify it.

I propose, in sum, that majorities of Americans view poor people sympathetically, that majorities view rich people resentfully, and that under predictable conditions, these attitudes toward the poor and the rich shape Americans' political preferences. These contentions directly contradict reigning myths about how Americans think about class. It is critical to note, therefore, that my claims are supported by a great deal of evidence, while the reigning myths are not.

My first source of evidence consists of ordinary Americans speaking in their own words. This is very different from the approach taken in most surveys, in which respondents are asked to select from predetermined options (e.g., "Do you 'Strongly Agree,' 'Agree,' 'Disagree,' or 'Strongly Disagree' with each of the following statements?"). Instead, interviewers ask Americans to think aloud – to discuss what comes to mind when they think about a candidate for office or a political party. The American National Election Studies (ANES) time series surveys of nationally representative samples of adult citizens routinely include these questions, but scholars do not often analyze these questions with respect to what they reveal about American attitudes about class.[12] I analyze a series of these studies dating back to 1992, and the results point in a clear direction. Contrary to accounts of class indifference, ordinary people routinely discuss the poor and the rich when talking about policies, candidates for office, and political parties. This is not just a recent phenomenon; it predates the Great Recession. When Americans form their judgments about political entities, the poor and the rich are often on their minds.

Furthermore, the character of ordinary Americans' thinking about the poor and the rich contradicts existing claims in political science. Those individuals who mention the poor in their responses to these survey questions do not typically say that they worry about government giving the poor free handouts. Instead, they express the concern that government is *not doing enough* to help poor people get by. Those who mention the rich, meanwhile, do not usually worry that government is strangling innovation by overtaxing "job creators." Rather, they complain that rich people are not paying their fair share in taxes. Of course, the opinions of people who mention the poor in unfavorable ways or the rich in favorable ways are in the data also. But these people are like black swans: they are the exception, not the rule. In general, when we take Americans on their terms by analyzing their own words, we see that they tend to discuss poor people in sympathetic ways and rich people in resentful ways.

The second source of evidence comes from responses to survey questions I developed to measure attitudes toward the poor and the rich. In a series of national surveys, I ask ordinary individuals across the country whether they feel that poor people have less or more than they deserve. I also ask how often they feel sympathy, compassion, anger, and resentment toward poor people and toward rich people. The results are clear: nationally representative samples of Americans are more likely to express sympathetic views – and less likely to express resentful views – toward the poor than toward the rich. These findings belie the common contention that most of the American public views the poor as deserving of their low status, and the rich as deserving of their high status.

Sympathy for the poor and resentment of the rich are also tightly connected to a wide range of political preferences. This may be surprising to some political scientists, who routinely exclude measures of attitudes toward the poor and the rich from their models of policy opinion. To be sure, findings from Larry Bartels' landmark book *Unequal Democracy*,[13] as well as similar results from the disciplines of political science and social psychology,[14] suggest that the poor are viewed more favorably, and the rich less favorably, than is commonly believed. I extend these findings by demonstrating that in many cases, those who sympathize with the poor are more likely than those who do not to support government programs intended to transfer resources to those at the bottom of the economic distribution. Resentment of the rich, meanwhile, is often positively associated with support for increased taxes on those at the top of the economic distribution.

The survey analyses also reveal that sympathy for the poor and resentment of the rich help explain why Americans vote the way they have in recent elections. For example, these class group attitudes are powerfully associated with vote choice in the 2012 presidential election and the 2016 presidential primary (but not in the 2016 general election). These findings shed new light on a topic central to the study of American democracy: how voters decide which candidates will represent them in public office.

Critically, I find that relationships between attitudes toward class groups and political preferences endure after holding constant other political variables such as partisanship, ideological principles, racial prejudice, beliefs about income inequality, beliefs about upward economic mobility, and demographics. In comparison, relationships between beliefs about income inequality or upward mobility and public opinion are relatively weak. Finally, the relationships between attitudes toward class groups and political preferences do not appear to be driven by self-interest, as they remain when respondents who might be considered to be poor or rich themselves are excluded from the analyses. These results lend additional support to my argument that in many cases, Americans base their judgments about politics in no small part on their attitudes toward poor people and rich people.

The third and final source of evidence comes from survey experiments, in which I randomly assign subjects into different groups and assign each group to receive a different version of a survey question. This allows me to have confidence that any difference in the responses among the groups arises from the differences I have created in the survey questions. In one such experiment, I reconsider the claim, made by Ann Schneider and Helen Ingram's widely-cited model of policymaking, that legislators who propose policies with harmful effects on the poor will become more popular as a result.[15] These scholars contend that the American public views the poor negatively and therefore rewards politicians' efforts to punish the poor. In contrast, I argue that majorities of Americans view the poor with sympathy, and therefore that politicians will actually become less popular if their policies are perceived to hurt the poor.

I use an experiment in order to adjudicate between these two perspectives. One group of experimental subjects reads a description of a politician whose policies transfer resources *away from* the poor, and another group reads a description of a second politician, otherwise identical to the first, whose policies transfer resources *to* the poor. Then I compare the popularity of the politician across the two groups of respondents, to see whether hurting the poor or helping them is more effective at winning public support. The results are clear: the politician is more popular in the condition in which he helps the poor, especially among those individuals who view the poor sympathetically. This finding is a testament to the power of sympathy for the poor over Americans' evaluations of candidates for public office.

These three sources of evidence – Americans' own words, their responses to original survey questions, and their behavior in an experimental setting – all lead to an unambiguous conclusion. Sympathy for the poor and resentment of the rich are widespread, and under predictable conditions these attitudes powerfully influence the political preferences of the American public.

LATE TO CLASS

Journalists are not the only ones who have overlooked the importance of attitudes about class to American politics. With few exceptions, political scientists omit measures of attitudes toward class groups from their analyses of public opinion and electoral behavior. A content analysis[16] of three top journals in political science, *APSR*, *AJPS*, and *JOP* from 1980 to the present, yielded not a single article that examines the effects of attitudes toward class groups on vote choice.[17] As I will show, this oversight warps our understanding of American politics.

How did so many of us miss such a central element of American thinking about politics? The answer is that many intelligent and talented scholars have been focused on research questions that allow little room to uncover the influence of sympathy for the poor and resentment of the rich on public opinion.

For example, one question that dominates scholarly thinking is: Why is there so little socialism in the United States?[18] From this perspective, the development of the American welfare state has taken a very different path from that of welfare states in many Western European democracies. The welfare state in the United States is often described as a "laggard"[19] – slow to develop, small in scope, miserly in its protection of the poor, and vulnerable to cutbacks. Scholars who find the American welfare state to be less socialist than welfare states in Western Europe design their research to determine how this state of affairs arose. One explanation leaps, perhaps too easily, to mind: government does not do much to help its poorest citizens because Americans want it that way.[20]

The problem with this simple explanation is that there is a great deal of evidence against it. For example, Benjamin Page and Larry Jacobs show that majorities of Americans support a wide range of downwardly redistributive policies, defined for the purposes of this book as either government programs that transfer resources to the poorest citizens or government increases in taxes on the rich.[21]

A skeptic might respond that if the public *really* wanted government to do more to aid the poor or take from the rich, government would do so.[22] Such skepticism is only warranted if one assumes that in contemporary American democracy, what the public says goes. This assumption is belied by political outcomes in the United States today. If the government did whatever majorities of the public wanted, the United States military would be attacking North Korea. Government would ban atheists from teaching in public schools. Marijuana would be legal across the country, as would physician-assisted suicide for the terminally ill, and the government would be barred from taking private property for economic development through eminent domain.[23] To be sure, in many cases public policy is consistent with the public will – but in many cases it is not. The United States would be a very different place if the majoritarian public always had its way.

One reason the majority does not always dictate policy is that the framers of the American Constitution consciously crafted our institutions to filter and refine the will of the electorate.[24] They were cognizant of the possibility that some "passion" would seize a majority of the public – a dominant "faction" – which could then do injury to "the rights of other citizens, or to the permanent and aggregate interests of the community," as James Madison put it in the tenth of the Federalist Papers.[25] Our system of separated institutions sharing power,[26] with the concomitant checks and balances, staggered elections, and supermajority rules, are all aimed at mitigating against the possibility that an electoral majority will dominate policymaking.

It is strange, therefore, that scholars have not always been able to resist the temptation to infer public opinion from political outcomes. As Jacob Hacker and Paul Pierson observe, the idea that politicians must adopt the preferences of the majority has dominated the thinking of many political scientists since the publication of Anthony Downs' *The Median Voter* in 1957.[27] One of Downs' key predictions is – or at least is often interpreted to mean[28] – that in a two-party system, the parties will adopt nearly identical policy positions, positions that converge on the preferences of the "median voter," the midpoint of the ideological distribution. This rendition is admirable in its parsimony, but it bears little resemblance to the reality of American politics,[29] in which the policy positions of the two major parties have in fact been moving away from the median voter for decades.[30] The reasons for this polarization are complex, but scholarship makes clear that, surprising as it may seem to some, the public is not the only entity that influences the policies that legislators choose to pass. Interest groups, the media, donors, rules, legislators' preferences, inequalities in political participation, inequalities in representation, and additional factors often preclude majority public opinion from determining policy.[31]

To be sure, the question of why the United States government does not do more to assist its poorest citizens is an important one, and it will be discussed later in this book. For now, I submit that some of those who find fault with American government's efforts to increase aid to the poor or taxes on the rich have been too quick to assume a one-to-one correspondence between policy outcomes and public opinion.[32] This assumption is contra-dicted by the findings in Martin Gilens' book *Affluence and Influence*. Gilens concludes that, "under most circumstances, the preferences of the vast majority of Americans appear to have essentially no impact on which policies the government does or doesn't adopt."[33] We need to let go of the assumption that what the public wants, it gets.

Another question that has commanded much scholarly attention, thereby obscuring the influence of class attitudes on public opinion, is as follows: Why aren't class divisions more pronounced in American politics? Many political scientists have been puzzled by the lack of a major class divide in American public opinion and political behavior. For exam-ple, the economic policy preferences of employed Americans are not all that different from the preferences of the unemployed.[34] Similarly, the association between occupational status and political preferences is only moderate,[35] paling in comparison to other divides, such as the divide in political preferences between racial groups such as whites and blacks.[36] Scholarship about class has long proceeded in the shadow of Karl Marx, who predicted class-based revolution. From this perspective, the relatively small differences in public opinion among different class groups are especially puzzling. Researchers have attempted to address this puzzle, with notable successes.[37]

Yet efforts to explain circumstances when class is unimportant are ill-suited to provide us with tools to understand those circumstances when class *is* important. As I will show, Americans may not be divided very much by their class positions, but they are deeply divided by their class attitudes. That is, while poor people and rich people, on average, think a lot alike about politics, Americans think very differently *about* poor people and rich people. These attitudes toward the poor and the rich mark a major fault line in public opinion. They help us understand why the public supports certain policies and candidates while opposing others. Research on the absence of major conflict among class groups ought not blind students of American politics to the importance of class attitudes to public opinion.

Scholars' focus on explaining public opposition to welfare has also made it difficult for social scientists to recognize the prevalence of sym-pathy for the poor. In 1996, President Clinton signed a bill transforming Aid for Families with Dependent Children (AFDC) to Temporary Assistance for Needy Families (TANF), drastically reducing government benefits to poor families. This legislation enjoyed strong public support: cash or cash-like[38] welfare to able-bodied adults was, and is, unpopular.

But welfare is a unique case. Nearly every government program intended to channel resources to the poor that has ever appeared on a survey has enjoyed the support of large proportions of the American public, with welfare a lonely exception. An important one, to be sure, and one that deserves explanation – yet research has already identified reasons why welfare is uniquely unpopular. Chief among these reasons, Martin Gilens shows in *Why Americans Hate Welfare*, are widespread white prejudice against blacks and the related belief that many welfare recipients are lazy.[39] But TANF is not the only program in the world that channels resources to the poor: Gilens is careful to note that the Earned Income Tax Credit, Supplemental Security Income, Head Start, and Social Security all enjoy substantial public support, as does the general principle of government helping the poor.[40] Those who are tempted to conclude that Americans don't like aid to the poor based on public attitudes about welfare should beware of letting the rotten apple spoil the barrel.[41] Our tunnel vision on public opinion about cash welfare threatens to distort our perspective on the role of attitudes about class groups in American politics.

The takeaway from this discussion is that the answers social scientists get depend on the questions we ask. If scholars are focused on trying to explain why there isn't more socialism in the United States, why there isn't more of a class divide in public opinion and electoral behavior, and why welfare is so unpopular, we are unlikely to uncover much evidence of sympathy for the poor and resentment of the rich. In place of the traditional research questions in the literature, therefore, I ask: what do Americans think about poor people and rich people? And how, if at all, do their attitudes toward the poor and the rich organize their thinking about public policies and candidates for public office? As will be seen, this approach results in a more accurate understanding of attitudes toward class groups in the United States and their influence in American politics. My findings suggest that government has done less than it might have to redistribute wealth downward *in spite of*, not because of, American attitudes about the poor and the rich. Those engaged in the battle to create a more economically egalitarian society should view the American public not as an inevitable enemy but as a potential ally.

A LOOK AHEAD

In Chapter 1, I conduct an initial investigation of the possibility that attitudes toward poor people and rich people influence political preferences. I do so by analyzing nationally representative samples from four separate ANES surveys: those conducted in 1992, 1996, 2000, and 2008.[42] Contrary to claims of class indifference in American politics, the results reveal that respondents frequently mention poor people and rich people when discussing what they like or dislike about political parties and candidates for public office. Furthermore, their discussions of the poor are predominantly sympathetic in nature: respondents often complain that a given candidate for office, or a given political party, does not do enough to help the poor. Meanwhile, references to the rich typically take on a resentful tone: respondents often say that they dislike a candidate or a party because that party seems to favor the interests of the rich at the expense of the interests of the rest of America.

To place the findings of these analyses in context, I also assess how often the survey respondents mention "inequality." I do so because a vibrant strand of recent scholarship addresses the topic of how increasing economic inequality has affected public opinion in the United States.[43] While research in this tradition is important and has yielded valuable insights, much of it begs a key question: How much do Americans rely on the concept of economic inequality to make sense of politics in the first place? Interestingly, the open-ended responses reveal only a few instances in which ordinary individuals use terminology related to inequality. This is consistent with research from Eunji Kim, Rasmus Pedersen, and Diana Mutz, which finds that economic inequality is a highly abstract concept that is often misunderstood by individuals and not tightly connected to their political judgments.[44]

It is not at all clear, then, that ordinary individuals have economic inequality on their minds when forming their political preferences. But Americans do routinely refer to class groups such as the poor and the rich when talking about candidates for public office and political parties. The chapter concludes by charting the boundaries of the concepts "poor" and "rich" in the public mind, by asking ordinary Americans what these terms mean to them.

The responses to these open-ended questions are especially useful because they take Americans on their own terms, pointing a clear path forward for the remainder of the book. For example, I find that respondents rarely refer to subgroups of the poor (such as the "working poor," "poor children," or the "deserving poor"). While policymakers have often made use of such subcategories, it is not at all clear that ordinary individuals do the same. I therefore theorize and test propositions about public thinking about *broad* class groups – poor people and rich people – in the subsequent chapters.

Furthermore, the open-ended responses suggest that when it comes to thinking about politics, public views about poor people and rich people are unidimensional, centered on questions of deservingness. In theory, of course, it is possible for Americans to evaluate class groups along a variety of dimensions: one might, for example, resent the rich but also view rich people as talented, hard-working and intelligent. But in practice, those Americans who spontaneously mention these class groups tend to do so with one central consideration in mind; as Pamela Conover puts it, their political thinking about these groups is centered on "the desire to know who is getting what and whether they deserve it." Those class groups perceived to get less than they deserve (typically the poor) are viewed with sympathy, and those class groups perceived to get more than they deserve (typically the rich) are viewed with resentment. I therefore place sympathy for the poor and resentment of the rich at the center of the theory-building and empirical analysis of this book.

The development of a theoretical framework for this study of attitudes toward poor people and rich people in the United States is the task of Chapter 2. Here I grapple with four essential questions: How do Americans view the poor and the rich? Where do their attitudes about these class groups come from? Under what conditions do individuals link their class group attitudes to their political preferences? And how do attitudes toward poor people and rich people organize policy attitudes and candidate evaluations? The chapter concludes by presenting an overview of the data used to answer these questions, along with an overview of the tests of the empirical implications of the theory.

I examine the contours of public thinking about poor people and rich people in the United States in Chapter 3. The chapter begins by introducing and defending the strategy for measuring class group attitudes adopted here. Next, I examine responses to original survey questions in three national survey datasets. Consistent with the results of the analysis of open-ended responses in Chapter 1, the findings demonstrate that sympathy for the poor and resentment of the rich are pervasive, though far from universal, in American society today – and this has probably been true for decades. Furthermore, the multiple survey questions that are used to measure attitudes toward the poor and the rich yield similar results, leading to greater confidence in the findings.

Next, I show that sympathy for the poor and resentment of the rich are stable over time. They are also distinct from such standard fixtures in contemporary accounts of public opinion as partisanship, ideological principles, beliefs about economic inequality, beliefs about economic mobility, and demographics. I find that racial prejudice plays an important role; those whites who hold negative stereotypes about blacks express less sympathy for the poor than those whites who do not. This is consistent with the finding from Chapter 2 (and other scholarship) that many people overestimate the percentage of the public that is black. But the power of racial prejudice is limited; while it places an upper bound on sympathy for the poor, sympathy for the poor nonetheless remains widespread.

Once we recognize the importance of sympathy for the poor and resentment of the rich, the scales fall from our eyes, and we see the landscape of American politics more clearly. In particular, the insights about class group attitudes gained from the analyses in Chapters 1, 2, and 3 equip us admirably to address the long-standing puzzle[45] of public support for downwardly redistributive policies: those policies that aid those at the bottom of the economic distribution or take from those at the top. Chapter 4 begins by showing that consistent with the findings of past research, support for downwardly redistributive policies is high and stable over time, as revealed through descriptive analyses of secondary survey datasets of nationally representative samples of Americans over decades. I also scrutinize existing explanations for public opinion about downwardly redistributive policy. Research has made important advances, illuminating the importance of such factors as economic self-interest and core values or principles such as individualism and egalitarianism. Yet even after taking these factors into account, widespread American support for downwardly redistributive policy remains puzzling, particularly in the context of a few important cases in which Americans actually oppose downward redistribution. My task, therefore, is to explain both the pattern of support for downwardly redistributive policies and the exceptions to this pattern.

To do so, I conduct statistical analyses of original survey data, uncovering strong associations between class group attitudes and opinion about a wide range of policies. I also simulate what public opinion about downwardly redistributive policy would look like in the absence of sympathy for the poor and resentment of the rich. The results show that class group attitudes help explain American support for downward redistribution. In comparison, beliefs about economic inequality and beliefs about upward economic mobility are only weakly associated with policy opinion.

But the survey data also suggest that in some key cases such as the federal estate tax and the homeowners' mortgage interest tax deduction, wide swaths of the American public are not informed about the distributive consequences of policy. I test the consequences of this ignorance through a series of embedded survey experiments in Chapter 5: some subjects, but not others, are randomly assigned to exposure to information about who benefits from, and who pays the costs of, these policies.[46] I find that among those subjects exposed to information, downward redistribution is much more popular than among those subjects not exposed to information. Furthermore, this effect is driven by those individuals who are high on sympathy for the poor and resentment of the rich.

Taken together, these findings imply that sympathy for the poor and resentment of the rich bolster support for downward redistribution – but only when one key condition is met. When Americans know which class groups are the likely beneficiaries (or victims) of a policy, they are able to bring their attitudes toward these class groups to bear on their opinion about the policy. In such cases, sympathy for the poor and resentment of the rich lead many Americans to support downwardly redistributive policies. But for an important set of policies, it is not clear to most Americans who reaps the benefits and who pays the costs. In these cases, Americans are unable to bring their class group attitudes to bear on their policy opinions, and support for downward redistribution remains low. Sympathy for the poor and resentment of the rich help us understand why – and when – majorities of Americans support downward redistribution.

The influence of class group attitudes extends beyond the domain of policy opinion. In many cases, sympathy for the poor and resentment of the rich organize public thinking about political candidates as well. In Chapter 6, I present the results of original survey experiments that isolate the effects of a hypothetical candidate's legislative record on public support for the candidate. Contrary to reigning myths about how Americans think about class, the results suggest that a candidate actually becomes *more* popular if his record indicates that he is likely to use government to transfer resources to the poor. Critically, these results do not appear to be driven by social desirability pressures – that is, by the desire for survey respondents to conform to social norms.

Building on these experimental results, the chapter next moves outside the laboratory, examining the effects of attitudes toward poor people and rich people on vote choice in real-world elections. I begin by returning to the open-ended survey responses presented in Chapter 1, this time focusing on the 2008 presidential election. In the nationally representative 2008

American National Election Studies time series survey, respondents were asked to say in their own words whether there is anything about Obama that would make them want to vote for him (or make them *not* want to vote for him), and respondents were also asked the same about McCain. I focus on those responses that include mentions of poor people and rich people, and the results add up to a clear advantage for Obama. While there is important variation in these responses, on balance they reveal confidence that Obama would look out for the interests of the poor, combined with fear that a McCain presidency would benefit the rich. This analysis is not definitive, but it does corroborate the evidence provided in the experiments; Americans tell us that all else equal, they will reward those candidates who seek to help the poor or hurt the rich.

Next, I analyze the role of class group attitudes in the presidential election of 2012. By the time of this election (unlike in 2008), I had developed measures of sympathy for the poor and resentment of the rich. This makes possible a quantitative analysis of associations between class group attitudes and vote choice, again through the use of nationally representative ANES survey data. As discussed above, those social scientists who study vote choice rarely include class attitudes in their analyses. My findings suggest that this omission leads to a pinched sense of the considerations that influence Americans' voting decisions. After holding constant standard political variables such as partisanship, ideological principles, racial attitudes, and demographics, I find that attitudes toward class groups were tightly bound up with the voting decisions of American citizens in the 2012 presidential election. On balance, it appears that class group attitudes benefited Obama: sympathy for the poor and resentment of the rich bolstered his vote share at the expense of Romney's.

Finally, a statistical analysis of the 2016 election reveals that resentment of the rich helps explain Sanders' unlikely run in the Democratic presidential primary; however, attitudes toward the poor and the rich had little impact on the general election between Clinton and Trump. In key instances, then – though not in all – class group attitudes help Americans decide who they want to represent them in public office.

The findings discussed so far reveal important evidence in support of the proposition that sympathy for the poor and resentment of the rich are important ingredients in the stew of considerations that influence public thinking about policy and candidates for public office.[47] But as powerful as sympathy for the poor and resentment of the rich are, they have not proven potent enough to abate rising economic inequality. Why is the gap between the poor and the rich increasing so rapidly, seemingly unabated by government action? Chapter 7 reviews a number of possible answers to this question from existing literature and also explores two additional possibilities. First, it is likely that public officials and interest groups have made the same mistake as academics, misperceiving the American public's attitudes toward class groups. It is for this reason, I argue, that many candidates for public office avoid talking about poverty and wealth in the contemporary United States:[48] they underestimate the extent, and the power, of sympathy for the poor and resentment of the rich. Second, even when political elites perceive public attitudes toward class groups correctly, they do not necessarily heed the wishes of the public. Rather, political elites attempt to shape public opinion about policy by *framing issues in ways that downplay the relevance of class*. In an additional survey experiment examining opinion about the estate tax, I show that this strategy makes it less likely that the public will bring sympathy for the poor and resentment of the rich to bear on policy opinion, thereby decreasing mass support for downward redistribution. Due to the misperceptions and strategic actions of political elites, then, sympathy for the poor and resentment of the rich can coexist with increasing economic inequality.

Donald Trump's election to the presidency represents another key case in which attitudes toward poor people and rich people proved politically unimportant. In contrast to the 2012 presidential contest between Obama and Romney, neither Trump nor Clinton provided the public with clear, consistent messages about the likelihood that their policy proposals would help or hurt poor people or rich people. On numerous occasions, Trump suggested that he would raise taxes on the rich and increase spending on a variety of social welfare programs. Clinton, meanwhile, rarely talked about poverty and wealth – while her primary opponent, Bernie Sanders, had made increased taxes on the rich the centerpiece of his campaign. This is not to say that class was irrelevant to the election. It is possible, for example, that Donald Trump won over much of the white working class on his behalf, although Nicholas Carnes and Noam Lupu's analysis of recent survey data suggests that this is unlikely; the best available evidence suggests that Trump's victories were with white people in general rather than with class subgroups of white people in particular.[49] In any case, more important for the purposes of this book is that in the 2016 presidential election, clear cues about where the candidates stood with respect to poor people and rich people were not easily found. As a result, I find, sympathy for the poor and resentment of the rich had little effect on Americans' voting decisions. This finding further reinforces my contention that the political importance of these attitudes toward class groups is variable.

I draw all of these various results together and explore their implications for the character and quality of American democracy in the book's conclusion. One of the primary purposes of democratic forms of government is to represent the will of the people. For this reason, foundational theories in political science hold that in democratic forms of government, economic inequality should be low, as majorities of Americans will vote to redistribute wealth downward. Yet the book illuminates a disconnect between American political preferences and policy outcomes: while majorities of Americans believe the poor to have less than they deserve and the rich to have more, the gap between the richest and the rest has been widening for decades, and government does much less than it might to aid its poorest citizens. The concluding chapter discusses reasons for this breakdown in majoritarian democracy. It also examines the implications of this book's findings for scholars' understanding of a range of important topics, including public opinion and political behavior, economic inequality in the contemporary United States, race and welfare state policy, and unequal government responsiveness to American citizens. I conclude on an optimistic note, identifying a path forward for activists and policymakers who, like me, are troubled by abject poverty in the midst of decadent wealth.

I

In Their Own Words

In this chapter, I begin my consideration of the possibility that people think about the poor and the rich when forming their political preferences. Here I examine open-ended responses to questions about what citizens like and dislike about political entities, relying on four separate nationally representative ANES survey datasets. If my argument is correct that evaluations of the poor and the rich figure into political preferences, open-ended evaluations of the major political parties and candidates for president should include mentions of the poor and rich. The benefit of this approach is that it meets individuals on their own terms, examining the language they actually use rather than prescribing options to them in a closed-ended survey.

The analyses in this chapter are preliminary. After all, they can only go so far: the ANES only provides the data in restricted format, for ethical reasons. That is, so that respondents cannot be identified, the ANES only provides their open-ended responses, and does not include any other information about the people providing these responses. But the data can still give a sense, broadly speaking, of whether individuals are thinking about their attitudes toward class groups when forming their political preferences. They also provide an important descriptive overview of the phenomenon under investigation. As such, I use the open-ended responses as inductive material to inform the theoretical framework of class group attitudes presented in the subsequent chapter.

After showing that mentions of the poor and rich are frequent in the open-ended responses, I push further. In addition to a simple count of how often the terms "poor" and "rich" are used in the responses, I also code for whether these terms are discussed in favorable or unfavorable ways. Next, I compare how often respondents use class terminology to how often they use terminology related to economic inequality, since American attitudes about inequality are such a common topic of study in political science.

I also examine whether people tend to mention broad class categories (e.g., "the poor") or class subgroups (e.g., "the working poor"). The history of social welfare policy in the United States reveals that policymakers have often differentiated between the "deserving poor" and the "undeserving poor." It is an open question whether ordinary Americans do the same when thinking about politics.

While these responses to open-ended questions tell us how frequently Americans use class terminology, they cannot tell us what Americans mean by this terminology. In the final analysis of this chapter, I examine responses to an original national survey, designed to get a basic sense of what the ambiguous terms "poor" and "rich" mean to ordinary Americans. The chapter concludes by discussing how the analyses of these open-ended responses motivate the remainder of the book.

HOW AMERICANS TALK ABOUT CLASS AND POLITICS

If I am correct that Americans possess meaningful and politically relevant attitudes toward the poor and the rich, they ought to mention the terms "poor" and "rich" spontaneously when talking about politics. I begin, therefore, by taking respondents at their word, examining open-ended responses to survey questions. Here I present the results of a content analysis, with the assistance of a team of students,[1] examining responses to open-ended questions in the 2008 American National Election Studies (ANES) time series survey. These questions ask respondents what, if anything, they like and dislike about each of the two major parties as well as each of the presidential candidates representing these parties.[2]

I also place this approach in context by comparing it to the approach of much of the existing research on this topic, which is to examine public responses to survey questions about economic inequality.[3] I do so because inequality is a concept scholars use to characterize the growing gap between the richest and the rest over the last few decades, and scholars often study public reactions to increasing economic inequality. I seek to determine whether a complementary approach might also prove useful. Decades of research findings have shown that one primary ingredient of mass political thinking is attitudes toward social groups.[4] In addition to asking Americans whether they approve of economic inequality, therefore, analysts might also do well to ask Americans how they feel toward the poor and the rich.

In order to conduct a difficult test of my proposition that attitudes toward the poor and the rich play a role in Americans' political thinking, I count only the exact terms "poor" and "rich," excluding synonyms for these terms. Furthermore, for purposes of comparison to the approach of existing research on this topic, I also code for mentions of "inequality" and related terms: "equality," "equal," "unequal," and "equivalent." Finally, responses are coded as "1" if any part of the response mentions the relevant term and "0" otherwise; multiple mentions of the term within a response are not counted. Results are collapsed across like/dislike categories and parties at this point; distinctions among these categories will be taken into account later.

Consistent with my expectations, Figure 1.1 reveals that meaningful proportions of Americans make references to the terms "poor" and "rich." Just over one thousand respondents typically answered the like/dislike open-ended questions about the parties (the actual number varied across the questions): of those who did respond, 170 mentioned the term "poor" and 195 mentioned the term "rich." In contrast, only 20 respondents used terms related to inequality. Similarly, in responses about the presidential candidates, 65 respondents used the term "poor," and 64 used the term "rich," while 8 used terms related to inequality.

Because this analysis adopts such strict criteria for what counts as a mention of "poor" or "rich," it underestimates – by design – the prevalence of attitudes toward the poor and the rich in Americans' political thinking. This is done in order to conduct a difficult test of my contention that class group attitudes influence the formation of political preferences. The estimate of the number of references to the poor and rich in responses to the party like/dislike questions would have nearly doubled had I adopted a more inclusive coding strategy, including such terms as "lower class" (63 mentions), and "wealth" or "wealthy" (48 mentions).

Furthermore, this analysis may overestimate the extent to which the concept of economic inequality figures into Americans' political judgments, since I have cast a wide net: terms related to "inequality" might refer to economic inequality but might also refer to inequality along other dimensions such as race, gender, or sexual orientation. This test, in sum, intentionally stacks the deck against a class group account of American public opinion and in favor of an account that emphasizes attitudes about inequality. Yet the findings still yield a stark imbalance in favor of the class group account: respondents often refer to the poor and rich, unprompted, when discussing political entities, and they almost never make references to economic inequality.

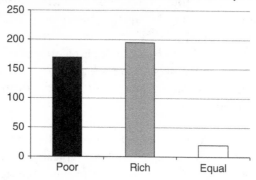

Open-ended Responses to Questions about the Two Major Parties

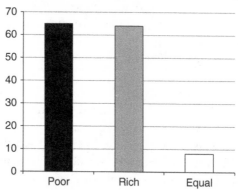

Open-ended Responses to Questions about Presidential Candidates

FIGURE I.I Respondents routinely invoke the terms "poor" and "rich" when asked what they like or dislike about political entities. Source: 2008 ANES survey *Survey respondents were asked if there is anything they like or dislike about each of the two major parties and each of the presidential candidates representing those parties. This analysis collapses across all mentions of "poor," "rich," and "equal." The y-axis values indicate the number of responses including each of these terms. All of the following qualify as including the term "equal": equality, inequality, equal, unequal, and equivalent. This analysis reveals that many respondents mention class groups when talking about what they like or dislike about political entities. They are also much more likely to talk about specific class groups than to talk about economic inequality.*

One might wonder whether these results are exceptional because the survey from which they are taken was conducted in the middle of a recession – indeed, the worst recession since the Great Depression. Perhaps at that time class issues were particularly salient. To address this possibility, I also examine the results of ANES surveys in all other years for which I was able to obtain these restricted data: 1992, 1996, and 2000. As the Appendix shows, the results reveal similar patterns to those found in 2008; mentions of "poor" and "rich" are frequent, while use of inequality terminology is practically nonexistent.

FAVORABLE AND UNFAVORABLE MENTIONS OF THE POOR AND THE RICH

Next, I attempt to get a sense of how favorably (or unfavorably) disposed Americans are toward poor people and rich people, continuing with the 2008 ANES open-ended survey data and focusing on the open-ended questions about what respondents like or dislike about the two major political parties. Of course, these questions do not directly ask respondents how they feel about poor people and rich people. Yet respondents often disclose their views of the poor or the rich by implication, praising or criticizing a political party for helping them.

For example, in answer to the question of what the respondent likes about the Democratic Party, responses include: "They are for the poor people," "They want to help the poor," "They do a lot of things better for the poor," "I like their original creed of helping the underman – the poor," "They're for poor folks," and "They are more geared to helping poor American people."[5] If political parties that help the poor are to be praised, the obvious implication of this claim is that poor people deserve help.

These responses reflect a broader pattern: the open-ended survey responses indicate, on balance, the belief that parties and candidates are preferred to the extent that they help poor people. To some extent, both the Democratic and Republican parties are recipients of this praise: for example, in answer to the question of what the respondent likes about the Republican Party, one response was "For the poor people." But praising the Republican Party in this regard is relatively rare; the perception that the Republican Party is good at helping the poor does not appear to be widely shared.

Indeed, one common criticism of the GOP is that it does not do enough to help the poor. In answer to the question of what the respondent dislikes about the Republican Party, replies include: "They are not for the poor people," "They are unconcerned for the poor people," "They are hard on poor people," and "They do nothing for poor people but make it worse." Taken together, these findings suggest that many Americans believe that poor people deserve more than they get. Furthermore these Americans view a political party more favorably if they perceive it to help than if they do not.

In contrast to the mentions of poor people in the data, mentions of rich people are largely unfavorable. The following criticisms of the GOP are telling: "All for the rich and the rich just get richer," "They like rich people," "Inclined to favor the rich people," and "They seem to help the rich people." Some of these mentions combine negative mentions of the rich with positive mentions of the poor, such as: "Don't like that they favor the rich and not the poor people," "They are in there just for the rich and not concerned about the poor people," and "Want the rich to get richer and the poor to get poorer." The Democratic Party meanwhile, is praised for *not* helping the rich: "Don't just focus on the rich," and "They are more for the poor than they are for the rich."

The responses presented here are illustrative rather than exhaustive; there are instances in which the poor are discussed in unfavorable terms or the rich in favorable terms. For example, one respondent complains about the Democratic Party that, "All they talk about is poor people and giving money to them." Another praises the Republican Party for their "loyalty to the rich." But these responses cut against the grain. In 2008, the poor were mentioned favorably 213 times and unfavorably only 5 times; 17 mentions were ambiguous. The rich, meanwhile, were mentioned favorably 6 times and unfavorably 228 times; 29 mentions were ambiguous.[6] The patterns are similar for each of the other available years: 1992, 1996, and 2000.[7] While the number of times each class group is mentioned changes throughout the years (perhaps in part due to fluctuations in ANES sample size across those years), the dominant pattern is to mention the poor in favorable ways and the rich in unfavorable ways.

These patterns also hint at a potential source of "issue ownership": these class considerations may tend to be a winning issue for the Democratic Party.[8] That is, the survey responses suggest that one advantage that Democrats have is that much of the public believes them to help the poor more, and to help the rich less, than Republicans do. In Chapter 6 I test the durability of this Democratic advantage.

SUBGROUPS OF THE POOR AND THE RICH?

The open-ended responses presented above are also illustrative in another sense: respondents tend to refer to class groups as a whole rather than to subsets of these class groups. One might have expected that majorities of responses would refer to subgroups such as the working poor (to distinguish them from the nonworking poor) or to the idle rich (to distinguish them from the self-made rich).

Strikingly, however, respondents tended to focus on the larger class categories. Only three references to subgroups of the poor ("working poor," "working poor," and "poor working class") and only two references to subgroups of the rich ("very rich" and "ultra rich"[9]), were evident in the 2008 ANES. Similar patterns were evident in the other years of the ANES survey data. In the 1992 ANES, only four responses mentioned subgroups of the poor ("working poor," "working poor," "poor working people," and "poor underpaid people"[10]) and only one response mentioned a subgroup of the rich ("independently rich"). In the 1996 ANES, only one response referred to a subgroup of the poor ("working poor") and only one response mentioned a subgroup of the rich ("elite rich"). The same is true in the 2000 ANES; only one response mentioned a subgroup of the poor ("working poor") and only one response mentioned a subgroup of the rich ("unethical rich").[11] In the hundreds of times that respondents talked about poor people and rich people, they *almost never* mentioned subgroups within these class categories.

The finding that Americans tend to focus on the superordinate category of "poor people" in their responses is especially important because it is unanticipated by scholarship on the history of welfare state policy. For centuries, policymakers have categorized poor people into two groups, one portrayed as worthy of government assistance and one portrayed as unworthy.[12] Throughout the history of the United States, political elites have relied heavily on this deserving/undeserving poor distinction when structuring the provision of social benefits.[13]

For this insight and for many more, we have scholars of welfare state policy to thank; but some otherwise careful researchers have been a bit too quick to generalize beyond the scope of their findings, assuming a one-to-one correspondence between the views of political elites and the views of the public without actually examining public opinion data.[14] The findings presented here reveal that mentions of subgroups of the poor are surprisingly rare, and mentions of the superordinate group – "the poor" or "poor people" – are common. While elite discourse about poverty has often been dominated by a deserving/undeserving distinction, this may be yet another case in which political elites think about politics very differently from the masses.[15] When talking about what they like and dislike about parties and candidates for public office, ordinary Americans seem to focus not on subgroups of poor people but on the superordinate category – on "the poor" *writ large*.

WHO COUNTS AS POOR? AS RICH?

Terms referring to social groups, at least as they are used in everyday conversation, do not invoke clearly bounded categories. Certainly a policymaker or an economist might specify a bright line between two social groups, as in the case of the official federal poverty line. But to follow their example would undermine rather than advance the current project, since the goal here is to identify concepts as they actually exist in the minds of the mass public. It would not be productive, for example, to ask the following survey question: "How often do you feel sympathy for those families of four who make less than $24,250 per year?"[16] This question would assume an attitude that respondents are unlikely to possess, and the intention is not to impose categories on the thinking of ordinary Americans but rather to examine the categories they already use.

To understand what it means to analyze the power of attitudes toward social groups that are not clearly differentiated from each other, consider attitudes toward racial groups. Prejudice against blacks powerfully predicts public opinion,[17] vote choice,[18] and turnout.[19] These findings persist despite the fact that the boundaries of racial categories are far from clear: at exactly what point does someone cease to belong to one racial group and begin to belong to another? Indeed, there is widespread public disagreement about the race of one of the most prominent political figures in the United States, former president Barack Obama; surveys routinely show that a majority of whites claim that Obama is mixed-race, while a majority of blacks claim that he is black.[20] In short, social group categories, as they exist in the public mind, may have ambiguous boundaries and still powerfully shape public opinion about politics.

That said, however, social group categories must have at least some shared meaning if we are to interpret their influence on public thinking. Here, therefore, I briefly examine the range of this shared meaning for the class group categories of "poor" and "rich." Because existing survey datasets do not typically include questions asking about what these terms mean to people, I conducted an original survey of a national sample of 800 adult, non-Hispanic white[21] U.S. citizens through the survey firm Qualtrics in April of 2017.[22]

First respondents are asked, "Suppose there is a person about whom you know ONLY ONE THING: the amount of money per year this person makes. How MUCH money would this person have to earn per year for you to conclude that the person is definitely POOR?" Respondents are next asked the same question except the word "poor" is replaced with "rich." This question elicited a range of responses, perhaps because – as some respondents pointed out in an open-ended section at the end of the survey – income is insufficient in the absence of information about wealth. Still, the median response for the "poor" question was $15,000, while the median response for the "rich" question was $250,000. Moreover, the 5th to 95th percentile ranges were nonoverlapping: for the poor, the range was from $1,000 to $35,000, while for the rich, the range was from $50,000 to $2 million. This suggests that while respondents did not necessarily agree on the point at which someone ceases to be poor (or rich), there was little overlap between the two categories: if one respondent viewed a person as poor, no other respondent was likely to view that person as rich.

Similar results were obtained for an additional question: "Now suppose there is a different person about whom you know ONLY ONE THING: the amount of money this person HAS IN THE BANK. How MUCH money would this person have to HAVE IN THE BANK for you to conclude that the person is definitely RICH?" Again, an additional question was asked with the term "POOR" replacing rich, and the purpose of these questions was to move beyond income, to begin to get at the possibility that perceptions of wealth also influence perceptions of who counts as poor or rich. Here too, however, as some respondents pointed out, the utility of the question is limited, as it is possible to be rich without having *any* money in the bank (e.g., all the money could be in stocks). Still, the medians for poor ($100) and rich ($500,000) were far apart, and the 5th to 95th percentile ranges were nearly nonoverlapping: $10,000 to $10 million for the rich, and $0 to $10,000 for the poor.

Next I turn to perceptions of the racial composition of the poor. I do so because if I find that many white Americans view the poor sympathetically, this might be because they use the term "poor" not to refer to all those at the bottom of the economic distribution but rather those poor people who are white. The final questions on the survey, therefore, ask: "Approximately what percentage of POOR people do you think are

WHITE/BLACK?" Consistent with research showing that media depictions of poverty have overrepresented blacks, I find that the mean percentage of poor people perceived to be black was 54, while the mean
percentage of poor people perceived to be white was 43. The term "poor
people" does not appear to be code for a subgroup of the poor such as
"poor white people." This is an important finding given that, as the next
chapter will show, sympathy for the poor is widespread among the
American public; this sympathy persists despite the fact that many whites
perceive the poor to be disproportionately black.

CONCLUSION

In this chapter, I have mapped out the territory ahead, providing a better
sense of the phenomena under investigation: American attitudes toward
the poor and the rich. This brush-clearing exercise is also important for its
own sake, as it yields important substantive insights. Chief among these is
that Americans seem to think about poor people and rich people fairly
often when forming their evaluations of political entities such as the two
major parties and candidates for public office. This is especially interesting
because a common scholarly approach to this topic is to conduct survey
analyses of American beliefs about economic inequality. Yet when we ask
Americans to talk about politics in their own words, they rarely use
inequality terminology, but mention "the poor" and "the rich" frequently. If I had only analyzed mentions of economic inequality,
I would have erroneously concluded that the American public does not
think about class when forming political judgments.

Additionally, ordinary Americans' discussions of poor people and rich
people follow consistent patterns. The most common portrayal of the
poor is as a group that receives insufficient assistance, such that
a political party or candidate who helps the poor merits accolades.
The rich, meanwhile, are often depicted as receiving too much help from
government; by this logic, a political party or candidate who channels
resources toward them warrants condemnation.

As will be seen, a key claim in this book is that sympathy for the poor is
widespread among the American public – to which a skeptic might
respond: "Which poor?" While subcategories of "deserving" and "undeserving" poor have dominated the discourse of policymaking elites, it is
not clear that the thinking of the mass public follows this distinction.
Political elites might well have a variety of subgroups in mind when they
design policy, such as "able-bodied poor people," "the working poor,"

"the white poor," or "poor children" – but the public at large appears to have a broader focus on poor people in general.

We also have a rough sense of what individuals mean by the terms "poor" and "rich." To be sure, people do not come to unanimous agreement on the precise boundary lines of "poor" and "rich" categories, and their conceptions of poverty overrepresent black people. But the boundaries of poverty do not need to be clear, accurate, or universally shared for attitudes about poor people to figure into mass political judgments.

Indeed, the evidence so far suggests that these attitudes toward class groups are bound up with how Americans think about politics. That is, the concepts "poor" and "rich" do appear to figure in the political judgments of at least some Americans. There appears to be potential, then, in an approach that places class attitudes front and center. In the next chapter, I develop a theoretical framework of attitudes toward the poor and the rich and the political consequences of these attitudes.

A Theory of Attitudes toward Class Groups and Their Political Consequences

In this chapter I turn to the task of developing a comprehensive theoretical framework of attitudes toward the poor and the rich. I use the findings in the previous chapter inductively, considering the ways that Americans talk about the poor and the rich as theoretical building blocks. I also attempt to identify what is most helpful, for my purposes, in the work of those who have already analyzed public thinking about class. While I argue that many explanations of public opinion have paid insufficient attention to attitudes toward class groups, some social scientists have considered these attitudes more thoroughly, and I attempt to extend their important research here. I argue that the findings of previous scholarship have pointed a way forward by suggesting that the poor are widely perceived to have less than they deserve and the rich to have more.

Integrating the findings from the previous chapter with the insights of existing research, I theorize two essential concepts: sympathy for the poor and resentment of the rich. I also discuss how these class group attitudes arise. Next, I develop expectations about the conditions under which individuals use attitudes toward the poor and the rich to form judgments about public policies and candidates for public office. The chapter concludes by describing the datasets and methods used to test my theoretical propositions.

A CURIOUS OMISSION: SCHOLARLY NEGLECT OF ATTITUDES TOWARD CLASS GROUPS

People are social animals. Humans make sense of life by dividing the world into social groups, where a "group" refers to any set of people experienced as a psychological entity by an individual.[1] An attitude toward a social group is an enduring tendency to evaluate the group with some degree of favor or disfavor.[2]

Scholarship on this topic consistently finds that attitudes toward social groups are central to mass judgments about public policies and candidates for public office.[3] Research in this vein has shown that public evaluations of both policies and candidates for public office are based on: (1) perceptions of which groups are thought to be most affected by these policies or candidates and (2) beliefs about whether these affected groups are deserving of the benefits provided (or the costs incurred) by these policies or candidates.[4] This "group-centric" line of inquiry has proved indispensable to political behavior research on matters of race,[5] gender,[6] religion,[7] sexual orientation,[8] civil rights,[9] and more.

Strangely, however, measures of attitudes toward class groups are rarely included in political scientists' models of public opinion, even opinion about economically redistributive policies. This is puzzling. Why would attitudes toward social groups, so critical to public thinking in a variety of domains including race, gender, sexual orientation, and more, suddenly be put on hold when it comes to class?

One possibility is that substantial numbers of Americans do not actually hold meaningful attitudes toward these class groups in the first place. There are many ways to aggregate and divide the billions of people on Earth, and individuals do not spend time thinking about all of these potential groupings. People are more likely to have long-standing, stable, crystallized affective reactions toward such groups as "Nazis," "black politicians," and "disabled veterans" than toward "red-headed bankers" or "coastal feminists." It should be proven rather than assumed that meaningful attitudes toward "poor people" and "rich people" exist.

But numerous studies in sociology and social psychology make clear how important class is to everyday life. Consider, for example, the findings of a study conducted by social psychologists Weeks and Lupfer: subjects who view a photo of someone they have never met before are just as quick to categorize the pictured individual in terms of class as in terms of race.[10] Further evidence of the salience of class is the common finding that being reminded of one's socioeconomic status affects one's performance on academic tests and self-ratings of one's intelligence.[11] Of particular interest to political scientists, as noted above, economic status is associated – albeit weakly – with policy opinion[12] and vote choice.[13] Additionally, research about the impact of social groups on public opinion and political behavior suggests that social groups become relevant to politics when they are "sites of persistent inequality"[14]; given limited economic mobility in the United States,[15] class clearly qualifies. Finally, the analyses in the previous chapter find that Americans routinely talk about class groups when discussing what they like or dislike about presidential candidates and the two major parties. The evidence is clear: class is a meaningful distinction to many ordinary Americans. We should not proceed as though it isn't.

Of course, I am not the first to consider the possibility that attitudes toward the poor and the rich influence public opinion and political behavior. Some research in political science has examined the importance of attitudes about the poor, although the interpretation attached to such findings tends to emphasize other factors such as individualism or racial prejudice.[16] Attitudes about the rich, meanwhile, have been analyzed by a few studies in psychology,[17] but these studies do not assess the consequences of these attitudes for policy opinion and political behavior.

One important work examining the political relevance of class attitudes in recent years is Larry Bartels' landmark *Unequal Democracy*.[18] Bartels analyzes feeling-thermometer scores, which measure how warm or cold people feel toward the poor and the rich,[19] along with perceptions of the adequacy of the tax burden shouldered by poor people and rich people. As will be seen, some of his conclusions are consistent with mine: "Insofar as the policy preferences of ordinary citizens are colored by their class sympathies, those sympathies are more likely to reinforce broadly egalitarian values to negate them."[20]

But just how far is "insofar"? Bartels is skeptical that public attitudes about class influence policy opinion and electoral outcomes in meaningful ways.[21] But he does not develop theory about the character of American attitudes toward class groups or about the consequences of these attitudes for public opinion. Instead he analyzes associations between class attitudes and policy opinion in a handful of available cases – and does not directly examine whether attitudes toward class groups are associated with individual-level vote choice. These decisions are appropriate for Bartels' research purposes, as *Unequal Democracy* casts a broad net, examining not only public attitudes about class but also a slew of other important topics.[22] Bartels' treatment of class attitudes in the mass public is therefore less extensive than it might be, and necessarily so given his broad research interests.

Similarly, consider Leslie McCall's *The Undeserving Rich*, a theoretically innovative and empirically rigorous book that promises to influence decades of research on public attitudes about economic inequality in the United States.[23] Despite its title, this book focuses less on public attitudes toward the rich than on attitudes about inequality and economic opportunity. The term "undeserving rich," as used by McCall, is intended to characterize "the particular configuration of inequality and opportunity in our day" – that is, the belief that economic inequality is undesirable because it results in restricted economic opportunities. Perhaps because McCall's primary interest is in beliefs about inequality and opportunity, she focuses less on survey questions that mention the rich directly and more on questions about inequality.[24]

Finally, scholars pursuing a related line of inquiry rely on survey questions asking individuals whether they approve of economic inequality. For example, one widely cited question developed by sociologists James Kluegel and Eliot Smith asks whether incomes should either be "completely equal, the same as they are now, or less equal than they are now."[25] In their study, only 3 percent of respondents say that incomes should be completely equal, leading the authors to conclude that, "very few Americans ... see strict equalities as just." Also in this study, when asked whether "it would be a good thing if all people received the same amount of money no matter what jobs they do," only 7 percent of respondents endorsed this proposition.[26] Citing this result (among others), Kay Schlozman, Sid Verba, and Henry Brady conclude that Americans "condone inequalities in economic rewards."[27]

But those who focus on attitudes about economic inequality rather than attitudes toward class groups may be missing out on an important piece of public thinking. Studies of public views of economic inequality, while important, do not necessarily capture the range of public opinion about class, as attitudes toward class groups may differ from attitudes about inequality in important ways. For example, one could agree in principle for unequal compensation for occupations requiring different skills but still resent the particular people who happen to be wealthy. The same logic could apply to attitudes about the poor; it is possible to believe that some level of inequality in outcomes is necessary to provide the incentives required for sustained economic growth while also believing that poor people have less than they deserve and that the government should do something to help them.

In sum, the dominant tendency in research on public opinion has been to pay little attention to attitudes toward class groups, excluding them from our explanations of public opinion and political behavior. In rare cases, scholars have incorporated measures of class group attitudes in their analyses, but as a secondary focus. As a result, what we have is a handful of important but fragmented findings about class group attitudes; what we lack is theory, validated survey measures, and extensive, rigorous testing of the political consequences of class group attitudes.

THEORIZING CLASS GROUP ATTITUDES AND THEIR EFFECTS

Political scientists often draw on research in social psychology that helps explain why individuals sometimes derogate low-status groups and extol high-status groups. But other research in social psychology has been often ignored. In particular, political scientists have made relatively few attempts to incorporate research in social psychology that can help us understand *sympathy* for low-status groups and *resentment* of high-status groups. This is the task I undertake here.

Sympathy for the Poor

Foundational American political thinkers, long understood to be purveyors of individualism at the expense of equality, were actually much more sympathetic to the poor than conventional accounts suggest. Adam Smith, for example, worried that economic inequality would have undesirable consequences. As Rasmussen notes, "There is now broad agreement among Smith scholars that he regarded poverty as deeply problematic and sought ways to combat it."[28] Similarly, Hanley observes that, "the fundamental departure point for Smith's defense of commercial society is its capacity to provide for the poor."[29] Some scholars have been slow to acknowledge sympathy for the poor in the history of American political thought; they have been slower still to acknowledge its presence among ordinary Americans.

Sympathy, often referred to as "empathic concern" in social psychology,[30] is defined as the belief that some person or group has suffered "undeserved misfortune" coupled with the feeling that this is a bad thing.[31] Sympathy for others is a widespread phenomenon[32] that leads to altruism,[33] motivating a wide variety of helping behaviors.[34]

Sympathy for low-status groups is consequential not only in private life but in political life as well. Whites who view black people sympathetically, for example, were disproportionately likely to vote for Barack Obama and support the policies he sponsored while in office.[35] Men who are sympathetic toward women, meanwhile, are more likely than their counterparts to support government efforts to improve the social and economic position of women.[36]

While research in political science has not rigorously investigated the extent of sympathy for the poor, what evidence does exist is suggestive. Consider Feldman and Zaller's analysis of the justifications that supporters of social welfare policies gave for their position in open-ended responses on the ANES.[37] Such policies were typically supported by majorities of Americans, and while social welfare policy supporters did not appear to rely on the core value of egalitarianism, they did often provide an "indication that certain people need assistance."[38] This suggests that many welfare policy supporters may view the poor sympathetically – in need and deserving of government aid. Similarly, as discussed above, Bartels' analyses of feeling-thermometer scores in the 2004 American National Election Studies time series survey reveals substantial warmth toward poor people.[39]

Certainly, some evidence suggests that subgroups of poor people can be viewed unfavorably under certain conditions – for example, when they are racialized as black and when they are portrayed by the media as lacking a strong work ethic.[40] But some scholars have been too quick to interpret existing findings as evidence that the American public typically views the poor unfavorably. Consider, for example, Gilens' finding that attitudes about the poor are strongly associated with opinion about welfare.[41] This finding has been cited by Don Kinder as evidence that "[O]pposition to social welfare programs derives from hostility toward the poor."[42] But the only measure that explicitly referenced the poor in Gilens' analysis is a 1 to 4 scale asking respondents why they think poor people are poor, where "1" represents "they don't get the training and education they need" and "4" represents "they don't try hard enough to get ahead."[43] The mean score on this measure is a 1.68, skewed heavily toward the sympathetic end of this spectrum. The more accurate interpretation of Gilens' findings is that most Americans attribute poverty to forces outside of poor people's control, resulting in higher support for policies to aid the poor than would otherwise be the case.

Resentment of the Rich

As Feather and Sherman write, "central to resentment is a feeling of injustice":[44] a feeling of hostility based on the judgment that some person or group enjoys advantage that is undeserved.[45] Resentment, and concomitantly the desire to "pull down" members of a successful outgroup, is a common phenomenon.[46] when high-status outgroups suffer misfortune, *schadenfreude*, pleasure resulting from the misfortune of others often occurs.[47]

Consider the "Millionaires' March" in New York, an example of the influence of resentment of the rich on public opinion and political behavior. Several hundred people, protesting the expiration of a state tax on those making over $250,000 per year, marched to the homes of several wealthy individuals in New York City, chanting "hey mister millionaire, time to pay your fair share!" One protestor was quoted as saying, "I'm out here because we're tired of a tiny number of Americans stealing off of us and not giving us our due."[48]

To be sure, this example comes from a time period during which resentment of the rich may have been especially high, in the midst of the Occupy Wall Street movement. Yet if we return to Bartels' analysis of feeling-thermometer scores in the American National Election Studies, we see that even in 2004, when the economy was performing well, a nationally representative sample of Americans rated the rich unfavorably.[49] Earlier still, findings from Kluegel and Smith's data reveal that 68 percent of respondents reported that they believe that "there are rich people in the U.S." because "The American economic system allows them to take unfair advantage of the poor."[50] An additional 67 percent cited, as another reason why there are rich people, "Dishonesty and willingness to take what they can get."[51] Finally, a series of studies in social psychology on convenience samples find that experimental subjects smile when hearing stories about an investment banker sitting in chewing gum on a bench, or a person in an Armani suit getting drenched by a taxi, or a yacht owner being pushed into the water.[52] While the evidence is incomplete, what evidence does exist is suggestive of widespread resentment of the rich among the public.

Distinct Outgroup Attitudes

In this section I argue that sympathy for the poor and resentment of the rich have three properties, each of which is represented by one of the following three words: *distinct outgroup attitudes*. I describe these concepts using the term *outgroup* because the theory developed here follows a key distinction that scholars have drawn between two types of group attitudes: outgroup attitudes, or attitudes toward groups to which one does *not* perceive oneself to belong, and ingroup attitudes. Outgroup and ingroup attitudes have distinct origins and differentiable consequences.[53] As Don Kinder and Allison Dale-Riddle observe, outgroups supply points of comparison, while ingroups provide opportunities for solidarity and coordination.[54]

While future scholarship would do well to explore ingroup class attitudes such as attitudes toward the middle class and the working class,[55] here I focus on outgroup attitudes: attitudes toward the poor and the rich. I consider these to be outgroup attitudes despite the fact that an economist might label substantial numbers of Americans as "poor" or "rich"; it is public thinking rather than economic reality that is my object of analysis, and the vast majority of Americans consider themselves to be neither poor nor rich. For these Americans the group labels "poor" and "rich" indicate groups of people to which they do not perceive themselves to belong, reflecting the insight from reference group theory that "people frequently orient themselves to groups other than their own."[56]

Attitudes toward these two groups are especially likely to be salient when Americans think about social welfare policy, but of course it is possible that attitudes toward such groups as the working class and the middle class are influential as well. This research project, therefore, should be seen as an initial step toward a broader agenda assessing the importance of class group attitudes to American politics: the concluding chapter discusses an possibilities for future scholarship on this topic.

I define sympathy for the poor and resentment of the rich as *attitudes* rather than emotions. Scholarship on group attitudes has demonstrated that outgroups judged to receive less than they deserve generate sympathy, while outgroups judged to receive more than they deserve are targets of resentment.[57] While these emotional states are fleeting, over an individual's lifespan they crystallize into enduring evaluative predispositions. These enduring predispositions, described by David Sears as "stored affective reactions to outgroup labels,"[58] are durable: stable over time.

Another reason not to view sympathy for the poor and resentment of the rich as emotions is that they contain cognitive elements. Research from social psychologists and political scientists shows that attributions make up a key cognitive component of many social group attitudes; that is, individuals attribute a group's position in society either to the actions of the members of the group or to external factors.[59] This is not a purely emotional process: individuals differ reliably with respect to their cognitive judgments about what causes poverty and wealth.

I define the concepts of sympathy for the poor and resentment of the rich, then, as attitudes – psychological tendencies to view the poor and rich as deserving or undeserving of their status, coupled with affective tags placed on these groups.

Finally, sympathy for the poor and resentment are *distinct*: they are independent of each other. The poor and the rich are conceived of as separate groups of people, and attitudes toward the two are likewise separable. Consider, for example, what one respondent to the 2008 ANES said when asked about what (s)he dislikes about the Republican Party: "they go overboard towards the wealthy, like the Democrats go overboard towards the poor." In this case the respondent appears to believe that both the poor and the rich receive undeserved benefits from government. While we have seen that this sort of response is the exception rather than the rule, it is nonetheless illustrative. It shows that resentment of the rich does not imply sympathy toward the poor: the two attitudes are independent.

Why Sympathy and Resentment? Why Not Other Attitudes?

Of course, sympathy and resentment are not the only possible orientations toward poor people and rich people. Human beings are capable of experiencing a wide range of emotions, any of which might be applied to a social group: admiration, disgust, envy, scorn, pity, fear, and more.[60] We also might think of a wide range of stereotypes that might come to mind when thinking about these class groups: perhaps the rich are perceived as especially competent, for example.[61] I hope that this book encourages our field to move toward a robust research agenda in which many scholars explore attitudes toward class groups and their importance to politics; it is certainly possible that this line of inquiry will discover an important role for one or more of these alternative attitudes toward the poor and the rich. That said, here I focus on sympathy and resentment for three reasons.

The first is a long-standing tradition in political science scholarship that finds that in the realm of politics, attitudes toward social groups are purposeful, based on "the desire to know who is getting what and whether they deserve it."[62] The public views those groups perceived to be getting less than they deserve with sympathy, and those groups perceived to be getting more than they deserve with resentment.[63]

The responses to the open-ended questions discussed in the previous chapter reinforce this traditional perspective. Readers may recall that respondents did not appear to express multidimensional attitudes toward the poor and the rich. Rather, they were centrally concerned with whether a political party or candidate for public office helps or hurts poor people and rich people. On balance, they praised those parties or candidates they perceived to help the poor and derogated those parties or candidates they perceived to help the rich. My second reason for focusing on sympathy and resentment, then, is inductive: the available evidence does not suggest that attitudes such as admiration of the rich are politically relevant.

Third, and finally, in research not presented here I have constructed and pilot-tested measures of additional possible attitudes, including admiration for the rich, negative stereotypes about the poor (that they use drugs, for example), positive stereotypes about the rich (that they are hard-working, for example), and more. Such measures appear to add little explanatory power to my models of policy opinion and candidate choice. I focus on sympathy for the poor and resentment of the rich in order to hunt where the ducks are.

Origins

Most of the empirical work that follows examines the consequences of sympathy for the poor and resentment of the rich. My primary concern is to examine whether attempts to explain public opinion would do well to take these class group attitudes into account. Still, it is worth taking a moment to provide at least a rudimentary theoretical account of where attitudes toward the poor and the rich come from. This account will be examined, to the extent possible, in the subsequent chapter.

Where we live and who we interact with matters – I begin this discussion of the origins of attitudes toward class groups, therefore, by placing context front and center. Social learning theory holds that much of what we believe comes from our interactions with "socialization agents" – we imitate, internalize, and reproduce the behaviors of those we know.[64] Parents play a particularly important role here. Certainly, parents provide our genetic inheritances, which might well contribute to our readiness to view some class groups favorably and other class groups unfavorably.[65] But parents are also the people we interact with most when our attitudes toward social groups are forming, before stabilizing in later years.[66] One's attitudes toward class groups might well be a function of the messages one receives from one's parents. College might serve as an important socialization agent as well; Tali Mendelberg, Katherine McCabe, and Adam Thal find evidence of associations between college experiences and class cultural norms.[67]

The class background of our friends also might influence our attitudes toward class groups. Benjamin Newman finds that those individuals with economically disadvantaged friends are more likely than those without such friends to perceive that the rich have undue influence in the political system. A number of studies have also found that contact with poor people leads to more positive intergroup attitudes: this research suggests that those with poor friends or with routine contact with poor people view poor people more sympathetically.[68] White people who live in areas with high proportions of poor blacks, however, may view poor people less sympathetically, due to extensive anti-black prejudice among whites.[69] Partisan context is likely to have an influence as well: if one's friends and preferred partisan elites are Democrats, one is more likely to encounter sympathetic depictions of the poor and resentful depictions of the rich.[70] Finally, context can be thought of not just in terms of geography but also in terms of media sources. It is likely that Fox News paints a less sympathetic portrait of the poor than MSNBC; media accounts that depict poor people in negative ways are likely to erode sympathy for the poor.

I now turn from context to predispositions, beginning with the possibility that core beliefs and values affect our attitudes toward class groups. Humanitarianism, a sense of obligation to help those in need,[71] might lead to sympathy for the poor. Egalitarianism, or the belief that formal equality is the right of all people, might reinforce both sympathy for the poor and resentment of the rich, since poverty and wealth violate this value.[72] Related to core values and beliefs are individual-level predispositions such as ethnocentrism and social dominance orientation. Ethnocentrism is a strong predisposition "to reduce society to us *versus* them," as Don Kinder and Cindy Kam put it.[73] Ethnocentric people tend to view outgroups negatively and ingroups positively. Ethnocentrism should thus erode sympathy for the poor even as it also bolsters resentment of the rich. Social dominance orientation, defined by Jim Sidanius and Felicia Pratto as the "degree to which individuals desire and support group-based social hierarchy and the domination of 'inferior' groups by 'superior' ones,"[74] might also affect class group attitudes. Those high on social dominance orientation – that is, those who tend to support group-based social hierarchy – should be relatively unlikely to sympathize with the poor, and also unlikely to resent the rich.

Finally, economic beliefs are likely to influence attitudes toward social groups as well. For example, attitudes toward poor people and rich people are likely to hinge on attributions for economic success (and failure). Those who believe that hard work rather than luck explains why people get ahead should be relatively unlikely to sympathize with the poor or resent the rich. Perceptions of one's own economic mobility are also likely to be a relevant factor: those who believe they are likely to become poor someday should be more likely to express sympathy for the poor, while those who believe they will one day be rich should be less likely to resent the rich.

Conditional Consequences

The principal purpose of this research project is to establish that attitudes toward the poor and rich play an important part in the formation of public preferences about politics. The importance of sympathy for the poor and resentment of the rich to public opinion is greater in some cases than in others. My aim here is to suggest two conditions under which attitudes toward class groups are activated: the first has to do with individuals' *political knowledge* and the second involves *framing* of policy issues and candidacies.

As noted above, political scientists have found that evaluations of social groups influence public opinion across a wide variety of domains.[75] This is consistent with predominant theories of human psychology and behavior indicating that social groups are critical to the way humans make sense of life.[76]

Attitudes about social groups are so important to public opinion in part because they provide an efficient means to sort through a complicated information environment to reach a decision. The masses' level of knowledge about political affairs is low relative to political elites.[77] Furthermore, even if levels of information were high it would take a long time to sort through that information to reach a considered judgment.

As a result, individuals tend to satisfice.[78] That is, constraints on information and time cause individuals to rely on time-saving decision strategies – heuristics – and attitudes toward social groups are an especially reliable and efficient heuristic.[79] Rather than putting in the time to obtain information and sort through it, one can reach an opinion more efficiently by thinking about which social group might constitute the "principal beneficiaries or victims"[80] of a proposed policy and bringing one's attitude toward the group to bear on one's opinion about the policy. From there the decision about whether to support the policy is relatively simple.

Consistent with this perspective, attitudes about social groups are strongly linked to opinions about policies that would affect these groups. For example, negative stereotypes about black people are associated with opinion about miscegenation laws, housing integration policies, and punitive criminal justice policies.[81] Similarly, support for civil liberties of a wide variety of social groups is powerfully influenced by evaluations of the groups under consideration.[82] A wide slew of research findings[83] corroborate Don Kinder and Allison Dale-Riddle's observation that, "Scores of studies show that public opinion on matters of policy is group-centric: that is, shaped in powerful ways by the attitudes citizens harbor toward the social groups they see as the principal beneficiaries or victims of the policy."[84]

My theoretical perspective is in line with this tradition of scholarship on group-centrism. Specifically, I argue that the influence of attitudes about social class groups on policy opinion hinges on two conditions. The first of these is that social groups must be linked to specific policies in the public mind for views about these groups to influence public opinion.[85] The key question, then, is whether a particular redistributive policy is actually known to be redistributive by the public – that is, whether it is perceived to benefit (or harm) the poor, the rich, or both. If so, the relevant class group attitude will be brought to bear on public opinion about the policy. However, in cases in which it is unclear who reaps a benefit of a given policy or who pays a cost, class group attitudes will be irrelevant to views of the policy.

The influence of attitudes toward class groups on public opinion also depends on how political issues and candidacies for public office are framed. Any political issue can be potentially understood in a number of ways. For example, consider the Patient Protection and Affordable Care Act, which is often referred to as "Obamacare." Under its official title, the public might view the policy in terms of its potential to keep health care affordable for the poorest Americans; under the "Obamacare" moniker, the public might view the policy more as a referendum on Barack Obama's presidential performance. Even those citizens who have learned that the Affordable Care Act transfers resources to the poor may not bring their attitudes toward the poor to bear on their opinion about the policy, if the "Obamacare" frame crowds out class considerations, bringing their attitudes toward Obama – and, relatedly, attitudes about race[86] – to the center.

Whether sympathy for the poor and resentment of the rich influence policy opinion, then, depends not only on knowledge of the policy's distributive consequences but also on framing – whether the policy under contemplation is described in terms that draw attention to its class beneficiaries or deflects attention away from them. Indeed, as will be discussed in Chapter 7, in many cases political elites have incentives to downplay class by framing issues in ways that evoke alternative considerations. This decreases the salience of sympathy for the poor and resentment of the rich, attenuating their influence on public opinion about policy – and, in turn, eroding public support for downward redistribution.

A similar logic can be applied to the question of when attitudes toward class groups affect public evaluations of candidates. Don Kinder and Allison Dale-Riddle's theory of attitudes toward social groups as "short-term forces" in elections holds that when "candidates are seen as standing for or against certain social groups, voters will be attracted or driven away, depending on their attitude toward the groups in question." Accordingly, one key consideration is the extent to which the public knows that a candidate for public office benefits (or victimizes) a class group. For example, in an election in which a candidate makes it clear on numerous occasions that he plans to increase taxes on the rich – as Bernie Sanders did during the 2016 presidential primary – it is especially likely that resentment of the rich will play an important role in public evaluations of the candidate.

At the same time, candidacies for political office are evaluated on multiple dimensions; it is possible that alternative considerations will dominate candidate evaluations even when clear class cues are present. Campaign strategy and media coverage determine how contests for political office are framed, and it is not a foregone conclusion that the dominant frames will invoke class issues. Generally speaking, people passively accept the frame they are given.[87] The question, then, becomes whether political elites frame elections in terms of class or not. The activation of sympathy for the poor and resentment of the rich is more likely when there is close correspondence between these attitudes toward class groups, on the one hand, and what is taking place in political campaigns that commands attention, on the other.[88]

DATA AND MEASUREMENT

I am centrally concerned with the influence of sympathy for the poor and resentment of the rich on the policy opinions and candidate evaluations of the American public. Yet, as argued above, existing survey data does not include theoretically motivated and empirically validated measures of attitudes toward class groups. Therefore, while I analyze publicly available survey data in many cases, the bulk of my analysis employs three separate sources of original data: the 2013 American National Election Studies (ANES) Study,[89] the 2013 YouGov Study,[90] and the 2014 Cooperative Congressional Election Studies (CCES) Module.[91] Each of these contains survey questions expressly designed for the purposes of this book, and each contains high-quality national samples of adult U.S. citizens (all analyses are weighted for national representativeness).

The merits of these studies will be discussed more thoroughly as they arise; for now, I note that two of them, the YouGov and the CCES study, include embedded experiments for the purpose of isolating causal effects.[92] Furthermore, these datasets allow me to describe the contours of public opinion and political behavior in three separate samples, all of which contain national cross-sections of the American population. Finally, when necessary I supplement these studies with original surveys that include national samples (conducted through the survey firm Qualtrics) or convenience samples (in which respondents are recruited from Amazon's Mechanical Turk platform). These rich sources of data position me well to examine sympathy for the poor, resentment of the rich, and their influence on the formation of political preferences in the United States.

CONCLUSION

In this chapter I have developed expectations about the character of two attitudes toward class groups and their importance to public opinion. The theoretical framework presented here integrates the open-ended responses discussed in the previous chapter, existing findings about class group attitudes from across the social sciences, and research on group attitudes from the discipline of social psychology. I argue that many Americans view the poor with sympathy and the rich with resentment. Sympathy for the poor and resentment of the rich are two distinct attitudes that are shaped by fundamental processes of social learning that vary across geographic contexts. These attitudes toward poor people and rich people have the potential to influence public evaluations of policies and political candidates in powerful ways. This potential is realized under two conditions. The first is when it is clear how the poor and the rich are affected by the policy or candidate under evaluation; the second is when issues are framed in ways that emphasize rather than downplay class considerations.

Much of the remainder of this book is devoted to testing the empirical implications of these theoretical propositions. In the next chapter, I examine whether sympathy for the poor and resentment of the rich are widespread, able to be measured reliably, and distinct from standard political predispositions. Then, in Chapters 4 and 5, I investigate my contention that sympathy for the poor and resentment of the rich influence opinion about redistributive policy, but only when the distributive consequences of policy are clear. In Chapter 6, I seek to determine whether sympathy for the poor and resentment of the rich influenced candidate evaluations in recent elections – those in which it was clear how the candidates would benefit or victimize these class groups. Finally, in Chapter 7 I analyze two recent instances in which political elites downplayed or obscured class considerations: in debates about the estate tax and in the 2016 presidential election. In these instances, I test my expectation that attitudes toward the poor and the rich had little influence on public thinking. Taken together, these analyses allow me to assess the empirical support for my claim that the sympathy for the poor and resentment of the rich powerfully influence public opinion, but only under certain political circumstances.

The theoretical claims I advanced in this chapter are inconsistent with prevailing conceptions of the mass public in the United States. One common view is that the American public is unconcerned with class, at least when considering politics. Indeed, the absence of attitudes toward class groups in canonical models of policy opinion and vote choice suggests, by implication, that class thinking is irrelevant to public opinion.[93] Another is that when public does think about class, it tends to do so in ways that derogate the poor and praise the rich. The argument I have put forward here will be tested against these rival understandings in the remainder of this book.

3

Attitudes toward the Poor and the Rich
in the United States

I have argued that under predictable circumstances, attitudes toward the poor and the rich powerfully influence the formation of political preferences among the American public. Having developed this argument in Chapter 2, here I introduce and explore measures of these attitudes toward class groups. One purpose is to establish that these measures are worth taking seriously. If they are, the tests of the political significance of attitudes toward the poor and the rich in subsequent chapters are worth taking seriously as well.

Another purpose is to assess the distribution of these attitudes. Contrary to many accounts of public opinion in an age of economic inequality, I show that on balance Americans tend to view the poor with sympathy and the rich with resentment; there is also important variation in these attitudes. In addition, I demonstrate that sympathy toward the poor and resentment of the rich are reliable, stable over time, and associated with other political factors in predictable ways.

In the next section, I present responses to original survey questions measuring class group attitudes in the United States and supplement these questions with analyses of available survey data. Then, indices of sympathy toward the poor and resentment of the rich are constructed, and the properties of these measures are examined. As discussed in the concluding section, the key finding of this chapter is that sympathy for the poor and resentment of the rich are widespread in the United States.

HOW AMERICANS VIEW THE POOR AND THE RICH

High-quality measures of attitudes toward the poor and the rich do not exist in available data. The American National Election Studies includes feeling-thermometer scores about these class groups, which are ratings of how the respondent feels toward these groups from 0 (cold) to 100 (warm). These measures are adequate and will be examined in the sections that follow, but they also have serious limitations. Chief among these is that it is not clear whether a person who rates a class group at a "70" actually feels less warmly toward the group than another respondent who rates the group at an "80."[1] Perhaps more importantly, such measures also fail to capture important "affective reactions differentiated beyond liking and disliking" – here, of course, the affective reactions I am interested in are sympathy and resentment.[2]

Accordingly, in this section I present the results of original surveys that measure attitudes toward the poor and the rich. Prior to conducting the research presented here, I administered a pilot study to a convenience sample of 135 adults (through Amazon's Mechanical Turk platform) in April 2012; subjects responded to open-ended questions about class politics in the United States, and I studied their responses in order to determine the vernacular through which attitudes toward poor people and rich people are expressed, so that I could develop question batteries.[3] Based on these responses as well as the open-ended responses to the ANES discussed in Chapter 1, and following Conover's "cognitive-affective model of the role of social groups in political thinking," I developed survey questions measuring attitudes toward the poor and the rich. These questions ask about deservingness – whether the poor and the rich have more or less money than they deserve – and about "stored affective reactions" to these class groups, including sympathy, compassion, anger, and resentment.[4] The questions are listed in Figure 3.1.

Conover writes that political thinking about social groups is dominated by "the desire to know who is getting what and whether they deserve it."[5] To some readers, it might go without saying that the poor have less than they deserve while the rich have more. Yet existing scholarship does not necessarily support this expectation. If the logic of individualism dominates public thinking – if, that is, sociologists Kluegel and Smith are correct that individuals are held "personally responsible" for their "economic fate" – we should expect that both the poor and the rich will be perceived to have exactly what they deserve: no more, no less.[6] Or, if Americans are persuaded by the *Wall Street Journal's*[7] description of the poor as "lucky duckies" (since they pay no federal income tax), and if they view the rich as "job creators" unfairly penalized by government, they should actually expect poor people to have *more* than they deserve and rich people to have *less*.

1. For each of the following groups, please say whether most people in the group have more money than they deserve, less money than they deserve, or about the right amount of money.

POOR PEOPLE, RICH PEOPLE

2. How often have you felt each of the following toward POOR PEOPLE?

Compassion, Sympathy, Anger, Resentment

3. How often have you felt each of the following toward RICH PEOPLE?

Compassion, Sympathy, Anger, Resentment

Notes: Response options for Question 1 are: A LOT MORE money than they deserve, SOMEWHAT MORE money than they deserve, SLIGHTLY MORE money than they deserve, About the right amount of money, SLIGHTLY LESS money than they deserve, SOMEWHAT LESS money than they deserve, A LOT LESS money than they deserve. Response options for Questions 2 and 3 are: Always, Most of the time, About half the time, Once in a while, Never. Furthermore, while the above is accurate for the 2013 YouGov Study and the 2014 CCES Module, the questions on the 2013 ANES Recontact Survey were different in two ways, because of changes to the question wording made by the ANES. First, the wording for Question 1 was "The right amount of money" rather than "About the right of money." Second, "Disgust" was asked rather than "Resentment" for Questions 2 and 3.

FIGURE 3.1 Question wording of sympathy for the poor and resentment of the rich

Leading theories in social psychology might also lead us to expect that the poor are viewed more negatively than the rich. According to social dominance theory,[8] for example, high-status groups maintain their position in the social hierarchy through "legitimizing myths" – widely shared cultural ideologies denigrating low-status groups (such as the poor) and extolling high-status groups (such as the rich). Relatedly, both just world theory[9] and system justification theory[10] argue that individuals possess a psychological motivation to view existing social arrangements as fair outcomes, leading them to view low-status groups as deserving of their inferior position and high-status groups as worthy of their privilege.

Against these common claims, I test my expectation that sympathy for the poor and resentment of the rich are widespread. I do so by analyzing the distribution of responses to the deservingness question for the poor in three studies: the 2013 ANES Recontact Survey, the 2013 YouGov Study, and the 2014 CCES Module (Figure 3.2). Consistent with my expectations, but inconsistent with claims from existing scholarship, in all three national samples majorities of respondents report that the poor have less than they deserve. That said, the figure also reveals substantial variation in

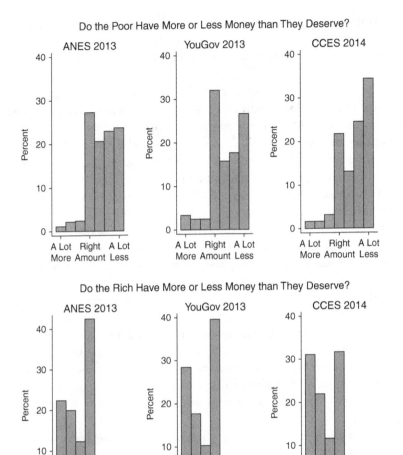

FIGURE 3.2 Perceptions of deservingness of the poor and the rich
y-axis values indicate the percentage of respondents that gave each response option (response options shown on the x-axis). The data source is given in the heading for each chart. Exact question wording is provided in Figure 3.1.

the responses. Some respondents appear to follow the logic articulated by Kluegel and Smith that people get what they deserve: across the three studies, between 20 and 35 percent of respondents claim that the poor have about the right amount of money.[11] Other respondents share the view of the editorial in the *Wall Street Journal* that the poor have more than they deserve – but these respondents only make up about 5 percent of the sample in each of the studies. The modal response, then, is that the poor have less than they deserve, while important heterogeneity also exists.

Also consistent with my expectations, the distribution of attitudes toward the rich approximates the inverse of the distribution of attitudes toward the poor. Majorities of respondents report that the rich have more than they deserve across all three studies. We also see heterogeneity in responses once again: between 30 and 45 percent of respondents claim that the rich have about the right amount of money. Finally, some respondents, albeit less than 5 percent in each of the three datasets, claim that the rich have less than they deserve.

I now turn to emotional reactions to the poor and the rich, presented in Figure 3.3. When interpreting these results, it is important to remember that as a general rule, survey respondents less often express negative attitudes than positive attitudes toward social groups.[12] It is not surprising, therefore, that subjects report feeling sympathy more often on average than resentment. Bearing this in mind, the comparisons between attitudes toward the poor and attitudes toward the rich are instructive. Across the three studies, respondents are about four to six times as likely to express sympathy toward the poor as toward the rich. Furthermore, respondents are only about half as likely to express resentment toward the poor as toward the rich. The additional emotions questions reveal similar patterns.

One might wonder whether the finding that the poor are viewed more positively than the rich is limited to the early twenty-first century, which includes one of the biggest recessions in American history as well as the Occupy Wall Street movement. While I cannot of course ask respondents from previous points in history survey questions that I developed recently, I can use what measures exist in available data. Relying on American National Election Time Series cross-sectional surveys dating back to 1993 (the earliest year containing a thermometer score for the rich), I compare feeling thermometer scores toward the poor and the rich in Figure 3.4.

The results show that on balance, the American public views the poor more warmly than the rich across the period of examination, even during the period of welfare reform in the early- to mid-1990s. It is also important to note that while at first it might seem that the rich are still viewed somewhat favorably – above the midpoint of "50" in all years – this appears to reflect a general tendency for respondents to resist

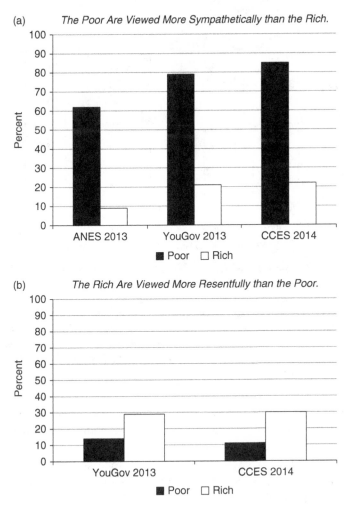

FIGURE 3.3 Sympathy and resentment toward the poor and the rich
y-axis values indicate the percentage of respondents feeling the indicated emotion "always," "most of the time," or "half the time." The ANES 2013 Recontact Study is not included in the second figure because it asks about "disgust" instead of "resentment."

reporting cold feelings toward groups. As Larry Bartels has noted, placing these attitudes in context with attitudes toward other groups reveals that the poor are rated relatively high, on par with other popular groups such as Christians and the military, while the rich are rated quite low, in company with other unpopular groups such as atheists and feminists.[13]

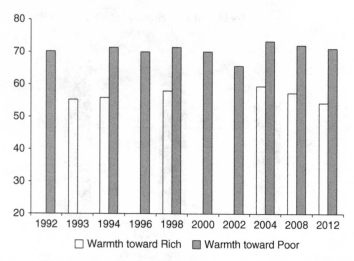

FIGURE 3.4 The poor have been viewed more warmly than the rich for decades
Source: American National Election Time Series Surveys. *Bars represent average feeling thermometer scores (0–100; high scores indicate greater warmth) for all respondents in a given year; analyses are weighted to approximate national representativeness. Missing bars indicate that feeling thermometer questions about the group were not asked in that year. Also, terminology varies somewhat across years for the rich: in 1993 and 1994, the term "wealthy" is used, while in the other years, the term "rich" is used.*

   In sum, the results are remarkably consistent. Whether the survey question asks about deservingness, emotional reactions, or warmth, the dominant attitude toward the poor is one of sympathy and the dominant attitude toward the rich is one of resentment – across multiple nationally representative samples and across multiple points in time. Again, important variation in these attitudes also exists: later chapters will examine whether this variation is politically consequential.

ASSESSING THE VALIDITY OF MEASURES OF SYMPATHY FOR THE POOR AND RESENTMENT OF THE RICH

It is important to be certain that the questions used here are valid measures of attitudes toward the poor and the rich. I therefore combine the questions about deservingness and emotional reactions to these groups (weighted equally) into two separate indices – one measuring sympathy for the poor and another measuring resentment of the rich – and then subject these indices to validation tests.[14]

One way to assess the validity of an index of survey questions is to assess the extent to which responses to one question in the index correlate with responses to another question in the index. For example, those respondents who report that they feel sympathy for the poor should also be likely to claim that the poor have less than they deserve. Indeed, the indices hang together well across all three national datasets. The Cronbach's alpha for the index of sympathy for the poor is 0.74 in the YouGov 2013 sample, 0.72 in the CCES 2014 sample, and 0.72 in the 2013 ANES sample; the Cronbach's alpha for the index of resentment of the rich is 0.79 in the YouGov 2013 sample, 0.76 in the CCES 2014 sample, and 0.73 in the 2013 ANES sample. These tests of internal reliability support the conclusion that the indices presented here are valid measures of attitudes toward the poor and rich.

Another validation test is to examine whether these indices of class group attitudes are stable over time. This is especially important given the theoretical expectation, developed in the previous chapter, that attitudes toward the poor and rich are predispositions: meaningful and stable attitudes, not fleeting top-of-the-head considerations. The three national surveys presented above were too expensive to allow me to interview the same respondent at more than one point in time, but I did conduct a two-wave panel survey of a convenience sample of Mechanical Turk respondents (n = 1,585) between June and August of 2012; the time between the waves ranged from six to twelve weeks. For the sympathy for the poor index, the wave 1-wave 2 correlation is 0.73, and the correlation for the resentment of the rich index is 0.69. This is an admittedly brief time period, but it does speak to the test-retest reliability of the measures. By comparison, the correlation for a standard index of questions measuring another important and stable predisposition, the value of limited government, is 0.73.[15]

To examine further the question of whether class group attitudes are stable over a longer time period, I now turn to the 2000–2002–2004 American National Election Studies panel, which uses a nationally representative sample. The survey contains an identical feeling-thermometer measure of attitudes toward the poor (but not the rich), which allows me to compare responses from the same individuals across different points in time. As Table 3.1 shows, responses to the feeling thermometer about poor people at one point in time are moderately associated with responses to same question at another point in time, up to four years later. Critically, these over-time correlations are of similar magnitudes to over-time correlations of measures of attitudes well known to be stable over time: attitudes about race.

TABLE 3.1 *Continuity of Individual-Level Attitudes toward the Poor*
(2000–2002–2004 ANES Panel)

	Poor people	Whites	Blacks	Hispanic-Americans	Asian-Americans
2000–2002	0.37	0.35	0.35	0.40	0.37
2002–2004	0.36	0.32	0.38	0.46	0.40
2000–2004	0.46	0.38	0.41	0.43	0.45

Cell entries are Pearson's correlation coefficients between warmth (0–100 feeling thermometer) toward the indicated social group in one year and in another (see left-most column). This analysis reveals that attitudes toward poor people are as stable as attitudes toward racial and pan-ethnic groups.

As a final series of tests of the validity of the measures of class group attitudes developed here, I examine whether these measures relate to other variables in predictable ways. I begin by noting that sympathy for the poor and resentment of the rich appear to be independent attitudes, as correlations between the two are low to moderate: 0.20 in the YouGov 2013 Study, 0.21 in the CCES 2014 Module, and 0.25 in the ANES 2013 Survey. This is as expected, since at least some antecedents of sympathy for the poor and resentment of the rich should be different; for example, personality traits we would expect to facilitate sympathy, such as trait empathic concern,[16] are independent of those that we would expect to facilitate resentment, such as trait aggression.[17] Similarly, we might expect that ethnocentrism, or the general tendency to prefer ingroups to outgroups, should be negatively associated with sympathy for the poor but positively associated with resentment of the rich.[18] The low correlations are also consistent with a small proportion of open-ended responses (Chapter 1): some survey respondents express negative sentiments toward both the poor and the rich, arguing that the poor get help from government, the rich do not need help, and the middle class get left out.

Next, I examine associations between attitudes toward class groups and an array of traditional variables of interest to political scientists in Table 3.2. These analyses rely heavily on the 2013 ANES Recontact Survey, supplementing when necessary from the 2013 YouGov Study and the 2014 CCES Module. The table, which presents bivariate Pearson's correlation coefficients, indicates that those respondents who subscribe to negative stereotypes about blacks or report indifference to black suffering are somewhat less likely to feel sympathy to the poor.

These racial attitudes are not tightly associated with resentment of the rich, however. This is consistent with expectations, given that the poor are disproportionately perceived to be black (Chapter 1).

Associations between class group attitudes and partisan ideological orientations also yield predictable results. Republicans and conservatives are less likely than Democrats and liberals to report both sympathy for the poor and resentment of the rich. Those with humanitarian principles are more likely to report sympathy for the poor (but no more likely to report resentment of the rich), consistent with the contention that humanitarianism captures the belief that concrete groups are in need of assistance.[19] Those with egalitarian principles, meanwhile, are more likely than their counterparts to report both sympathy for the poor and resentment of the rich. This is also as expected, given that extreme poverty and wealth are likely to be perceived to violate egalitarian principles. Finally, those who believe in the value of limited government are relatively unlikely to sympathize with the poor and resent the rich; while I did not anticipate this result, it may be that beliefs about the proper size of government are contingent on perceptions of which groups are perceived to benefit from government action. In sum, those who sympathize with the poor and resent the rich are more likely to stake out liberal positions when it comes to evaluations of the parties, ideological self-identification, and core values or principles. Yet the strength of these relationships is moderate at best: class group attitudes appear independent of these standard political variables.

Existing research has also illuminated the importance of beliefs about economic outcomes, and here we see limited relationships between such beliefs and attitudes toward class groups. Those who believe that income inequality is a bad thing, for example, are slightly more likely to sympathize with the poor and resent the rich. Those who believe success is the result of hard work rather than luck, meanwhile, are relatively likely to resent the rich and relatively unlikely to sympathize with the poor, although the correlation here is weak. Perceptions of economic mobility are also related to class group attitudes: those who think they are likely to become rich someday are less likely to resent the rich and (very slightly) less likely to feel sympathy for the poor, while those who think they are likely to become poor are somewhat more likely to sympathize with the poor and resent the rich. Attitudes toward class groups, then, are related to, yet differentiable from, beliefs about economic outcomes.

Finally, demographic characteristics are not tightly bound up with class attitudes. Income is slightly negatively correlated with sympathy for the

TABLE 3.2 *Correlates of Sympathy for the Poor and Resentment of the Rich*

	Racial Attitudes		
	Stereotypes	Racial Resentment	Indifference to Black Suffering
Sympathy for the Poor	−0.23	−0.23	−0.26
Resentment of the Rich	−0.06	−0.17	−0.12

	Partisan and Ideological Predispositions				
	Party ID (Rep.)	Ideology (Cons.)	Humanit.	Egalit.	Limited Govt.
Sympathy for the Poor	−0.26	−0.21	0.44	0.35	−0.27
Resentment of the Rich	−0.31	−0.33	0.10	0.26	−0.26

	Beliefs about Economic Outcomes			
	Income Inequality Is Bad	Success Result of Work	Likely to Become Rich	Likely to Become Poor
Sympathy for the Poor	0.17	−0.13	−0.08	0.10
Resentment of the Rich	0.18	−0.30	−0.20	0.21

	Demographics					
	Educ.	South	Inc.	Male	Age	White
Sympathy for the Poor	−0.01	0.08	−0.07	−0.10	0.08	−0.12
Resentment of the Rich	−0.02	−0.01	−0.12	0.04	−0.16	−0.05

Cell entries are Pearson's correlation coefficients. The primary data source is the 2013 ANES; the 2013 YouGov Study and the 2014 CCES Module are used to supplement when questions are not available in the 2013 ANES. Republican, Conservative, Humanitarianism, Egalitarianism, Limited Government, Education, and Income indicated respectively by abbreviations.

poor and resentment of the rich, but no other consistent patterns are evident. Sympathy for the poor and resentment of the rich pervade social divisions among the mass American public.

CONCLUSION

This chapter has shown that many Americans view the poor with sympathy and the rich with resentment. Furthermore, these class group attitudes can be measured reliably: the indices hang together well, they are stable over time, and they correlate with other variables in predictable ways. Finally, there is important variation in attitudes toward the poor and the rich. I now turn to the task of assessing whether this variation is consequential for Americans' political preferences.

4

Why So Many Americans Support Downward Redistribution

Public support for social welfare programs in the United States has never been easy to understand.
— Stanley Feldman and Marco Steenbergen, 2001

Why do citizens support the welfare state? The answer remains as elusive as the question is fundamental.
— Philipp Rehm, Jacob S. Hacker, and Mark Schlesinger, 2012

The belief that most Americans do not support downward economic redistribution is one of the defining myths of our time. It dominates the op-ed pages and pervades the airwaves. It even animates entire research agendas; some scholars design their research based on the incorrect premise that only a small proportion of the American public supports policies intended to give to the poor or take from the rich. As common as this approach is, it is nonetheless misguided. The available data have indicated practically since the advent of survey research that majorities of Americans consistently support a wide variety of measures intended to redistribute wealth downward. The real question, then, is not why support for social welfare state programs is so low but why it is so *high*.

When I mention this commonplace fact to social scientists, many respond, "That can't be right – I learned from Gilens that Americans hate downward redistribution!" Unfortunately, Martin Gilens' classic *Why Americans Hate Welfare* is often misunderstood.[1] He does *not* argue that most downwardly redistributive welfare state policies are unpopular. To the contrary, Gilens begins his book by noting that, "Large majorities of Americans ... think the government should be spending more money to fight poverty and homelessness, to improve our nation's education and health care, and to assist displaced workers and the elderly." He then attempts to explain why public opinion about welfare is an important exception to this long-standing pattern of public support for welfare state policies. As Gilens writes, "The aim of this book is to understand why Americans seem to hate welfare *even while they embrace most other elements of the welfare state*" (emphasis mine). His exemplary scholarship achieves this aim, providing a powerful explanation[2] of opinion about "welfare," or a limited set of programs involving cash payments to able-bodied adults. Gilens thus explains a key exception to the pattern of American support for welfare state programs – but scholars have yet to explain the pattern.

Years after the publication of Gilens' research, many pundits and political analysts continue to claim that downwardly redistributive government programs tend to be unpopular with the American public. Again, this claim is belied by the data. Decades of public opinion surveys show that majorities of Americans support welfare state programs – not just "inclusive" programs from which middle-class Americans directly benefit such as Social Security, but also downwardly redistributive, "means-tested" programs for which one has to demonstrate poverty to be eligible, such as Supplemental Security Income, the Earned Income Tax Credit, and Head Start. Majorities of Americans also support increased taxes on the rich, and have done so even prior to the Great Recession and Occupy Wall Street.[3] Support for increased taxes on the rich might be explained by economic self-interest – but self-interest cannot easily explain majority support for means-tested programs that only benefit the poor directly.[4] Furthermore, support for downward redistribution is routinely found across partisan, ideological, and socioeconomic groups. Why, then, do so many Americans love downwardly redistributive social welfare programs? As the epigraphs to this chapter indicate, we are still searching for answers.

By investigating the long-standing puzzle of public support for downward redistribution, this chapter reverses the approach of scholarship in comparative politics on the topic. Such research often attempts to explain why public support for government-led downward redistribution is lower in the United States than in other Western industrialized democracies. Valuable studies have illuminated a number of factors: for example, Americans are more antigovernment than the citizens of many Western European countries. They are also more likely to attribute economic success to hard work than luck. Furthermore, the United States is a postslavery society with continuing racial prejudice, driving down white support for some forms of downward redistribution such as food stamps and welfare cash payments – indeed, the influence of prejudice against blacks on white opinion grew significantly in the Obama years.[5]

Extant scholarship, then, provides no shortage of explanations for why the level of support for downward redistribution is lower in the United States than in most Western European countries. But the findings of existing research also deepen the puzzle presented here. In a land of antigovernment sentiment, individualistic ideals, and the mythology of the American Dream, in a nation in which the media disproportionately represent poor people as black and in which white prejudice against blacks abounds, it is striking that *any* Americans – let alone majorities of Americans – support so many forms of government-led downward redistribution, especially when only the poorest appear to benefit directly.[6] Taken as a whole, then, this line of research is more notable for what it does not explain than for what it does. It contributes to our understanding of the opinions of a minority of Americans but does little to help us understand the opinions of the majority. I complement existing scholarship by reversing the research question, explaining why so many Americans support downward redistribution.

The explanation I put forward lies in a fundamental aspect of American public opinion that has often been overlooked: attitudes toward the poor and the rich. As discussed in previous chapters, political scientists do not often examine how Americans view class groups, even though the effects of social welfare programs clearly vary across class groups. It is even less common for political scientists to examine how attitudes toward class groups inform the public's opinions about policy. In this chapter, I remedy these omissions, and by doing so identify an important piece of the puzzle of majority American support for downwardly redistributive welfare state programs.

A PUZZLING PATTERN

Why are so many welfare state programs so popular in the United States? As scholars have argued for decades,[7] and as confirmed by my original data in Table 4.1, majorities of Americans prefer increased government spending on the elderly, making college affordable, and improving public health. They also support tax breaks on college expenses, student loans, and health care expenses. Perhaps these policy attitudes could be explained by self-interest, if Americans are thinking of themselves as likely to become elderly (if they are not elderly already), to attend college or have

TABLE 4.1 *Public Support for Downward Redistribution, and Key Exceptions*

	Policy	% Support	% Oppose	Difference
Government Spending	Assistance to the elderly[a]	68	5	63
	Making college affordable[a]	64	13	51
	Improving public health[a]	58	16	42
	Assistance to the unemployed[a]	45	25	20
	Aid to the poor[a]	53	27	26
	Subsidizing housing for the homeless[a]	67	15	52
	Aid to the homeless[a]	61	17	44
	Welfare[c]	14	49	−35
	Aid to blacks[b]	15	59	−44
Taxes and Breaks	Tax break on health care expenses[a]	71	8	63
	Tax break on children's college expenses[a]	59	16	43
	Tax break on student loans[a]	58	15	43
	Tax break on those with low incomes[a]	50	23	27
	Tax break on home mortgages[a]	77	7	70
	Taxes on $250k+ earners[c]	68	17	51
	Taxes on millionaires[c]	76	11	65
	Estate Tax[a]	17	49	−32
General Principles	Eliminate poverty line[b]	47	37	10
	Reduce gap between rich and poor[b]	48	38	10

[a] 2014 CCES Module;
[b] 2013 YouGov Study;
[c] 2013 ANES Recontact Survey.

children or grandchildren who will attend college, or to become ill. But we also see that pluralities, and often even majorities, of Americans also support policies that do not appear to benefit them directly: increased government spending on aid to the poor and the homeless as well as tax breaks on low-income earners. Furthermore, the strong tendency even among Republicans and conservatives is to support these policies, although support is somewhat reduced among these groups. The results also do not change much if the analyses are restricted to respondents in the top third of the income distribution. Widespread public support for downward redistribution in the United States cannot easily be explained by partisanship, ideology, or self-interest.

One might interpret support for government efforts to redistribute wealth downward as consistent with past findings that Americans subscribe to on one hand a general, philosophic conservatism and on the other a pragmatic liberalism when it comes to specific policy programs.[8] While this interpretation undoubtedly fits many aspects of public opinion, it falls a bit short here. Majority support for increased government efforts to redistribute wealth downward extends beyond specific policy programs to general orientations,[9] such as the objective of reducing the gap between the rich and poor and the broad goal of bringing all families up to the poverty line. Public support for downward redistribution is evident in both practice and principle.

More puzzling still is that the findings in the table show important exceptions to the dominant pattern of American "strong and sustained support for concrete policies that would expand opportunity and reduce economic inequality."[10] As previous research has found, some forms of government spending are unpopular, such as welfare and aid to blacks. This exception has been explained by existing scholarship[11] as follows: a subgroup of the poor, welfare recipients, are commonly viewed as lazy and therefore undeserving, in part due to white prejudice against African Americans and racialized depictions of poverty. But there are additional exceptions, such as the federal estate tax on large inheritances; this downwardly redistributive policy is also unpopular, a fact that scholars have struggled to explain.[12] Its unpopularity cannot be explained by either resistance to taxes generally[13] or resistance to taxing the wealthy in particular; the table also shows that taxes on those making more than $250,000 per year, as well as taxes on millionaires, are quite popular. Neither does the popularity of these downwardly redistributive taxation policies cohere easily with widespread support for the home mortgage tax interest deduction, a highly *upwardly* redistributive policy.[14] What we need is an explanation of not only the pattern of support for downward redistribution but also important exceptions to this pattern.

SELF-INTEREST?

Some may not believe that support for downward redistribution requires explanation, arguing as follows: the majority of Americans would benefit from taking resources from the rich, and therefore should be expected to support government-led downward redistribution.[15] This argument rests on the premise that political behavior is shaped by self-interest – that people will support policies that materially benefit them and oppose those that do not.

However, the extent to which self-interest influences public opinion is the subject of continuing debate. A plethora of research findings have suggested that in many cases, self-interest is a weak predictor of public opinion and political behavior across a wide variety of domains.[16] That said, methodological advances in a couple of recent studies have enabled scholars to detect more self-interest effects than had been previously evident.[17] Additionally, scholars have broadened the concept of self-interest – to include longer time-horizons for example[18] – or accepted that self-interest often does not predict public opinion or political behavior well and begun the search for the conditions under which self-interest matters most.[19]

Consistent with the findings of previous scholarship, the following patterns suggest that the role of self-interest should not be taken for granted. Consider opinions about government spending held by those in the top third and the bottom third of the income distribution, taken from the American National Election Studies' (ANES) nationally representative survey data from 1992 to 2008.[20] Responses to these questions are scaled from 0 to 1, where 1 represents the most extreme position in favor of increasing spending, 0 represents the most extreme position in favor of decreasing spending, and 0.5 represents the position that spending should be kept the same. Mean responses, weighted for national representativeness, are presented in Figure 4.1a–d.

Aggregate support for increasing federal spending on aid to the poor is both high and stable (Figure 4.1a). This finding is consistent with thorough analyses of nationally representative survey data, which have routinely found majority support for a wide range of downwardly redistributive policies – including not only support for policies intended to aid the poor but also support for policies that would take from the rich.[21]

Critically, even well-off Americans appear to support increased aid to the poor: additional analyses, which pool across this time period, show that Americans in the top third of the income distribution are nearly four times as likely to say that federal spending on aid to the poor should be increased (44 percent) as to say it should be decreased (12 percent; the remainder say funding levels should not be changed). Restricting the analysis to the top 5 percent of income earners yields similar results: respondents are nearly three times as likely to say aid to the poor should be increased (39 percent) as to say it should be decreased (15 percent). Finally, while an income gap in support for downward redistribution is evident, suggesting some role for self-interest, this effect is quite small. Indeed, as Figure 4.1b shows, even homeless people are generally viewed as deserving of increased government aid, again with very little differences across income levels. These patterns cannot be written off to a general pattern of support for increased government spending, as government aid to groups other than the poor – foreigners (Figure 4.1c) and blacks (Figure 4.1d) – is not nearly as popular.

This evidence of the weak relationship between self-interest and income is consistent with those of political scientists Benjamin Page and Larry Jacobs, whose original, nationally representative survey uncovers substantial support for a wide variety of policies that would downwardly redistribute wealth *even when the respondent is told that (s)he would have to pay increased taxes, and even when the respondent is relatively well-off.*[22] Yet scholars subscribing to the self-interest premise rarely address this apparent violation.

Of course, the analysis presented here is illustrative, not exhaustive. There are more ways of conceiving of downward redistribution than federal spending on aid to the poor and the homeless. There are also alternative ways of measuring self-interest besides income: measures of wealth, for example, or subjective measures such as individual perceptions of one's own economic mobility. A wider range of concepts and measures will be considered in the analyses to come; for now, I note that this brief presentation, in combination with the results of previous studies, suggests that it is unlikely that explanations premised on self-interest will be sufficient to make sense of public support for downwardly redistributive social welfare policy.

PRINCIPLES?

Another set of factors with the potential to shape public opinion about downward redistribution are "principles" or "core values." Scholars have paid especial attention to *individualism*, a concept that encompasses a range of principles such as economic self-reliance, laissez-faire

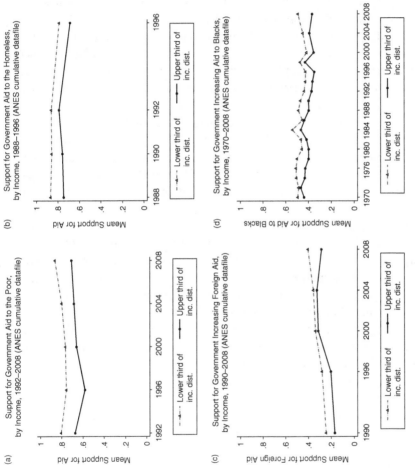

FIGURE 4.1 Opinion about welfare state policy over time

63

capitalism, and a limited role for government. Kluegel and Smith refer to these principles, taken together, as the "dominant ideology" – not in the sense of a coherent belief system but rather a widespread perception that "opportunity for economic advancement based on hard work is plentiful" and the concomitant judgment that individuals are "personally responsible for their own economic fate."[23] Individualistic principles have a long tradition in American political thought[24] and undergird public opposition to many forms of downward redistribution.[25]

But the prevalence of individualism and its strong ties to public opinion make the puzzle presented here harder, not easier, to solve. If "[a]dherence to the dominant ideology" of individualism is so "widespread,"[26] why do majorities of the American public support such a wide range of downwardly redistributive government programs?

A different principle (or core value), egalitarianism, has more promise to address the puzzle of public support for downward redistribution. Like individualism, the concept of egalitarianism, or support for equality, has a long history in the United States,[27] and its deceptive appeal can conceal a variety of meanings.[28] Analyses of survey data indicate that at least in some cases, those Americans subscribing to egalitarian ideals are more likely to support downward redistribution.[29] However, other studies give reason to doubt the ability of egalitarianism to account for American support for downward redistribution. Feldman and Zaller's examination of open-ended responses to "stop-and-think" prompts on the ANES finds that "supporters of social welfare are hardly more likely to invoke egalitarian values than welfare opponents."[30]

In response to the limitations of an egalitarianism explanation for public support for downward redistribution, one study conducted by Stanley Feldman and Marco Steenbergen identifies another principle that might underpin support for social welfare policies, humanitarianism: "the belief that people have responsibilities toward their fellow human beings and should come to the assistance of others in need."[31] Feldman and Steenbergen analysis of survey data indicates that humanitarianism predicts support for poverty relief and other forms of aid for those in need but does not explain the (less common) belief that government should take a more active role by "intervening" in the economy.

These studies suggest that principles are an important part of the story of American opinion about downward redistribution. But on balance, the effects of principles appear mixed: humanitarianism is counterbalanced by individualism, and egalitarianism is inconsistently applied.

Moreover, the application of principles to public opinion may hinge on attitudes toward social class groups. Don Kinder and Lynn Sanders argue that the effects of principles "have a contingency and specificity about them that are out of keeping with the common portrayal of principles as unstoppable forces that level all opposition," and that social groups account for their "contingency and specificity."[32] On this point, Cara Wong persuasively argues that the principles "often operate corralled by community boundaries."[33] Kinder and Sanders frame the question as follows: "When Americans say that they are unhappy that not everyone is given an equal chance, do they really have an abstract 'everyone' in mind, or just some particular ones?[34] When Americans say that the nation would be better off if people were treated more equally, are they thinking of people in general, or particular kinds of people?" Wong's answer, anticipated by Kinder and Sanders, is that principles are applied differentially depending on the social group under consideration. For example, neighbors are seen as more deserving of humanitarian aid than denizens of distant lands: "Contributing help to ease distant suffering, such that little time or money remains to help a neighbor, would be strongly sanctioned by most of the most common value systems."[35] We must look beyond principles to social groups if we are to come to terms with public opinion about redistributive policy, it seems reasonable whether public opinion about downward redistribution is shaped by public attitudes toward the class groups affected by downwardly redistributive policies.

CLASS GROUP ATTITUDES AND PUBLIC OPINION

To examine associations between attitudes toward class groups and public support for downward redistribution, I conduct a series of ordinary least squares regression analyses.[36] The independent variables of interest are the measures of sympathy for the poor and resentment of the rich developed and validated in the previous chapter. The dependent variables are questions capturing respondent support for a variety of social welfare policies. These policies vary in the extent to which they are explicitly redistributive. That is, some policies consist of government assistance to a group, such as the poor or homeless, or increased taxes on a group, such as those making more than $250,000 per year. For these policies, it is either not made explicit where the money is coming from, in the case of government spending, or not made explicit where the money is going, in the case of increased taxes. In contrast, the question that asks whether government should take an active role in reducing the gap between rich and poor clearly spells out both the winners and losers of the policy. For all policy attitudes in this set of analyses, at least one class group is explicitly named as a potential beneficiary (or victim).

At first it might seem self-evident that attitudes toward the poor and the rich are relevant to responses to survey questions about policy that explicitly reference those at the bottom or the top of the economic distribution. Here it is worth quoting Converse's response to a similar critique: "If this conclusion seems self-evident, it is worth reflecting on the constancy with which it is ignored ..."[37] That is, models of public opinion about redistributive policy almost never include attitudes toward class groups. This is a strange omission given that in other domains, group attitudes have been known for decades to be among the strongest determinants of public opinion.[38] For example, attitudes toward racial groups shape opinion about policy relevant to race,[39] while attitudes about gender influence opinion about policy relevant to gender.[40] Scholars do not provide grounds for an expectation that public opinion about policy relevant to class would be exempt from this pattern, yet measures of attitudes toward class groups are routinely omitted from their analyses.

While control variables differ somewhat depending on the study, measures of key ingredients of opinion about redistributive policy are evident across the three surveys: racial attitudes, partisanship, ideology, principles, perceptions of economic mobility, attributions for economic success, and demographics. Given concerns about regression models with long arrays of controls,[41] it is important to note that the results are robust to a variety of specifications, including specifications without a single control variable. Indeed, the relationships between class group attitudes and policy opinion typically increase if a control variable or set of control variables is excluded. The magnitude of the relationships between attitudes toward class groups and policy opinion is presented in Figures 4.2 and 4.3.

I begin with two dependent variables that are broad policy orientations related to downward redistribution (2013 YouGov Study). The first of these is the ambitious goal of making sure no families fall below the poverty line – in a nation purportedly dominated by antipoor sentiment, it is striking that this goal is endorsed by a plurality of Americans, as was shown in Table 4.1 above. As one would expect, self-identification as Republican and conservative is negatively associated with support for this policy goal, consistent with previous research. Those who self-identify as poor are also somewhat more likely to support this policy goal, consistent with explanations based on self-interest; demographic characteristics, meanwhile, are not meaningfully associated with opinion about the policy after taking other considerations into account.

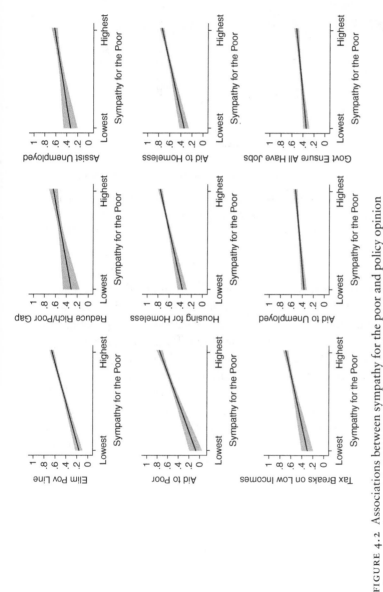

FIGURE 4.2 Associations between sympathy for the poor and policy opinion

The y-axis values are predicted probabilities or predicted values based on regression analyses; regression coefficients can be found in the Appendix (4a, 4b, and 4c). The analysis shows that sympathy for the poor is positively associated with public support for a wide range of downwardly redistributive policies.

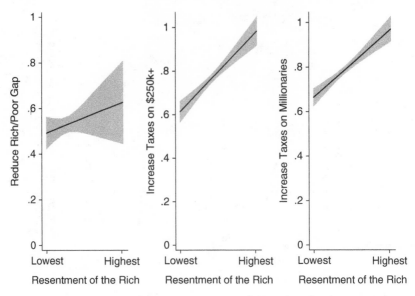

FIGURE 4.3 Associations between resentment of the rich and policy opinion
The *y*-axis values are predicted probabilities or predicted values based on
regression analyses; regression coefficients can be found in the Appendix
(4a and 4c).

Turning to the independent variables of central interest: the coefficient
on sympathy for the poor is statistically significant and is the largest
coefficient in the model (all regression coefficients in the Appendix). After
taking into account conventional explanations for public opinion, support
for bringing all families above the poverty line is positively and strongly
associated with sympathy for the poor. Resentment of the rich, meanwhile,
is not meaningfully associated with opinion about the poverty line, which is
not surprising given that this question does not explicitly invoke the rich.

Next we turn to opinion about the policy goal of reducing the gap
between rich and poor. Those political observers who have characterized
Americans as supportive of economic inequality should note that this goal
is endorsed by a plurality of Americans as well (again as previously seen in
Table 4.1).[42] Here too Republicans and conservatives are less likely to
subscribe to this goal. The elderly are also less likely to say they support
government efforts to reduce the gap between rich and poor, while black
people are more likely to do so; other demographics provide little explanatory power.

Critically, both sympathy for the poor and resentment of the rich are positively associated with support for government efforts to reduce the gap between the rich and the poor. The coefficients are among the largest in the model, rivaling those on partisanship and ideology. This finding substantiates the argument that broad public orientations in favor of downward redistribution are bolstered by sympathy for the poor and resentment of the rich. The patterns across these two questions are also consistent with the contention that the measures developed in the previous chapter tap not into some broader orientation toward government spending but rather into attitudes toward specific class groups, as intended; here the coefficient on resentment of the rich pops up when the rich are indicated by the policy question and not otherwise.

I now build on these analyses by including a more extensive series of control variables: racial resentment, principles of humanitarianism and egalitarianism, respondent perceptions of economic mobility, attributions of economic success, income, and labor force participation (2014 CCES Module). All of these variables are plausibly correlated with both class group attitudes and opinion about redistributive policy; each, therefore, represents an alternative explanation for the associations between class group attitudes and policy opinion found above. I also examine a different set of dependent variables: respondents are asked whether they support increased government spending on assistance to the unemployed, aid to the poor, subsidized housing for the homeless, and aid to the homeless. Respondents are also asked whether they would support a tax break on low-income earners; recall from Table 4.1 that all of these policies were supported by a plurality, and in most cases a majority, of respondents.

The coefficients on the control variables reinforce the findings of previous research (see the Appendix). Prejudice against blacks is fairly consistently associated with public opposition to downward redistribution.[43] Republicans and conservatives are also less likely to support downwardly redistributive policies.[44] Those who subscribe to the principles of humanitarianism[45] and egalitarianism,[46] meanwhile, are more likely to support downward redistribution. Perceptions of economic mobility also play a role: people who (perhaps unrealistically) think they are going to become rich are less likely to support aid to those at the bottom of the economic distribution in three of the five cases. The belief that economic success is the result of hard work rather than luck is also associated with opposition to downward redistribution. Finally, some apparent self-interest effects are evident as well: higher-income respondents are more likely to say they oppose downwardly redistributive policies, although labor force participation is inconsistently related to opinion about such policies. Racial attitudes, partisan and ideological identifications, principles, and self-interest: each contributes to our understanding of public attitudes about downwardly redistributive policy.

Yet after taking all of these factors into account, the relationship between sympathy for the poor and policy opinion remains strong and statistically significant in all five cases. The magnitude of the relationship is large: movement across the range of the sympathy for the poor scale is associated with a twenty-nine percentage point increase in support for assistance to the unemployed. Associations between sympathy for the poor and policy opinion are even larger in the other four cases; in fact, for opinions about all of the five policies analyzed here, the coefficient on sympathy for the poor is the largest in the model. By ignoring sympathy for the poor, previous scholarship has neglected one of the most important determinants of public opinion about downwardly redistributive policies.

Interestingly, in some cases resentment of the rich is also positively associated with support for government aid to those at the bottom of the economic distribution. This unanticipated result appears to reflect that some respondents make sense of poverty by contrasting it to wealth. For example, consider open-ended responses from the April 2012 Mechanical Turk survey, in which, after expressing their opinions about government spending on policies related to helping the poor, respondents were asked why they had given the answers they did. One respondent wrote, "A lot of people are struggling. It seems like those with the most just keep getting richer, while some people are barely scraping by." Another said, "Because we have an enormous disparity of wealth." And a different respondent pointed out that "there are people with millions, and there are people going hungry." For these respondents, increased aid to the poor is necessary not only because the poor need help in absolute terms but also in relative terms: it is wealth that casts the ills of poverty into sharp relief. Some respondents went farther still, claiming that poverty is the direct result of wealth, in the sense that the rich are perceived to have reached their position by taking from others. For example, in responses to another question in the 2014 CCES asking about the causes of homelessness, a full 60 percent of respondents reported that "greedy rich people" are a cause of homelessness in the United States.[47]

I now assess the relationship between class group attitudes and policy opinion further by examining the viability of two alternative explanations not yet considered: beliefs about income inequality and the value of limited government. It might be, in other words, that the relationships between attitudes toward class groups and policy opinion found in the preceding paragraphs are an artifact of associations between these two variables and concerns about income inequality in general (rather than attitudes toward class groups in particular). And it might also be that those respondents low on sympathy for the poor and resentment of the rich are less supportive of downward redistribution not because of these class group attitudes but because such respondents are also likely to believe that government is too big and interferes in the operation of the economy too much. To assess these possibilities, I now turn to the 2013 American National Election Studies (ANES) Internet Recontact Survey, which includes measures of beliefs about inequality and the role of limited government. A second advantage of the ANES is its address-based sampling method, which may increase confidence in the generalizability of findings from this dataset to the national population of American citizen adults.[48] Finally, the ANES allows us to examine a broader range of dependent variables, including questions about policies that explicitly single out those at the top of the economic distribution.

Consistent with previous research,[49] my analyses reveal that concern about income inequality is positively associated with support for increased taxes on those at the high end of the economic distribution (coefficients in the Appendix). Furthermore, those who value limited government are less likely than their counterparts to support increased government spending and increased taxes across the board. Standard variables also behave as expected once again; conservatism is negatively associated with both support for government aid to those at the low end of the economic distribution and support for taxes on those at the high end of the economic distribution, while associations between egalitarianism and policy opinion run in the opposite direction.

Most importantly for the purposes of this project, sympathy for the poor and resentment of the rich demonstrate strong predictive power after taking these alternative explanations into account. Sympathy for the poor is positively associated with support for government aid to the unemployed, as well as subscription to the goal of government ensuring that everyone has a job. Also as expected, sympathy for the poor does not predict opinion about policies affecting those at the top of the income distribution. Resentment of the rich, meanwhile, is also positively associated with support for government aid to the unemployed and subscription to the goal of government ensuring that everyone who wants a job has one, consistent with the results above. Notably, the coefficient on resentment of the rich is substantially larger when the policy under consideration is increased taxation on those who earn over $250,000 per year, as well as when the policy is increased taxation on millionaires. Indeed, resentment of the rich is more tightly bound up with support for increased taxes on those at the top of the economic distribution than is any other variable measured here.

Across three national datasets, in sum, and after taking into account an extensive set of potential alternative explanations, the analyses reveal strong, consistent associations between attitudes toward class groups and policy opinion. This is consistent with the argument that downwardly redistributive policies are popular because of sympathy for their beneficiaries and resentment of their victims.

IF SYMPATHY FOR THE POOR AND RESENTMENT OF THE RICH WERE TO EVAPORATE, WHAT WOULD HAPPEN TO PUBLIC OPINION ABOUT REDISTRIBUTIVE POLICY?

An additional implication of the argument that attitudes toward class groups explain the popularity of downwardly redistributive policy is as follows: if sympathy for the poor and resentment of the rich were to evaporate, public support for downwardly redistributive policy would decline precipitously. In order to assess this implication, I now generate simulated values of policy opinion based on the regression models presented above. All control variables are set to their means, and sympathy for the poor and resentment of the rich are set to their lowest values.[50]

The results of these simulations, presented in Figure 4.4, suggest that sympathy for the poor and resentment of the rich play an important role in bolstering public support for downward redistribution. The y-axis of the figure presents average opinion; since the coding is transformed onto a 0 to 1 scale, values greater than 0.5 indicate that average opinion is favorable toward the policy, while values less than 0.5 indicate that average opinion is unfavorable. The black bars indicate actual average opinion about each policy, while the gray bars indicate simulated opinion: what the average opinion about each policy would be in the absence of sympathy for the poor and resentment of the rich.

A comparison between the black and the gray bars suggests that the average level of support for these downwardly redistributive policies would plunge in the absence of sympathy for the poor and resentment of the rich. Support for increased government spending on aid to the unemployed, for example, would be cut by more than three-quarters, dropping from 0.61 to 0.13. Support for government efforts to reduce the gap

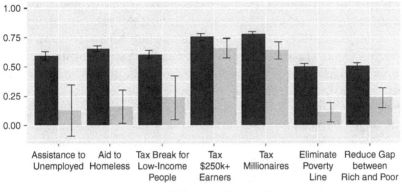

FIGURE 4.4 Simulating support for social welfare policies in the absence of sympathy for the poor, resentment of the rich
Black bars indicate the respondents' average level of support for each policy, transformed on a 0 to 1 scale, where 0 is the lowest and 1 the highest level of support. Gray bars represent the respondents' average level of simulated support for each policy when sympathy for the poor and resentment of the rich are set at the lowest possible value, based on regression analyses presented in the Appendix (4a, 4b, and 4c).

between the rich and poor, meanwhile, would be halved, declining from 0.50 to 0.24. Other policy changes are of similar magnitudes, with two exceptions: for taxes on those who make more than $250,000 per year and taxes on millionaires, support does not drop as precipitously.[51] Still, the balance of the findings indicates that support for a wide range of downwardly redistributive policies would decline substantially if sympathy for the poor and resentment of the rich were to disappear. Sympathy for the poor and resentment of the rich help explain why Americans support downward redistribution.

ALTERNATIVE EXPLANATIONS

I have presented a wide range of findings indicating the powerful effects of sympathy for the poor and resentment of the rich on support for downwardly redistributive programs. Notably, the power of sympathy for the poor and resentment of the rich is sustained even after taking standard explanations of policy opinion into account. One such explanation is self-interest: I have therefore presented models in which typical demographic indicators of self-interest, such as socioeconomic status, are included as covariates. Furthermore, I have moved beyond this standard approach, accounting for perceptions of economic mobility (CCES 2014 Module) and class identity (YouGov 2013 Study). Finally, in supplemental analyses I have excluded those who identify as poor and/or those who identify as rich, or break out the analyses by income group. In no case does the relationship between attitudes toward class groups and policy opinion meaningfully change.

Partisan commitments and ideological principles constitute another potential alternative explanation for associations between class group attitudes and public opinion. Up to this point I have presented models controlling for partisan identification, ideological identification, egalitarianism, humanitarianism, beliefs about the desirability of income inequality, and attributions for economic success. Following up on this approach, in additional supplementary analyses I also break out the results by partisanship (Democrat, Independent, Republican) or ideology (liberals, moderates, conservatives), and again the results are not sensitive to this decision.

Sympathy for the poor and resentment of the rich, then, have substantial associations with opinion about a wide range of policies, even after taking wide range of potential alternative explanations into account. Indeed, the models presented here may be more extensive than is ideal, overcontrolling by including covariates that are shaped by attitudes toward class groups. For example, beliefs about the desirability of income inequality may depend on one's views of the class groups most directly affected by inequality. This potential for "posttreatment bias," however, does not affect the overall conclusions put forward in this chapter. I have conducted additional analyses that exclude a single covariate, a set of covariates, or all covariates; the associations between class group attitudes and policy opinion typically increase in these more parsimonious models.

Indeed, the associations between sympathy for the poor, resentment of the rich, and policy opinion presented here are so strong, and so consistent, that one might be tempted to wonder whether the measures of attitudes toward class groups developed here in fact tap into some broader orientation related to taxation and spending. One argument against such a conjecture is that analyses presented later in this book show that associations between class group attitudes and opinion are attenuated or absent when respondents lack information about the consequences of proposed policies for class groups. In addition, elite-driven issue framing can attenuate the impact of class group attitudes on policy opinion

(Chapter 7). Furthermore, in supplementary analyses I also find that sympathy for the poor and resentment of the rich are *not* associated with opinion about economic policies that are not clearly relevant to class groups in the United States, such as government spending on science, government spending on the Food and Drug Administration, and others (2013 ANES Recontact Survey). The effects of sympathy for the poor and resentment of the rich, then, are powerful and wide-ranging, but they have limits. They do not extend to policies unrelated to class groups, nor do they extend to policies that are related to class groups in ways that are hidden from the American public.

Originally, I thought that the influence of attitudes toward class groups would be curbed further by the principle of limited government.[52] After all, it is perfectly possible to believe that the poor have less than they deserve without also believing that government efforts would be effective in improving the lot of the poor or without also believing that aiding the poor falls within the scope of legitimate government duties. For example, one respondent to the 1987 ANES says in an open-ended follow-up to the government services question that on one hand, "we have lots of poor people," but on the other, "government gets too involved in things they shouldn't be involved in." This respondent would likely agree with another respondent that "Some of the churches are feeding the poor; I think it's more of people and churches who should do it rather than have the government have the whole load." I expected, therefore, that the effects of class group attitudes would be strongest among those open to large government programs. But the results of analyses testing this hypothesis yielded inconsistent effects. The impact of class group attitudes on opinion about redistributive policy may not be conditioned by the value of limited government.

CONCLUSION

I have argued that political scientists have yet to provide a compelling account of support for downward redistribution in the United States.[53] To be sure, social scientists have conducted valuable analyses of the determinants of public attitudes about economic inequality and government-led downward redistribution.[54] However, this line of research has been more productive at explaining *opposition* to down- wardly redistributive policies than *support* for such policies, even though the latter is much more common.

Therefore, I have presented a powerful explanation for the long-standing puzzle of widespread public support for downward redistribution. When it is clear how a policy will benefit (or hurt) the poor or the rich, sympathy for the poor and resentment of the rich bolster support for downward redistribution. But in other cases, the public is ignorant about the distributive consequences about the policy under consideration. What happens in these cases? The next chapter investigates this question.

5

The Role of Political Knowledge

We have now seen that in many cases, sympathy for the poor and resentment of the rich powerfully influence how Americans think about policy. The findings in the previous chapter are especially important because they help us resolve a central puzzle in the study of public opinion: why so much of the public so often supports downwardly redistributive policies.

However, one limitation of the analyses presented so far is that many of the survey questions that have been analyzed up to this point make the connection between the policy and the affected class group explicit. What happens when this connection is not as clear? After all, in many cases political elites discuss policies without doing so in terms of how they affect class groups. I argue that in these cases, only politically knowledgeable individuals should understand the distributive consequences of the policies under consideration – and, therefore, only these individuals will be able to bring their attitudes toward class groups to bear on their opinions about these policies.

In this chapter's initial test of this argument, I analyze opinion about four additional policies: the provision of government services (as a general matter), the Affordable Care Act, government spending on education, and government actions to discourage corporate campaign contributions. I show first that sympathy for the poor and resentment of the rich are associated with opinion about these policies – but the associations are weaker than the associations reported in the previous chapter. Second, and as expected, these associations between attitudes toward class groups and policy opinion are driven by those respondents high in political knowledge. In the absence of clear cues about the relationships between policies and class groups, only sophisticated citizens are able to make the connections for themselves.

Next, I analyze two important exceptions to the long-standing pattern of public support for downward redistribution discussed in the previous chapter. These exceptions are the unpopular federal estate tax (which only taxes the rich) and the popular home mortgage interest tax deduction (which disproportionately transfers resources to the rich). While attitudes toward these two policies are well worth explaining in their own right, I am primarily concerned with the estate tax and the home mortgage interest deduction (HMID) as additional test cases of the proposition that the impact of attitudes toward class groups on policy opinion hinges on political knowledge. Indeed, the findings suggest that when it comes to the estate tax and the HMID, ignorance about who benefits from (and who is hurt by) these policies precludes many Americans from bringing their attitudes toward the poor and the rich to bear on their political judgments.

Taken together with the results from the previous chapter, these findings explain not only *why* but also *when* the public supports downwardly redistributive policies. When the class implications of public policy are spelled out for ordinary Americans, they bring sympathy for the poor and resentment to bear on their political preferences, leading many individuals to support downwardly redistributive policies. But in key instances in which the class implications of policy are unclear, political ignorance inhibits the activation of attitudes toward class groups, and as a result public support for downward redistribution is lower than it would otherwise be.

THE ROLE OF POLITICAL KNOWLEDGE

The analyses conducted so far have examined "most likely" test cases of the proposition that sympathy for the poor and resentment of the rich bolster public support for downwardly redistributive policies. Survey questions that spell out class consequences of public policy satisfy a critical condition for the influence of group attitudes on public opinion: as Phil Converse explains, "the actor *himself* must perceive some meaningful link between membership in a particular group and preference for a particular party or policy alternative."[1] Group attitudes are most likely to be associated with responses to survey questions about policy opinion when the link "is made explicit by the very nature of the situation," as they have been in the survey questions analyzed as dependent variables so far. To be sure, such survey questions are perfectly appropriate, as they reflect many real-world policy debates. For example, on November 5, 2014, voters in four states, Alaska, Arkansas, Nebraska, and South Dakota, passed legislation raising the minimum wage. It is likely that as in the survey questions asked here, voters perceived the minimum wage to benefit the poor, since the policy explicitly singles out those at the bottom of the economic distribution as beneficiaries. The analyses conducted up to this point, then, reflect an important subcategory of real-world political activity.

But when the link between class groups and policy opinions is less explicit, political knowledge plays a critical moderating role. Converse argues that the following condition is necessary for group attitudes to shape an individual's evaluation of a policy:

[T]he individual must be endowed with some cognitions of the group as an entity and with some interstitial "linking" information indicating why a given party or policy is relevant to the group. Neither of these forms of information can be taken for granted, and our key proposition is that, as the general bulk of political information declines, the probability increases that some key pieces of information relevant to this group-politics equation will not show up.[2]

Following this logic, the argument advanced here is that when the policy under consideration does not explicitly invoke class considerations, only highly knowledgeable respondents will be able to bring their class attitudes to bear on their policy views, since only they follow politics enough to observe linkages between class groups and policy.

INITIAL TEST CASES

I now begin to assess this argument empirically, examining whether sympathy for the poor and resentment of the rich are associated with public support for four additional policies: government increasing services (instead of reducing spending), the Affordable Care Act, government increasing spending on education, and government discouraging corporate campaign contributions. Critically, in none of these cases is a class group explicitly singled out as a beneficiary or victim of the policy.

Yet each of these policies might be perceived to have redistributive consequences for class groups, at least among those who follow politics on a regular basis. In support of the expectation, consider the following responses to open-ended questions on the 1987 ANES Pilot Study. After being asked whether they favored government increasing services, some respondents were asked to "tell me what ideas came to mind as you were answering that question."[3] Consider the following responses: "Just because people are poor, doesn't mean that they shouldn't get this kind of help;" "They should spend more on helping the poor;" "For the poor people, the poverty, so many people are unemployed, and a lot of jobs the pay is small and I don't know how they can support their families." For these respondents, it appears, attitudes toward the poor influence their thinking about increasing government spending in order to expand services – even though no class groups were explicitly mentioned in the survey question.

Consistent with these open-ended responses, the regression models of the 2013 ANES Recontact Survey presented in Table 5.1 indicate that class group attitudes are associated with opinions of each of the four economic policies examined here. Notably, these associations are not as large in magnitude as the associations in the analyses conducted previously; again, this is consistent with expectations, given that class groups are not explicitly mentioned in the policy questions. Still, sympathy for the poor is positively, and meaningfully, associated with support for government services and support for government spending on education. Sympathy for the poor is not associated with support for the Affordable Care Act, possibly because partisan and ideological associations with this controversial policy crowded it out, as suggested by the fact that the coefficients on partisan and ideological identification are largest in this model (although see the results below that are broken out by political knowledge).

We also see that support for the government limiting corporate campaign contributions is bound up with resentment of the rich (but, as expected, not with sympathy for the poor). Indeed, the coefficient on resentment of the rich is the largest coefficient in the model. Resentment of the rich is also associated with support for increased government services and increased government spending on education. This result was not expected, but it is consistent with results presented above as well as with additional open-ended responses from the 1987 ANES. One respondent who supports increased spending on government services complains that "Poor are getting poor and rich are getting richer," while another supporter of increased spending argues that "the super rich [and others] ... have taken control of so many aspects of the economy." For these respondents, government spending is necessary not just to help the poor in an absolute sense but also in a relative sense: the poor deserve to have more in part because the rich have so much.

TABLE 5.1 *Class Group Attitudes Predict A Wide Range of Policy Opinions (2013 ANES Recontact Survey)*

	Govt. Services	Affordable Care Act	Govt. Spending on Education	Limit Corporate Contributions
Sympathy for the Poor	0.10**	0.01	0.08*	−0.03
	(0.04)	(0.05)	(0.04)	(0.07)
Resentment of the Rich	0.09**	0.03	0.10*	0.19***
	(0.04)	(0.06)	(0.05)	(0.07)
Inc. Ineq. Is Bad	−0.05	0.05	0.00	0.14***
	(0.03)	(0.03)	(0.03)	(0.04)
Prejudice against Blacks	−0.05	−0.04	0.07*	0.03
	(0.03)	(0.04)	(0.04)	(0.06)
Party ID (Rep.)	−0.10***	−0.29***	0.02	−0.05
	(0.04)	(0.04)	(0.04)	(0.05)
Ideo. Self-ID (Cons.)	−0.12**	−0.27***	−0.20***	−0.13*
	(0.05)	(0.06)	(0.06)	(0.07)
Egalitarianism	0.28***	0.28***	0.29***	0.03
	(0.04)	(0.06)	(0.06)	(0.08)
Limited Government	−0.16***	−0.20***	−0.07***	0.04
	(0.03)	(0.03)	(0.03)	(0.04)
Age	0.03	−0.00	−0.06*	0.17***
	(0.03)	(0.04)	(0.03)	(0.05)
Education	−0.04	0.11***	0.01	0.12**
	(0.03)	(0.04)	(0.03)	(0.05)
Male	0.00	−0.01	−0.01	−0.05*
	(0.01)	(0.02)	(0.02)	(0.03)
South	0.00	0.02	0.01	0.00
	(0.01)	(0.02)	(0.02)	(0.02)
Income	−0.10***	−0.01	0.07**	0.08*
	(0.03)	(0.04)	(0.03)	(0.05)
Own Home	0.01	−0.01	0.01	−0.02
	(0.02)	(0.03)	(0.02)	(0.03)
Constant	0.51***	0.63***	0.47***	0.48***
	(0.07)	(0.08)	(0.08)	(0.10)
N	1,344	1,425	1,426	1,425
R-squared	0.50	0.54	0.23	0.10

*** $p < 0.001$; ** $p < 0.01$; * $p < 0.05$; cell entries are ordinary least squares regression coefficients (standard errors in parentheses). All variables are coded from 0 to 1. The column headings indicate dependent variables. Analyses weighted for national representativeness.

The finding that class group attitudes are less strongly associated with policy opinions when the survey questions do not explicitly invoke class categories is consistent with the argument that in these cases, only the politically knowledgeable are able to connect their class group attitudes to the policy in question, depressing aggregate associations. In order to test this argument further, I break out the sample by political knowledge in Figure 5.1 (regression coefficients in the appendix). The figure displays the associations between class group attitudes and policy opinion separately for low-knowledge and high-knowledge groups.[4] We see that for those with low levels of political knowledge, the associations between class group attitudes and policy opinion are statistically indistinguishable from zero in all four cases. In sharp contrast, however, we see that for those with high levels of political knowledge, strong associations between class group attitudes and policy opinion are evident. Indeed, in the case of the Affordable Care Act, the null aggregate relationship between sympathy for the poor and policy opinion presented earlier actually masks a relationship among highly knowledgeable respondents.

WHY IS THE ESTATE TAX SO UNPOPULAR?

I now turn to two prominent exceptions to the pattern of public support for downwardly redistributive policies: opinion about the federal estate tax and the home mortgage interest deduction (HMID). I begin with the estate tax, a federal tax on large inheritances.[5] Previous research has shown that this policy is unpopular.[6] I argue that this is because many people are not aware that only the richest Americans pay the costs of the estate tax; they are therefore unable to bring resentment of the rich to bear on their opinions. If the public were better informed, resentment of the rich would become activated, increasing support for the estate tax.

The proposition that Americans are not aware who pays the costs of the estate tax follows existing research. Bartels' analysis of the 2003 NPR/Kaiser Foundation/Kennedy School survey, for example, finds that "two-thirds of the American public apparently failed to recognize the single most important fact about the estate tax: that it is paid only by very wealthy people."[7] That said, my argument that ignorance about the estate tax helps explain its unpopularity directly contradicts some prominent scholarship on the topic. For example, Graetz and Shapiro's comprehensive account of estate tax repeal in 2001 argues that ignorance about the estate tax had little to do with public opinion: "folk wisdom in Washington, which attributes the widespread support for repeal to the

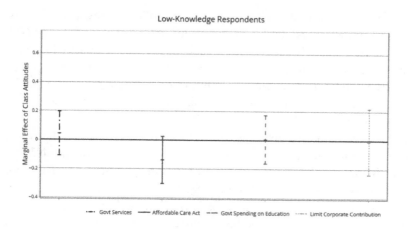

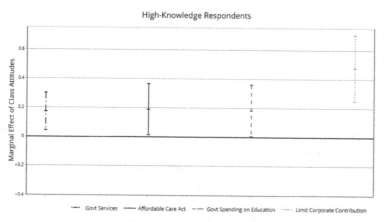

FIGURE 5.1A Associations between class group attitudes and policy opinion are driven by those who score high on political recall questions (2013 ANES Recontact Survey)

For all policy attitude questions, the marginal effect displayed (y-axis) is that of sympathy for the poor except for the question about limiting corporate contributions; in this case the marginal effect of resentment of the rich is displayed. The marginal effects are based on the regression analyses reported in Table 5.1.

gap between belief, rhetoric, and reality, misses the real story"[8] – which, they argue, is the success of conservative groups at framing the estate tax as a moral issue. Graetz and Shapiro do not provide rigorous analysis of survey data in support of their claims; but Bartels does, and he reaches similar conclusions about the irrelevance of political knowledge. Bartels' observational analysis finds that "better-informed people in the 2002 NES survey were actually slightly *more* likely than those who were less well-informed to favor repeal."[9] He concludes that, "even if the entire public somehow became splendidly well-informed about politics and public affairs, the overall distribution of public opinion about estate tax would change rather little."[10]

Yet because Bartels' analysis relies on the 2002 ANES, it is not possible for him to include a measure of knowledge about the estate tax. Neither can his analysis include a direct measure of more general knowledge about politics; as Bartels laments, "Unfortunately, the 2002 NES survey did not include [a] battery of factual questions about politics." He therefore understandably relies on the best available measure, which consists of interviewer assessments of respondents' political information. But serious critiques of the interviewer assessments have emerged, leading some scholars to conclude that they should be significantly modified or abolished entirely.[11]

To build on this important line of scholarship, therefore, I conducted a survey experiment[12] in the 2014 CCES Module. Of the experimental subjects analyzed here, half were randomly assigned to the Ask Condition, which includes a direct measure of knowledge about the estate tax. These respondents were asked, "What percentage of Americans have a large enough estate to be affected by the federal 'estate tax' on inheritances?" The other half, in the Tell Condition, were informed that "only the wealthiest 0.14 percent of Americans, those individuals who have over $5.25 million, have a large enough estate to be affected by the federal 'estate tax' on inheritances." Next, all respondents were asked whether they favor or oppose the estate tax.

This approach improves on previous research by measuring the impact of information on opinion about the estate tax with substantially more precision. It enables an assessment of the impact of ignorance about the estate tax in two complementary ways: correlational, by looking within the Ask Condition for associations between ignorance and opinion about the estate tax, and experimental, by comparing opinion about the tax across the Ask and Tell Conditions.[13]

Beginning with the correlational approach, I look within the Ask Condition, in which no respondents were informed that only the wealthiest respondents are affected by the estate tax. Consistent with the findings of previous research, the tax is unpopular: only 17 percent of respondents support the tax, while 49 percent oppose it (the remainder

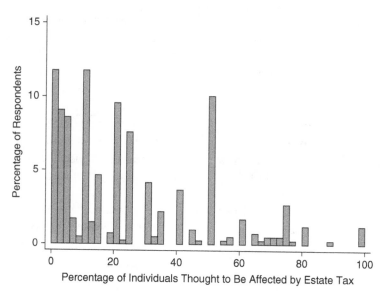

FIGURE 5.2 Widespread ignorance about who is affected by the Federal estate tax (2014 CCES Module)
Respondents are asked what is the percentage of individuals who are wealthy enough to be subject to the federal estate tax. Very few respondents correctly report that less than 1 percent of individuals have to pay this tax.

neither support nor oppose). Also reinforcing previous results is the finding that ignorance about the estate tax is widespread, as shown in Figure 5.2. Less than 13 percent of respondents correctly respond that less than one percent of individuals were eligible for the estate tax.

Next, we see that this more fine-grained measure of knowledge about the estate tax in the 2014 CCES Module allows me to detect some effects that elided some previous research on the topic. Among those respondents who incorrectly respond that more than 1 percent of households are eligible for the tax, only 15 percent support the tax, while 50 percent oppose it (again, the remainder neither support nor oppose). In contrast, among those who respond that only the wealthiest 1 percent (or less than the wealthiest 1 percent) of households are eligible, a narrow plurality support the tax, 36 percent, while 35 percent oppose it. Contrary to some existing claims,[14] those who are aware that few households are eligible for the estate tax are substantially more likely to support it.

Further analyses suggest that the effects of information about the estate tax operate by activating resentment of the rich. Figure 5.3 plots the effects of resentment of the rich on policy opinion (*y*-axis) across different levels of information about the estate tax (*x*-axis). Among those respondents who correctly perceive that a very small percentage of individuals are wealthy enough to be affected by the estate tax (seen on the left side of the *x*-axis), the effects of resentment of the rich on policy opinion are enormous, associated with nearly half the range of the dependent variable. In contrast, among those respondents lacking this knowledge (on the right side of the *x*-axis), the effects of resentment of the rich fade to zero.

These findings are consistent with the explanation of the estate tax's unpopularity advanced here. It appears that knowledge that only the

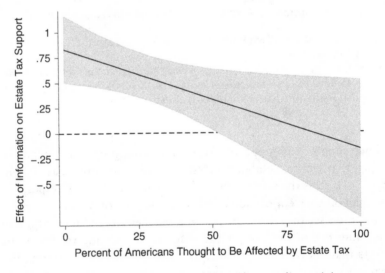

FIGURE 5.3 The effects of resentment of the rich on policy opinion are only evident for those who know that the estate tax does not affect a majority of Americans (2014 CCES Module)

This figure reports the marginal effects of resentment of the rich on public support for the estate tax (y-axis), by the percent of Americans that the respondent perceives to be affected by the estate tax (x-axis). Results are based on an ordinary least-squares regression analysis in which the dependent variable is support for the estate tax and the independent variables are (1) resentment of the rich; (2) the percent of Americans thought to be subjected to the estate tax; (3) the interaction of the two. Only respondents in the control condition ("Ask Condition") are analyzed here.

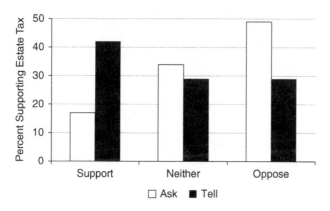

FIGURE 5.4 Information increases support for the estate tax (2014 CCES Module)
This figure plots the percentage of respondents (y-axis), broken out by experimental condition (x-axis), who report that they support the estate tax, oppose the estate tax, or neither support nor oppose the estate tax. Differences across experimental conditions are statistically significant at p < 0.001.

wealthy are affected by the estate tax is necessary for respondents to bring resentment of the rich to bear on their opinions about the tax. But many respondents lack this necessary knowledge – and among these respondents, resentment of the rich lies dormant and the estate tax remains unpopular.[15]

To build on these correlational analyses, I now analyze the results of the experimental approach, comparing those respondents who were informed that only the wealthiest have to pay the estate tax to those respondents who were not informed. Figure 5.4 shows that in the Ask Condition, in which experimental subjects are not told who is affected by the task, only 17 percent of the respondents support the tax, while 49 percent oppose it. But in the Tell Condition, in which subjects are informed that only the wealthiest pay the tax, 42 percent of respondents support the tax, and only 29 percent oppose it. Providing information about those affected by the estate tax profoundly changes the distribution of public opinion about it.

Furthermore, the effects of information on support for the estate tax are driven by those individuals with high levels of resentment of the rich. Figure 5.5 displays predicted values of support for the estate tax (y-axis) by resentment of the rich (x-axis), broken out by experimental condition (regression coefficients in the Appendix). The figure shows that the

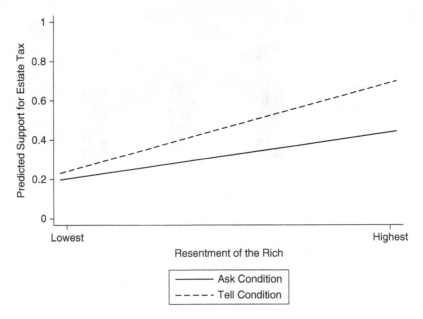

FIGURE 5.5 Informing respondents who is affected by the estate tax activates
resentment of the rich (2014 CCES Module)
The figure plots predicted support for estate tax (y-axis) by resentment of the rich
(x-axis), broken out by experimental condition (dashed and solid lines). Predicted
values are based on regression coefficients in Appendix 5b.

association between resentment of the rich and support for the estate tax is
nearly twice in large in the Tell Condition than in the Ask Condition.
These results suggest that if the public were more informed about the
distributive consequences of the estate tax, the influence of resentment of
the rich on public opinion would grow, and the estate tax would become
more popular as a result.

WHY IS THE HOME MORTGAGE INTEREST DEDUCTION
SO POPULAR?

I now turn to an additional exception to the pattern of American preferences for downward redistribution: the Home Mortgage Interest
Deduction (HMID). While this policy is highly upwardly redistributive,
research suggests that much of the public is unaware of this.[16] Parallel to
the case of the estate tax discussed above, I argue that ignorance depresses
the impact of resentment of the rich on public opinion. That is, if more

people were aware that the benefits of the HMID accrue to those at the top of the economic distribution, resentment of the rich would be activated, eroding support for this upwardly distributive policy.

To assess this proposition, I analyze another experiment embedded in the CCES 2014 Module. In the first wave of the survey, all respondents are asked their opinion about the policy: "Do you favor, oppose, or neither favor nor oppose the Home Mortgage Interest Deduction?" In the second wave of the survey, and in an extension of an experiment designed by Suzanne Mettler and Matt Guardino,[17] half of the respondents are assigned to an Information Condition, in which they are provided information about the distributive consequences of the policy.[18]

Now, here is some information about the federal Home Mortgage Interest Tax Deduction. This policy is a tax benefit for homeowners. It allows them to reduce the amount they pay in income taxes based on the amount they pay in interest on their home mortgage. The people who benefit most from this policy are those who have the highest incomes. In 2005, a large majority of the benefits went to people who lived in households that made $100,000 or more that year.

Respondents in the Information Condition also receive a graphic display of information about the distributive consequences of the policy (Figure 5.6). Respondents assigned to the Control Condition, meanwhile, receive no such information. Finally, all respondents are asked their opinion about the policy once again. The analytic approach enabled by this experimental design is a difference-in-differences that capitalizes on variation both within-subjects and across-subjects: I examine whether there is a difference in respondent opinion across the two waves of the survey that itself differs by information exposure.

We see first that consistent with Mettler's conclusions, informing people that the benefits of the HMID accrue disproportionately to the wealthy has the effect of drastically decreasing support for the policy. This effect is displayed in Figure 5.7. In wave 1, support for the HMID is high, and does not meaningfully vary across the Control Condition and the Information Condition: in the Control Condition, 77 percent of respondents say they support the policy, and in the Information Condition, 72 percent of respondents support the policy. This 5 percentage point difference is statistically indistinguishable from zero, which is as expected, since no respondent received additional information until wave 2. It is in the analysis of wave 2 that we see meaningful differences across conditions: in the Control Condition, 61 percent support the policy, while in the Information Condition, only 38 percent support the policy. This

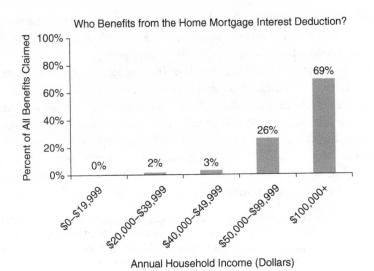

FIGURE 5.6 Design of the Home Mortgage Interest Deduction experiment (2014 CCES Module)
Subjects assigned to the treatment condition ("Information Condition") are asked to look at this graph and are then asked their opinion about the home mortgage interest deduction. Students assigned to the control condition are not shown this graph before being asked their opinion about the home mortgage interest deduction. This design extends the research of Suzanne Mettler and Matt Guardino (Mettler 2011).

statistically significant, 23 percentage point difference crosses the majority threshold of policy support. Furthermore, the change between support for the policy in wave 1 and wave 2 varies substantially across experimental conditions: among those assigned to the Information Condition, support drops by a statistically significant 18 percentage points more than it does among those in the Control Condition. As expected, information about distributive consequences decreases support for the home mortgage interest deduction.

Now we turn to the question of central interest here: whether the information effect observed above is driven by those respondents who resent the rich. The answer can be seen in Figure 5.8; the figure plots the marginal effect of assignment to the Information Condition on policy opinion (y-axis) by resentment of the rich (x-axis; regression coefficients in the Appendix). Among those respondents with high levels of resentment of the rich (right side of the x-axis), assignment to the Information Condition is strongly, and negatively, associated with support for the HMID. But among those with low levels of resentment of the rich (left

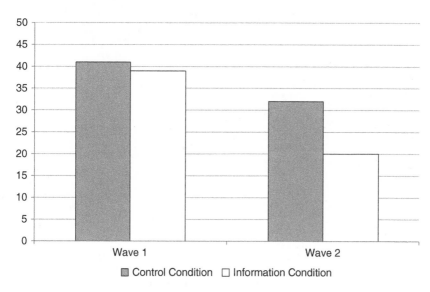

FIGURE 5.7 Information decreases support for the Home Mortgage Interest Deduction (2014 CCES Module)
The figure plots the percentage of respondents who support the Home Mortgage Interest Deduction (y-axis), by survey wave and experimental condition (x-axis).

side of the *x*-axis), assignment to the Information Condition has a null relationship with policy opinion.[19] This finding is consistent with my argument that who resent the rich would hold drastically different opinions about the HMID if they were aware of the extent to which its benefits accrue to the economically well-off; those who do not resent the rich, meanwhile, would remain unaffected. Ignorance suppresses the influence of resentment of the rich once again.

I have also conducted additional studies of the Earned Income Tax Credit and the Retirement Tax Savings Deduction, two additional policies whose distributive consequences are largely hidden from the public; to avoid redundancy I do not present the findings here, but the results follow the same pattern.[20] That is, ignorance about the Earned Income Tax Credit suppresses the impact of sympathy for the poor on opinion about the policy, and ignorance about the Retirement Tax Savings Deduction suppresses the impact of resentment of the rich. The two cases I have presented here are not unique: in key cases in which distributive consequences of policy are unknown, class group attitudes lie dormant, and downward redistribution is less popular than it would otherwise be.

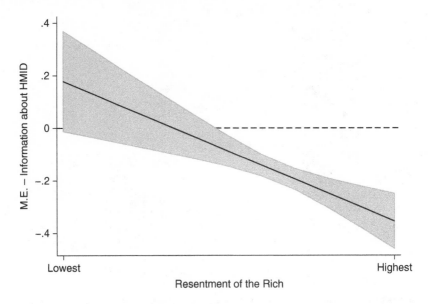

FIGURE 5.8 HMID information only changes opinions among those who resent the rich (2014 CCES Module)
The figure plots the marginal effect of assignment to the Information Condition (in which respondents are informed of the distributional consequences of the Home Mortgage Interest Deduction – see Figure 5.6) on predicted support for the Home Mortgage Interest Deduction (y-axis), by resentment of the rich (x-axis). The figure is based on the regression analysis reported in Appendix 5c.

CONCLUSION

In many cases, sympathy for the poor and resentment of the rich organize public opinion about redistributive policy. In other cases, they do not. I have shown that the power of these attitudes toward class groups on political thinking hinges on information. When it is clear that a policy will either transfer resources to the poorest Americans or increase taxes on the richest Americans, the policy is likely to be popular, because in this case attitudes toward class groups are especially likely to influence public opinion. But when the distributive consequences of a policy are unclear, citizens are not able to connect sympathy for the poor or resentment of the rich to the policy. In these instances, downwardly redistributive policies enjoy less support from the public than they otherwise would.

These findings identify an important condition under which the public supports downwardly redistributive policies. The obvious implication for activists seeking to increase public support for policies that would reduce economic inequality is to talk about class – to discuss which class groups benefit from, and which class groups are victimized by, the public policies under consideration.

The results also shed light on the power of sympathy for the poor and resentment of the rich in contemporary American politics. The previous chapter analyzed important circumstances in which these attitudes toward class groups shape policy opinion. Building on those findings, in this chapter I have revealed important instances in which the potential for these attitudes toward class groups to influence political thinking remains unrealized.

I now turn to the following question: Do the effects of these class group attitudes extend beyond policy opinion to vote choice? If sympathy for the poor and resentment of the rich affect how Americans think about policy, but not how they think about political candidates, we might not expect politicians to respond much to class group attitudes. If, on the other hand, sympathy for the poor and resentment of the rich do influence electoral choice, but government still does little to redistribute wealth downward, this might lead to disturbing conclusions about the quality of representation in the United States. The next chapter, therefore, examines the potential of sympathy of the poor and resentment of the rich to shape candidate evaluations.

6

Effects of Class Group Attitudes on Vote Choice

So far I have shown that sympathy for the poor and resentment of the rich explain majority support for downwardly redistributive policies – but only under predictable conditions. This chapter pushes further, examining whether sympathy for the poor and resentment of the rich also shape evaluations of candidates for public office.

I begin by presenting a survey experiment addressing the relationship between sympathy for the poor and candidate evaluations. The experiment isolates the effect of a fictional candidate's record – specifically, whether he has helped or hurt the poor while in the state legislature – on support for the candidate. The experiment also varies the partisanship of the candidate, in order to assess whether class group attitudes can benefit Republican candidates as well as Democrats.

The chapter then builds on these experimental findings by moving outside the laboratory to examine the role of class group attitudes in three recent presidential elections. First, I return to the open-ended responses to questions about the 2008 presidential candidates from the ANES. This approach again takes individuals on their own terms, assessing whether survey respondents spontaneously bring up their attitudes toward poor people and rich people when discussing what they like and dislike about Obama or McCain. Next, I analyze the role of sympathy for the poor and resentment of the rich in the 2012 presidential election. Analyzing original survey questions administered in the 2013 ANES Recontact Survey, I examine the possibility that attitudes toward class groups bolstered Obama's vote share at the expense of Romney's. Finally, I analyze evaluations of Democratic candidates in the 2016 presidential primary, relying on a diverse national sample to assess the hypothesis that Bernie Sanders' candidacy – but not Hillary Clinton's candidacy – benefited from widespread resentment of the rich.

As will be seen, the analyses of recent elections and the survey experiment reveal that many Americans seek to reward candidates who help the poor and to punish candidates who help the rich in the voting booth. Attitudes toward class groups influence not only which policies Americans support but also which leaders they choose to represent them in public office.

ISOLATING THE EFFECTS OF SYMPATHY FOR THE POOR EXPERIMENTALLY

Experiments have a key advantage: they are well-suited to test hypotheses about causation, as they are designed to isolate effects.[1] The experiment presented here focuses on the role of sympathy for the poor. I seek to determine whether candidates who are perceived to help the poor are preferred to otherwise identical candidates who are perceived to hurt the poor. The experiment is also designed to assess whether sympathy for the poor can be activated, shaping candidate evaluations.

In the survey experiment, respondents from the 2013 YouGov Study were asked to read a description of a fictitious candidate for US Congress named Bob Taylor and then asked their level of support for the candidate. Afterward, respondents answered the questions measuring sympathy for the poor (see Chapter 2).[2]

The logic behind the design of this experiment is straightforward. If majorities of Americans indeed view the poor with sympathy, and bring that view of the poor to bear on their candidate evaluations, a candidate should be more popular when he is portrayed as likely to help the poor. Accordingly, in the experimental component of the survey, I manipulated whether the description of a hypothetical candidate for US Congress indicated that he would be likely to "help" rather than "hurt" the poor, based on his record in the state legislature. The candidate's partisanship was also manipulated: either no partisan cue was provided, the candidate was a Democrat, or the candidate was a Republican. This manipulation of partisanship allows us to observe whether sympathy for the poor affects candidate evaluations even when additional information is provided about the candidate. It also enables me to determine whether sympathy for the poor shapes evaluations about candidates across different partisan backgrounds.

One potential problem with this design is that any effects of the manipulation might reflect respondent reactions to the words "help" and "hurt" rather than respondent attitudes about the poor, since both of these are manipulated simultaneously. Therefore, two placebo conditions were also included that suggest that the candidate might "help" or "hurt" the district as a whole, allowing me to isolate the impact of this help/hurt terminology on candidate evaluations. The experimental conditions and sample text from the stimuli are presented in Figure 6.1, and all of the following analyses are weighted for national representativeness.

Does Aiding the Poor Help or Hurt Candidates for Public Office?

In August of 2011, *The New York Times* editorial board wrote of a "New Resentment of the Poor" among high-profile Republican officials at that time such as Minnesota Congresswoman Michele Bachmann, Texas Governor Rick Perry, and Indiana Senator Dan Coats, all of whom complained that the poorest Americans do not pay federal income tax.[3] Similar to many other media accounts, the article gave the impression that the views of these political elites are widely shared among the public.

This impression is promulgated by academics as well. In Ann Schneider and Helen Ingram's (1993) widely cited model of policymaking in the *American Political Science Review*, for example, the authors claim that the public views the poor negatively, as "lazy and shiftless," and that when a public views a powerless group negatively, politicians will pursue "punishment policies" targeting these groups in order to curry favor with the public.

These common conceptions of public views toward the poor lead to a rival hypothesis: that the candidate will be rewarded in conditions in which he would be likely to decrease aid to the poor. Of course, alternatives are also possible. If Americans are ambivalent about government helping the poor,[4] or indifferent to class considerations when evaluating political candidates, the candidate might be evaluated similarly across the experimental conditions.

I argue, however, that while some Americans may view the poor negatively, the dominant view of the poor is one of sympathy. I also argue that attitudes toward class groups can figure prominently in public evaluations of candidates for public office. The expectation presented here, therefore, is that the public will actually view the candidate more favorably, not less favorably, when he helps the poor.

FIGURE 6.1A *Conditions*

	No Party Cue	Democrat	Republican
Helped poor	X	X	X
Hurt poor	X	X	X
Helped district	X	–	–
Hurt district	X	–	–

The experiment is not fully factorial; those conditions that are included in the survey are marked with an "X."

FIGURE 6.1B *Sample text*

Help Poor/Republican Condition

Would Bob Taylor help the poor in our district?

Bob Taylor is a member of his state's House of Representatives who is planning to run for the United States Congress in 2014. A member of the Republican Party, and a practicing attorney, Taylor describes himself as a family man: he has two daughters.

While in the state legislature, Taylor's initiatives were often designed to increase government aid to the poor, attracting both praise and criticism.

Hurt Poor/Nonpartisan Condition

Would Bob Taylor hurt the poor in our district?

Bob Taylor is a member of his state's House of Representatives who is planning to run for the United States Congress in 2014. A practicing attorney, Taylor describes himself as a family man: he has two daughters.

While in the state legislature, Taylor's initiatives were often designed to decrease government aid to the poor, attracting both praise and criticism.

Help District/Nonpartisan Condition

Would Bob Taylor help our district?

Bob Taylor is a member of his state's House of Representatives who is planning to run for the United States Congress in 2014. A practicing attorney, Taylor describes himself as a family man: he has two daughters.

While in the state legislature, Taylor's initiatives attracted both praise and criticism.

FIGURE 6.1 Experimental design (2013 YouGov Study)

The findings are consistent with this expectation. Figure 6.2, which presents the average level of support for candidate Taylor on a 0 to 1 scale, shows that Taylor is more popular in the experimental conditions in which his record indicates that he would be likely to help the poor. This pattern is evident regardless of whether Taylor is nonpartisan, a Democrat, or a Republican; while effect is larger for the Democratic candidate than for the Republican candidate, the difference-in-differences across these partisan categories is not statistically significant ($p < 0.30$). The magnitude of this effect is substantively meaningful: Taylor enjoys more support when he helps the poor by about 6 to 13 percentage points across the nonpartisan, Democratic, and Republican conditions ($p < 0.05$). The results of the experiment suggest that all else equal, candidates who are perceived to help the poor are more popular than candidates perceived to hurt the poor.

Why Helping the Poor Benefits Candidates for Public Office

I now turn to the question of *why* helping the poor increases the candidate's popularity. My argument is that when it appears that the candidate has helped the poor in the past and is therefore likely to do so in the future, sympathy for the poor becomes activated, increasing public support for

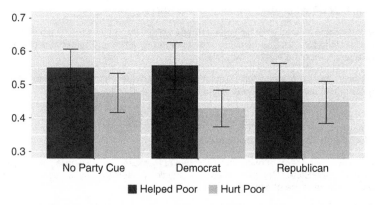

FIGURE 6.2 Effects of candidate's record on mean support for the candidate (2013 YouGov Study)
The figure plots respondents' mean support for the Congressional candidate, transformed onto a 0 to 1 scale, where 0 represents the lowest possible value and 1 represents the highest possible value (y-axis), broken out by experimental condition. Regardless of the candidate's partisan affiliation, respondent's support for the candidate is higher if the candidate's record includes initiatives designed to help the poor than if the candidate's record includes initiatives designed to hurt the poor.

the candidate. If this is correct, it should be those respondents who score high on sympathy for the poor that are driving the experimental effects presented above. Next, therefore, I examine associations between sympathy for the poor and support for candidate Taylor across the different experimental conditions. To do so, I estimate a series of ordinary least-squares regressions in which the dependent variable is support for the candidate, and the key independent variable is the interaction of sympathy for the poor and assignment to experimental condition (see Appendix for regression coefficients). The goal here is to assess whether descriptions of Taylor as likely to help the poor dispro-portionately increase support for Taylor among those high in sympathy for the poor.

Furthermore, in order to address potential alternative explanations, in each of the models I include two additional interactions: one between experimental condition and partisanship, and another between experi-mental condition and the principle of limited government.[5] The reason for this decision is as follows: even if those who are sympathetic to the poor are more likely to support the candidate in conditions in which he would help the poor, this could result from independent inferences respondents make about the candidate. For example, respondents who are sympathetic to the poor are more likely to be liberal, and they might reasonably infer that a candidate who would help the poor is also liberal. This could result in a relationship between sympathy for the poor and candidate support that is spurious. Including the interaction between partisanship and experimental condition (or, in alternative specifications, the interaction between ideology and experimental condition)[6] controls for this possibility.

Similarly, those respondents who oppose big government might also be unlikely to sympathize with the poor. Such respondents might also oppose the candidate in the condition in which he helps the poor, not because of his position on the poor *per se* but rather because he supports increases in government spending. This too might lead to a spurious relationship between sympathy for the poor and candidate support, so I take that possibility into account in the analysis as well, by controlling for the interaction of support for limited government and assignment to experi-mental condition.

The relationship between sympathy for the poor and candidate support across experimental conditions is plotted in Figure 6.3.[7] The y-axis shows the marginal effect of random assignment to the condition in which candi-date Taylor will help the poor (relative to the condition in which Taylor will hurt the poor) on support for the candidate. The *x*-axis shows sympathy for the poor. This approach allows us to examine the expectation that manipulating the likelihood that Taylor would help the poor has different effects on those who are sympathetic to the poor than on those who are not.

I begin with those experimental conditions in which the candidate is nonpartisan (Figure 6.3a). For those respondents low on sympathy for the poor (the left end of the *x*-axis), the effect of the candidate helping the poor actually appears to be negative (as shown by the negative value on the *y*-axis). That is, among these respondents, a candidate who helps the poor actually attracts less support than an otherwise identical candidate who does not. However, this effect falls short of conventional standards of statistical significance; the 95% confidence interval includes zero. Moreover, very few Americans score this low on the sympathy for the poor scale.

Turning to those who score high on sympathy for the poor (the right end of the *x*-axis), we see that the effect of the candidate helping the poor is positive (as shown by the positive value on the *y*-axis). That is, among these sympathetic respondents, a candidate who helps the poor attracts considerably more support than an otherwise identical candidate who does not. The magnitude of the effect is substantial: among respondents at the high end of the sympathy scale, the candidate is evaluated more favorably by more than twenty percentage points in the condition in which he helps the poor.

Next I turn to the question of whether both Democratic and Republican candidates can benefit from sympathy for the poor. For example, suppose that a Republican candidate were to signal that if elected, his/her actions would benefit the poor. Such a strategy might marshal the powerful force of sympathy for the poor on the Republican candidate's behalf, as I have argued. Alternatively, it might be that the Democrats are perceived to "own" the issue of helping the poor to such an extent that this Republican candidate's strategy would not be effective.[8]

The findings are nearly identical in the conditions in which the candidate is a Democrat (Figure 6.3b) or a Republican (Figure 6.3c). The one difference is that in the condition in which candidate Taylor is a Republican, those low on sympathy for the poor are actually less likely to support him in the condition in which he helps the poor, and this finding is statistically significant. Again, this finding only applies to a small fraction of the population, but it is among these folks that the anti-poor rhetoric of politicians such as Michelle Bachmann is likely to be appealing.

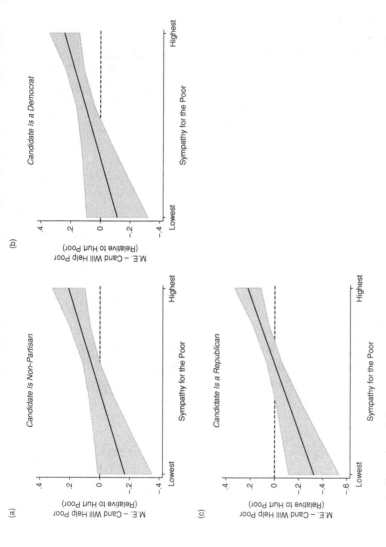

FIGURE 6.3 Marginal effect of candidate's record on support for the candidate, by sympathy for the poor (2013 YouGov Study) *y-axis values indicate the marginal effect of assignment to the "Help Poor" condition (in which respondents read that the candidate's initiatives are likely to help the poor) relative to the "Hurt Poor" condition (in which respondents read that the candidate's initiatives are likely to hurt the poor) on support for the candidate. x-axis values indicate sympathy for the poor. The figures are based on the multivariate regression analysis reported in Appendix 6a.*

This result suggests that prevailing accounts of public opinion as anti-poor are not wholly wrong – but they are mostly wrong.

This tidy pattern of findings reveals robust effects of sympathy for the poor on candidate evaluations. After providing information about the partisanship of the candidate, and after taking into account the possibility that the experimental manipulation differentially affected respondents with different partisan allegiances and beliefs about government, the relationship between sympathy for the poor and candidate support remains strong. These results are consistent with the argument advanced here. All else equal, candidates who help the poor are more popular than candidates who do not, because much of the public views the poor with sympathy.

Potential Alternative Explanations

Is it still possible that respondent partisanship is driving the results, given that Democratic individuals are moderately more likely than Republican individuals to express sympathy for the poor? Up until this point I have taken this possibility into account in two ways: by including the partisanship of candidate Taylor in the provided description of the candidate and by including an interaction between respondent partisanship and experimental condition in the model of support for the candidate. I now take an additional step, examining the results separately for Democratic and Republican respondents (regression coefficients in the Appendix).[9] This approach also allows me to examine a skeptical expectation that the range of the effects is limited: perhaps, for example, those Republicans who sympathize with the poor are open to helping the poor by donating to charity, but they oppose candidates who would increase government aid to the poor.

To the contrary, the results, presented in Figure 6.4, reveal that the effects of sympathy for the poor on candidate support are substantial among both Democratic and Republican experimental subjects. Also notable is that among Republican respondents – but not Democratic respondents – those low on sympathy for the poor actually penalize the candidate for helping the poor. This result suggests once more that for some Americans, the rhetoric of Michelle Bachmann and other Republican elites is compelling. Again, however, this slice of the population is a narrow one: 73 percent of Republican respondents in the 2013 YouGov Study score above the midpoint of the sympathy for the poor scale, and 91 percent of Democrats do the same. All else equal, candidates

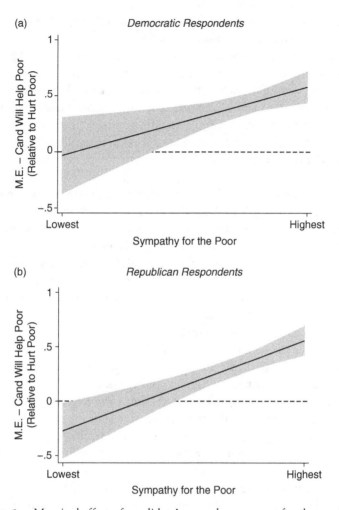

FIGURE 6.4 Marginal effect of candidate's record on support for the candidate, by respondent partisanship (2013 YouGov Study)

y-axis values indicate the marginal effect of assignment to the "Help Poor" condition (in which respondents read that the candidate's initiatives are likely to help the poor) relative to the "Hurt Poor" condition (in which respondents read that the candidate's initiatives are likely to hurt the poor) on support for the candidate. x-axis values indicate sympathy for the poor. The figures are based on the regression analysis reported in Appendix 6b.

from both of the two major parties can successfully appeal to their fellow partisans, on balance, by claiming to help the poor.

An additional possible alternative explanation for the results is that sympathy for the poor is associated with support for candidate Taylor not because the candidate helps the poor in particular but because he is a helpful person. On this account, those who score high on sympathy for the poor are probably more sympathetic people in general. Perhaps, therefore, they are more supportive of Taylor when he is portrayed as helpful in *any way*, not just when he is portrayed as helping the poor specifically.

The experimental conditions in which the candidate is described to be likely to either "help" or "hurt" the district were included with this possibility in mind. The effects of sympathy for the poor across these conditions are presented in Figure 6.5 (regression coefficients in the Appendix). The x-axis is identical to previous figures, in which low values indicate little sympathy for the poor and high values indicate a lot of sympathy for the poor. The y-axis is different from previous figures, however: here it represents the effect of being randomly assigned to the condition in which the candidate helps the district (relative to the condition in which the candidate hurts the district). The pattern of findings observed here is markedly different from the pattern observed in the previous analyses: sympathy for the poor is not associated with support for the candidate when the help/hurt manipulation refers to "the district." This suggests that it is not the candidate's stance toward helping in general, but rather helping the poor in particular, that drives the differences in candidate support observed across the experimental conditions discussed above. Those respondents who score high on sympathy for the poor do not disproportionately support candidates who are portrayed as generally helpful – but they do disproportionately support candidates who are portrayed as particularly helpful to the poor.

The final additional potential alternative explanation considered here is as follows. A subset of respondents might feel compelled by social norms to report that they are sympathetic to the poor (even though they really are not), and that same subset might, for the same reason, report that they would support a candidate who would help the poor (even though they really would not). In other words, it is possible that social desirability pressures bias self-reporting, leading to spurious relationships between sympathy for the poor and support for the candidate in the conditions in which the candidate is portrayed as likely to help the poor. In order to assess this possibility,

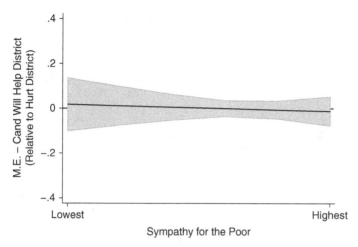

FIGURE 6.5 Marginal effect of candidate helping the district on support for candidate (2013 YouGov Study)
y-axis values indicate the marginal effect of assignment to the "Help District" condition (in which respondents read that the candidate's initiatives are likely to help the district) relative to the "Hurt District" condition (in which respondents read that the candidate's initiatives are likely to hurt the district) on support for the candidate. x-axis values indicate sympathy for the poor. The figures are based on the regression analysis reported in Appendix 6c.

I make use of an impression management scale[10] that identifies people who are strongly concerned with the impression they give off to others.[11] People who are concerned with impression management are relatively unlikely to give survey responses that are inconsistent with social norms; for example, those high on the impression management scale are less likely than those low on the scale to report racial prejudice.[12]

I reexamine the results presented above separately for those high on impression management and those low on impression management. In Figure 6.6, I split the sample at the median of the impression management scale,[13] following the approach of previous research (regression coefficients in the Appendix).[14] I begin by considering respondents high on impression management (Figure 6.6a). While the results are similar to those noted above, it is among these respondents that we should be most skeptical of any relationship between sympathy for the poor and candidate support, as these respondents are most likely to tailor their survey

(a)   *Respondents High on Impression Management*

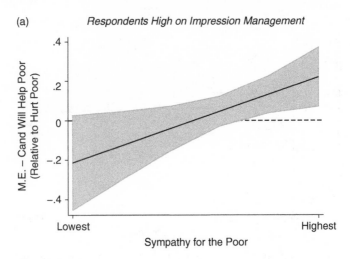

(b)

Respondents Low on Impression Management

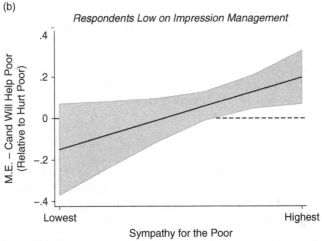

FIGURE 6.6 Marginal effect of candidate's record on support for the candidate, by impression management (2013 YouGov Study)
y-axis values indicate the marginal effect of assignment to the "Help Poor" condition (in which respondents read that the candidate's initiatives are likely to help the poor) relative to the "Hurt Poor" condition (in which respondents read that the candidate's initiatives are likely to help the poor) on support for the candidate. x-axis values indicate sympathy for the poor. The figures are based on the regression analysis reported in Appendix 6d.

responses in order to give off a favorable impression. Therefore, I next turn to respondents who are low on impression management (Figure 6.6b). Once again, a powerful relationship between sympathy for the poor and candidate support is evident. When candidate Taylor helps the poor, he becomes more popular – even among respondents unlikely to tailor their survey responses to conform to social desirability pressures – and this effect is driven by those respondents most sympathetic to the poor.

Discussion of Experimental Results

The findings from the experiment provide strong support for the argument that all else equal, candidates perceived to help the poor are more popular than candidates perceived to hurt the poor, due to widespread sympathy for the poor among the American public. These findings hold across nonpartisan, Democratic, and Republican experimental candidates, and they extend to both Democratic and Republican respondents. Moreover, these results cannot be explained away by either the "help/hurt" terminology employed in the experiment or social desirability pressures. These results suggest that sympathy for the poor can powerfully shape candidate evaluations. Furthermore, both Democratic and Republican candidates have the potential to activate sympathy for the poor to their benefit.

BEYOND THE LABORATORY: ASSESSING EFFECTS OF CLASS GROUP ATTITUDES IN RECENT PRESIDENTIAL ELECTIONS

If the main advantage of experiments is their ability to isolate effects, their main disadvantage is that it is difficult to know whether their findings hold outside the laboratory. In presidential elections, for example, individuals have access to substantially more information about the candidates than was presented to them in the survey experiment described above. It remains to be seen whether attitudes toward class groups influence candidate choice in the presence of the many competing potential considerations invoked by such information sources as campaign advertisements, news coverage, and everyday conversations about the candidates. In this section, therefore, I examine the role of class group attitudes in each of the last three presidential elections: 2008, 2012, and the 2016 Democratic primary. While the approach differs slightly across these elections depending on data availability, it will be seen that the pattern of findings is consistent: in each case, sympathy for the poor and resentment of the rich powerfully shape evaluations of presidential candidates.

McCain versus Obama in 2008: Taking Respondents on Their Own Terms Once Again

There were many potential factors on which voters in the 2008 presidential election could base their decision between the two major-party candidates. The Republican nominee for the 2008 presidential election was Arizona Senator John McCain, an experienced, familiar, elderly, white politician with a record of bipartisanship, a "maverick" reputation, and military experience. On the other side of the aisle was the first ever African American to capture a major-party nomination, the young and relatively inexperienced Democratic Illinois Senator Barack Obama. Obama's campaign centered on a message of "change we can believe in," in the context of remarkably low approval ratings of the current president, Republican George W. Bush, as well as an increasingly unpopular war in Iraq. Voters, then, encountered two dissimilar candidates, and could easily decide between them based on partisanship, race, age, experience, military record, domestic and foreign policy positions, association with the incumbent Bush, and more. Indeed, existing research suggests that voters had many of these considerations in mind when deciding between these two candidates.[15]

Among the many factors guiding voter decisions between McCain and Obama, I argue, were attitudes toward class groups. In the summer of 2008, the economy began to show signs of distress, and by Election Day, unemployment had risen, the stock market had tumbled, housing prices had fallen, industrial production had declined, and credit was drying up. Furthermore, late in the election cycle the economic collapse dominated the news,[16] making it more likely that voters would focus on considerations relevant to the economy, including their attitudes toward class groups. In particular, the increase in the salience of economic troubles likely activated sympathy for the poor, benefiting Obama at the expense of McCain, given the long-standing public belief that the Democratic Party is better than the Republican Party at helping the poor.[17]

The candidates' political rhetoric, combined with media coverage of the campaign, also promised to activate resentment of the rich. News outlets regularly reported that Obama's tax plan included eliminating the Bush tax cuts for those making more than $250,000 per year.[18] As *The New York Times* noted, Obama routinely drove this point home in speeches by "asking members of his audience to raise their hands if they made less than $250,000 a year."[19] John McCain, meanwhile, did himself no favors among those voters who resent the rich by admitting he did not know how many houses he owned, and shortly thereafter claiming that the fundamentals of the economy are strong, for which he was criticized heavily by media outlets and Obama campaign advertisements.[20] Most pointedly, at a rally in Chester, Virginia, Obama said, "I guess if you think being rich is you have to make $5 million a year and you have to think about how many houses you have, then you might think the economy is fundamentally strong."[21] Media analyses of the candidates' policy platforms also likely reinforced the perception that McCain would be more likely than Obama to look out for the interests of the rich, as in the *Wall Street Journal*'s claim that "upper-income taxpayers have the most to gain" from McCain's tax plan.[22]

Because I developed measures of sympathy for the poor and resentment of the rich after the 2008 presidential election took place, I cannot examine associations between these measures and evaluations of the two major-party candidates. However, I can return to the open-ended questions about the two major-party candidates asked in the 2008 ANES, which I previously analyzed in Chapter 1. Respondents were asked "whether there is anything in particular about McCain that might make you want to vote *for* him?" and also "whether there is anything that might make you want to vote *against* him?" The same questions were also asked about Obama.

We can get a sense of whether the expectation is correct that class group attitudes benefited Obama at the expense of McCain by examining the distribution of these open-ended responses (Figure 6.7). I begin with responses in which the poor are mentioned (Figure 6.7a). The pattern is clear: respondents are substantially more likely to invoke the poor when talking about what they dislike about McCain or like about Obama than when talking about what they like about McCain or dislike about Obama. Illustrative criticisms of McCain include: "Does not look out for the poor people," "Doesn't care about the poor," and "He's just like Bush . . . They don't think about the poor." Meanwhile, respondents praise Obama as follows: "Going to help the poor people," "Benefit the poor people," and "Going to make jobs better for the poor man." Recall Schneider and Ingram's claim that negative public views of the poor cause politicians to pursue "punishment policies" targeting the poor in order to win votes.[23] This claim was not based on any survey data, and the available evidence indicates the exact opposite pattern from what these accomplished scholars would predict: respondents criticize McCain for not doing enough to help the poor while praising Obama for looking out for the poor.[24]

Next, we turn to responses in which the rich are mentioned (Figure 6.7b). Here too the pattern is striking. Respondents are considerably more likely to invoke the rich when talking about what they dislike about McCain or like about Obama than when talking about what they like about McCain or dislike about Obama. Respondents often criticize McCain for his personal background, as in the claim that "He's rich," "He's friends with rich people." They criticize McCain for his policy positions as well, that he "goes toward the rich," that he "doesn't agree with making rich people pay higher taxes," and that he has an "attitude that he can solve problems by making the rich richer." Meanwhile, Obama is praised for his policy positions, including "I agree with his taxes on the rich," "Taking money from the rich," and "Taxing the rich." Praise for Obama that invokes the rich also takes the form of criticism for McCain or Republicans more generally: "he just seems like he will actually do something for the people instead of being for the rich people," and "To get Bush out, with these rich people."

In sum, it appears that in the 2008 election, some combination of a number of factors activated class group attitudes, bolstering Obama's vote share at the expense of McCain's: the economic crisis, the long-standing reputations of the two major parties on economic issues, the policy positions of the two candidates, and the dynamics of the electoral campaign. To date, no scholarly accounts of the 2008 election of which I am aware argue that attitudes toward class groups affected voting behavior, and the analysis here is hardly definitive, as it cannot easily address alternative explanations. But it is worth noting that the argument advanced here is shared by McCain's own pollster Bill McInturff, who said that the economic crisis "is a killer . . . it fed into a narrative which is, 'That's it. I've had it. The Republicans and George Bush have helped the rich. This doesn't work.'"[25] More importantly, this argument is supported by ordinary Americans themselves, many of whom told us in their own words what they liked and disliked about Obama and McCain.

Obama versus Romney in 2012

In many ways, the story of the 2012 presidential election is a familiar one. Barack Obama's victory is in no small part attributable to his status as a first-term incumbent with modest income growth in an election year; as

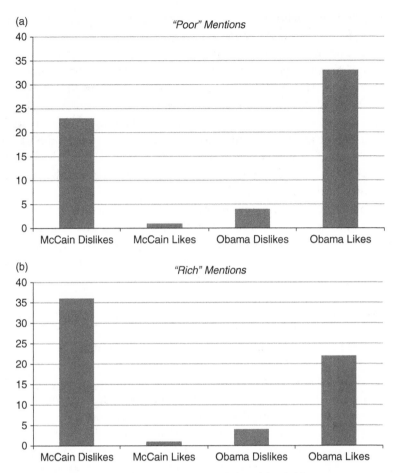

FIGURE 6.7 Open-ended responses to candidate like/dislike questions (2008 ANES)
Survey respondents were asked if there is anything they like or dislike about each of the presidential candidates representing the two major parties. The y-axis values indicate the number of responses including each of these terms. This analysis reveals that mentions of both the poor and the rich are more common among those providing reasons why they dislike McCain or like Obama than among those providing reasons why they like McCain or dislike Obama.

Larry Bartels writes, "any income growth at all is likely to be sufficient for reelection when a party has held the White House for only four years."[26] Furthermore, and as is so often the case, partisanship was central to the 2012 election; the power of allegiances to the two major parties was such that most people who turned out in 2012 knew how they would vote a year before the general election.[27]

In addition to these standard factors, existing scholarship shows that additional factors related to social groups also affected voting decisions. The two candidates were seen to represent two groups that are unpopular among much of the American public: black people and Mormons. Racial prejudice eroded Obama's vote share among whites, on balance, as it previously had in 2008,[28] and anti-Mormonism dampened support for Romney among religious conservatives and political liberals alike.[29] Meanwhile, racial and ethnic minorities, a growing share of the population, voted heavily in favor of Obama.[30]

Existing research, then, tells us much about why the 2012 presidential election unfolded as it did. Yet for the most part, scholars have overlooked the possibility that attitudes toward class groups affected the election.[31] The dynamics of the 2012 campaign provide powerful reasons to suspect that class group attitudes influenced the outcome.

I begin with sympathy for the poor. Romney's statements on the campaign trail made it clear that assistance to the poor was not high on his priority list. Most strikingly, during a CNN interview[32] Romney made it a point to claim that he was "not concerned about the very poor." Although Romney later backtracked somewhat, it is unlikely that the statement was a slip of the tongue; in the same interview, he said, "We will hear from the Democrat Party, the plight of the poor ... You can focus on the very poor, that's not my focus." Romney appeared to be making a strategic decision to contrast himself with Obama, calculating that whichever one of the two was perceived to help the poor more would lose the votes of the "90–95 percent of Americans" with whom Romney professed to be more concerned. Either as a result of these statements or as a result of the enduring reputations of the parties, Americans were considerably more likely in their responses to polls to say that Obama cares about the poor than to say that Romney cares about the poor.[33] I expect, then, that sympathy for the poor was activated in the 2012 presidential campaign, decreasing Romney's vote share.

I also expect that resentment of the rich undermined Romney's electoral prospects. The Obama campaign zeroed in on Romney's personal wealth and sought to define him, as *The New York Times* put it, as "a Wall Street 1 percent type."[34] For example, Democrats highlighted the experiences of workers who had been laid off from companies restructured by Bain Capital on Romney's watch. Romney, meanwhile, did himself no favors by publicly offering to bet Rick Perry $10,000, referring to his wife's "couple of Cadillacs," and mentioning friends who owned NFL and NASCAR teams. Late-night comedians routinely mocked Romney for his associations with the rich: Jay Leno joked that Romney considered million-aires to be an "endangered species," David Letterman quipped that Romney raised $76 million for his campaign when "he found it in an old sport-coat pocket," and John Oliver on *The Daily Show* said, "Everything about Romney tells the tale of a man who just fired your dad." The available survey data suggest that these messages were not lost on the American public.[35] Vavreck and Sides' YouGov survey revealed that 84% of respondents described Romney as caring about the wealthy, while 58% said the same about Obama.[36]

To test the expectation that class group attitudes benefited Obama at the expense of Romney in the 2012 presidential election, I return to the 2013 ANES Recontact Survey. The dependent variable, vote choice in 2012, is dichotomous – representing a vote for either Obama or Romney (all others excluded) – and I therefore conduct a logistic regression analysis. The independent variables of interest are sympathy for the poor and resent-ment of the rich. Control variables include those plausibly associated with both vote choice and class group attitudes: partisanship, ideology, beliefs about the desirability of income inequality, racial attitudes, and demo-graphics (regression coefficients in the Appendix). Many of the results of this regression analysis are consistent with previous findings; for example, partisanship shaped the vote more than any other single factor. Republicans were very likely to vote for Romney, and Democrats were very likely to vote for Obama. Ideological self-identification is powerfully associated with vote choice as well: conservatives were more likely than liberals to support Romney over Obama.

What is new in these results is that after taking standard explanations of vote choice into account, attitudes toward class groups matter as well. Sympathy for the poor is positively associated with the likelihood of voting for Obama, and this relationship is statistically significant. Furthermore, the size of the relationship is meaningful, as illustrated by a predicted probability plot (Figure 6.8a). Across the range of the sym-pathy for the poor scale, the predicted probability of voting for Obama rather than Romney rises from 0.46 to 0.56. Respondents high on sym-pathy for the poor were more likely than respondents low on sympathy for the poor to vote for Obama, by 10 percentage points.

Resentment of the rich is also positively associated with the likelihood of voting for Obama. The size of this relationship is again displayed in a predicted probability plot (Figure 6.8b). At the low end of the

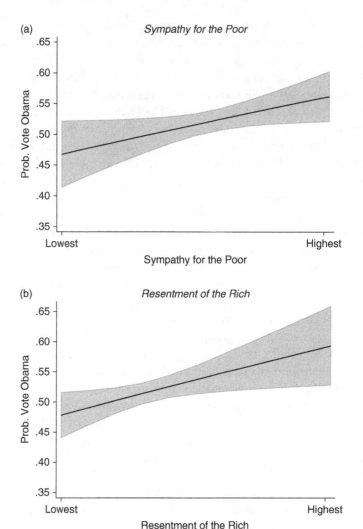

FIGURE 6.8 Class group attitudes benefited Obama in the 2012 presidential election (2013 ANES Recontact Survey)
The y-axis indicates predicted probabilities of voting for Obama (relative to Romney; all others excluded), and the x-axis indicates attitudes toward class groups. The figures are based on regression analyses reported in Appendix 6e.

resentment of the rich scale, the predicted probability of voting for Obama rather than Romney is 0.48, and at the high end of the scale, the probability of voting for Obama is 0.59. Resentment of the rich is thus associated with an increase in the probability of voting for Obama of

11 percentage points. Critically, the relationships between these class group attitudes and vote choice persist across a number of alternative specifications, such as models that include core values (e.g., egalitarianism, limited government) and models that include retrospective and prospective evaluations of the economy. Indeed, by controlling for partisanship and ideology, these results may actually underestimate the effect of class group attitudes on the election. That is, many Americans may identify as Democrats or as liberals precisely because they believe these partisan and ideological groups to be more likely to assist the poor and take from the rich.

In sum, and as expected, sympathy for the poor and resentment of the rich emerged as potent forces in the 2012 election. Faced with a choice between Barack Obama and Mitt Romney, voters were swayed by the usual and familiar play of factors – party identification, ideology, and racial prejudice, among others – but also by one unfamiliar factor: class group attitudes. The effects of attitudes toward the poor and the rich were significant, substantial, and robust. Obama's reelection in 2012 was attributable in part to the fact that many voters believe that the poor have too little, while the rich have too much.

"The Surprising Story of the Year": Sanders' Deep Run in the 2016 DNC Primary

Just a few weeks after Obama's reelection in 2012, media accounts began to proclaim Hillary Clinton as the Democratic nominee for the 2016 presidential election. *The New York Times* described her as "an instant presidential front-runner,"[37] the *Washington Post* claimed that most Americans want her to be a presidential candidate in 2016,[38] and many pundits agreed with Newt Gingrich that it would be "virtually impossible" for Clinton to lose the Democratic nomination if she sought it.

During most of Obama's first term, little happened to change this perception. Some attempted to recruit Elizabeth Warren to mount a challenge to Clinton from the left, but Warren refused. Vice President Joe Biden also considered running but eventually declined. Fringe candidates included former Senator Jim Webb, former Maryland Governor Martin O'Malley, and Harvard law professor Lawrence Lessig. None of them were believed to have strong electoral prospects – but then again, neither was Vermont Senator Bernie Sanders. His bid was described as "a long shot" by *The New York Times*,[39] and *The American Prospect* noted that he was "pegged as a fringe candidate."[40]

But by mid-October of 2015, *The Washington Post* (Wagner 2015a) described Bernie Sanders as "The Surprise Story of the Year."[41] His rally at the Boston Convention and Exhibition Center earlier that month had reportedly attracted a crowd of more than 20,000, more than twice the size of Obama's crowd at the same location in 2008 (Wagner 2015b).[42] During the same week, he reported raising $26 million in the past three months, comparable to Clinton's $28 million. By the beginning of 2016, Sanders had pulled neck-in-neck with Clinton in Iowa, held a considerable lead in New Hampshire, and appeared to be gaining in many of the remaining states. Clinton's national lead in the Democratic primary had apparently melted away.

Eventually, Clinton resurged, in no small part due to her advantages among primary voters from racial and ethnic minority groups.[43] Predictably, Sanders' candidacy was ultimately unsuccessful. The surprise is not that Clinton eventually won the Democratic nomination but that Sanders presented her with such a formidable challenge.

How did Bernie Sanders do it? How did that self-described socialist, that seventy-four-year-old, obscure, former Independent, that "strange bird out of Vermont,"[44] make such a deep run at the Democratic nomination? My answer to this question is that many Americans liked Sanders because he appealed to their resentful attitudes toward rich people. Sanders's campaign was centered on criticisms of the rich: he railed against the "billionaire class," promised to raise taxes on the wealthiest Americans, proposed limiting the ability of bankers to get rich from taxpayer bailouts of their institutions, assailed Hillary Clinton for her Wall Street speaking fees, and argued that a handful of very wealthy people determine who gets elected to public office. His campaign routinely and relentlessly depicted the rich as undeserving of their wealth, to the extent that Clinton (and others) sought to discredit him as a single-issue candidate.

Given the emphasis of his campaign, it may seem straightforward – perhaps overly so – to argue that resentment of the rich contributed to Bernie Sanders' public appeal. It is worth remembering, therefore, that many social scientists believe that Americans are tolerant of, or indifferent to, vast holdings of wealth in the hands of a view. Consider, for example, a 2002 essay in *Daedalus* by Yale political theorist Ian Shapiro: "Why the Poor Don't Soak the Rich." This essay argues that people do not concern themselves with the wealthy.[45] Instead, people in troubled economic circumstances blame others who are close to themselves in the social order for their plight rather than the wealthy.[46] Furthermore, they blame themselves for their circumstances rather than the wealthy and look inward rather than outward for solutions.[47] Alternative possibilities also discussed by the essay include the possibility that the poor and the middle class have unrealistic expectations about their own upward economic mobility and therefore hope to join, rather than soak, the rich, and the possibility that the rich are viewed as deserving of their wealth because capitalist economic markets are perceived to operate fairly as distributors of goods.[48]

None of these claims are based on any public opinion data, but they are claims I have often heard from political scientists, reporters, political pundits, friends, and graduate and undergraduate students. I draw attention to this essay not to single out Professor Shapiro for criticism but to remind readers of just how common it is to assume that negative attitudes toward the rich are scant or nearly nonexistent, even in the absence of supporting evidence. The clear implication of this assumption is that politicians who try to appeal to anti-rich sentiment are unheeded. From this perspective, Bernie Sanders was wasting his breath.

I challenge this account of public thinking about the rich, and Sanders' candidacy presents an opportunity to adjudicate between these two competing perspectives. I expect that resentment of the rich bolstered support for Sanders. To subject this expectation to empirical scrutiny, I examine the results of an original Qualtrics study conducted in March of 2016 on a nationally diverse sample of four hundred adult US citizens. The survey consisted of two waves. In the first wave, respondents answered questions about their attitudes toward the rich, as well as questions measuring control variables. In the second wave, respondents evaluated Democratic candidates Bernie Sanders and Hillary Clinton on a feeling thermometer scale ranging from 0 (coldest) to 100 (highest). I regress warmth toward Sanders and Clinton on resentment of the rich and control variables plausibly related to class group attitudes and candidate evaluations: partisanship, racial stereotypes, and demographics (regression coefficients in the Appendix).

The results reveal that standard factors behave consistent with expectations and existing poll results. For example, Democrats like Sanders and Clinton more than Republicans do. Young people like Sanders more than old people do, while age is not associated with warmth toward Clinton.

Black respondents view Sanders less favorably – and Clinton more favorably – than white respondents.

More important for the purposes of my argument is that resentment of the rich is associated with warmth toward Bernie Sanders. The magnitude of this positive and statistically significant relationship is presented in a predicted values plot in Figure 6.9a. At the low end of the resentment of the rich index, predicted warmth toward Sanders is 44 on the 0–100 scale, while at the high end of the resentment of the rich index, predicted warmth toward Sanders is 57. This relationship is not an artifact of the inclusion of control variables: excluding these variables nearly doubles the estimate of the magnitude of the effect of resentment of the rich on support for Sanders. Furthermore, the association between resentment of the rich and support for Sanders persists when the analysis is limited to Democratic respondents. At the same time, resentment of the rich is not associated with warmth toward Clinton, as Figure 6.9b shows. Contrary to the impression one might receive from the analyses presented earlier – those examining the 2008 and 2012 presidential elections – attitudes toward class groups do not benefit all Democratic candidates at all times. In the 2016 presidential primary, it appears, Sanders activated resentment of the rich while Clinton did not – this helps explain why Sanders did so well.

Until now, political scientists have been poorly equipped to assess the effects of Sanders' unique campaign strategy. Many of us would have joined political pundits in predicting that his anti-rich campaigning would fall on deaf ears. I know this because of reactions I encountered when presenting earlier versions of this research project. In early 2011, my survey analyses began to uncover evidence of widespread beliefs among the American public that rich people have more than they deserve, and I began to present these results to audiences of political scientists. One reaction I received from political scientists (and many others) was that these findings cannot possibly be correct. This skepticism was puzzling to me, so I would often ask why the survey results should be disbelieved. The most common response I received was that if most Americans did believe that rich people have more than they deserve, politicians would use anti-rich rhetoric to get elected. This criticism is reminiscent of the old joke in which a regular person and an economist are walking down the street, and the regular person says "Hey, look, there's a $20 bill!" to which the economist replies, "That's impossible. If it really were a $20 bill, somebody would have picked it up." In this analogy, the $20 bill –

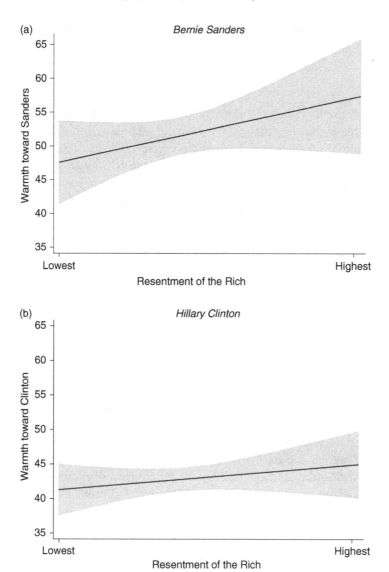

FIGURE 6.9 Resentment of the rich is positively associated with warmth toward Sanders but not warmth toward Clinton (2016 Qualtrics Survey)
The y-axis indicates predicted warmth toward Sanders (6.9a) and Clinton (6.9b); the x-axis indicates resentment of the rich. The figures are based on regression analyses presented in Appendix 6f.

anti-rich sentiment – was out there,[49] but many political scientists were unable to see it until Sanders picked it up.

CONCLUSION

Elections are thought to be the defining feature of democratic countries. They are, at least in theory, the "critical technique for insuring that governmental leaders will be relatively responsive to non-leaders."[50] Accordingly, political scientists often attempt to identify forces that shape voting decisions, and these attempts have often been successful. We know, for example, that voters are motivated to affirm their partisanship[51] and to reward or punish the governing party for its performance in office.[52]

Among the factors with the potential to influence vote choice, I argue, are attitudes toward class groups. Sympathy for the poor and resentment of the rich can motivate voters to support some candidates and oppose others. This chapter has shown that my argument is supported by a plethora of evidence. First, in survey experiments I activated class group attitudes by manipulating candidate legislative records, increasing support for those candidates perceived to assist the poor. Second, open-ended comments made by survey respondents about the 2008 presidential election indicate that some individuals were drawn to Obama because they perceived him to help the poor (and not the rich), and some were repelled by McCain because they perceived him to help the rich (and not the poor). Third, sympathy for the poor and resentment of the rich were associated with support for Obama over Romney in the 2012 presidential election, and fourth, resentment of the rich was also associated with support for Sanders over Clinton in the 2016 Democratic primary.

None of this discussion is intended to imply that sympathy for the poor and resentment of the rich *always* influence vote choice. This chapter has intentionally selected instances in which clear cues were provided to voters about the connections between candidates for public office and class groups. In the next chapter, I will examine a very different case: the 2016 general presidential election. For now it is sufficient to note that in many key instances, both in the laboratory and in recent presidential elections, voters tell us that they believe the poor have too little, while the rich have too much – and that they have these attitudes toward class groups in mind when choosing elected representatives.

These findings also build on the results from previous chapters. Earlier in the book I showed that sympathy for the poor and resentment of the rich are widespread, and that these attitudes explain why downwardly redistributive policies are so popular. Building on those results, this chapter has illustrated the depth of the public's commitment to assisting the poor and taking from the rich. Sympathy for the poor and resentment of the rich help determine not only which policies Americans support but also which public officials Americans choose to represent them.

At the same time, the findings of this chapter open up an important puzzle: Why does government not do more to redistribute wealth downward? If welfare state programs are popular, if sympathy for the poor and resentment of the rich are widespread, and if these class group attitudes influence vote choice, wouldn't it be in politicians' interest to cater to public opinion, redistributing wealth downward in order to win elections? Yet government does much less than it might to assist the poor and to take from the rich. The question of why this is the case will be taken up in the next chapter, which identifies important limitations on the power of sympathy for the poor and resentment of the rich.

7

Why Don't Politicians Listen?

> Political analysis must, then, proceed on two levels simultaneously. It must examine how political actions get some groups the tangible things they want from government and at the same time it must explore what these same actions mean to the mass public and how it is placated or aroused by them.
>
> —*Murray Edelman*[1]

On April 13, 2017, the Pew Research Center released poll results from a nationally representative sample in an article entitled: "Top Frustrations with Tax System: Sense that Corporations, Wealthy Don't Pay Fair Share." In that poll, 60 percent of respondents said that it bothered them "a lot" that "Some wealthy people don't pay their fair share," while only 20 percent said the same about the amount they themselves paid in taxes.

Thirteen days later, the Trump administration introduced its tax reform plan. While the plan was vague for the most part, sketching out broad strokes in its single page of bullet points, it did plan did make one thing clear: it proposed to reduce taxes on the wealthiest Americans, in direct contradiction to the expressed preferences of the mass public.[2]

Why don't the actions of elected officials more closely reflect the wishes of the people they are supposed to represent? I have shown that majorities of Americans believe the poor to have less than they deserve and the rich to have more. Furthermore, their sympathetic orientations toward the poor and resentful orientations toward the rich organize their opinions about policy and influence their voting decisions. Why, then, doesn't government do more to redistribute wealth downward? And why do Americans keep electing officials who do so little to help the poor or take from the rich?

I address these questions in this chapter, considering a range of possible answers. Central among these is that politicians face strong incentives to serve the interests of the wealthy. However, they risk being voted out of office if they go against the wishes of the general public. Many politicians attempt to balance these competing incentives by downplaying the importance of class, emphasizing other considerations instead. This allows politicians to serve the interests of the wealthy while still, in many cases, escaping punishment from the mass public.

In support of this argument, I present empirical evidence of two cases: a policy and a candidate. The first of these cases is the estate tax. As discussed earlier in this book, taxes on millionaires are generally popular, but the estate tax on large inheritances is an exception. As I have shown, part of the reason for the unpopularity of the estate tax is widespread public ignorance of the fact that it only affects rich people. I now argue that another reason for the estate tax's unpopularity is that many Americans think of the policy as a "death tax." I show in a survey experiment that framing the policy as a "death tax" deactivates resentment of the rich, in turn eroding public support for the policy. This is a key example of how emphasizing alternative considerations decreases the salience of class considerations, making downward redistribution less popular than it would otherwise be.

The next case is the election of Donald Trump to the presidency – he who released the plan to decrease taxes on the rich in April of 2017. If Americans harbor so much sympathy for the poor and resentment of the rich, it seems strange that they elected a man whose policy proposals have attempted to transfer wealth from the poor to the rich. As I will show in this chapter, the story for the 2016 presidential election is similar to the story of the estate tax: class attitudes did not have much influence on the public because they were crowded out by other considerations. Clinton missed an opportunity to emphasize class as an area of profound advantage – perhaps because she is not exactly a class warrior herself. Trump, meanwhile, obscured matters by giving contradictory and vague pronouncements, including suggestions that he would actually *increase* taxes on the rich. The election, as a result, became a referendum on a number of issues, including the two major parties, race and ethnicity, religion, gender, and more – but not about the poor and the rich. Unlike in other previous presidential elections, sympathy for the poor and resentment of the rich were not associated with candidate evaluations in 2016.

Political elites, then, seek not only to respond to public opinion but also to shape it. Those elites who do not favor downward redistribution attempt to downplay class considerations when pushing favored policies or when running a campaign. In many cases, this means that government officials do much less than they might to redistribute wealth downward, while still managing to stay in power.

A DEMOCRATIC DISCONNECT

Studies of American democracy often take for granted that what the public wants influences what the government does. Chris Achen and Larry Bartels summarize this view as follows: "Democracy makes people the rulers." As Achen and Bartels (2016) then show, however, this assumption about democracy is inconsistent with many political outcomes in the real world. For my purposes, it is sufficient to note that when it comes to the redistribution of wealth, the influence of the public is limited indeed.[3]

I have shown that many Americans view the poor with sympathy and the rich with resentment. Furthermore, in many cases these class group attitudes exert substantial influence on their policy decisions and on the ballots they cast. In word and in deed, Americans tell us that the poor have less than they deserve while the rich have more – and that government should do something about it.

What, then, does government do? More than it might, certainly: the effects of such programs[4] as the Earned Income Tax Credit and Medicaid should not be underestimated.[5] Neither should the effects of progressive taxation.[6] But the United States government does far less to assist those in poverty than the governments of many other industrialized nations – and, as we have seen, far less than majorities of the American public would prefer.[7] Andrea Campbell notes that one in seven Americans live below the official poverty line, and that the official poverty line is so low that it does not cover many Americans who have low incomes. Furthermore, while the GDP grew by 18 percent between 2000 and 2011, the median income for working-age households actually fell by 12 percent.[8] Fewer people are enrolled in means-tested social programs these days, the benefit levels of these programs are meager, and their experiences with these programs are often stigmatizing and demoralizing.[9]

Meanwhile, wealthy Americans pay substantially less in taxes than they did decades ago. Economists Thomas Piketty and Emmanuel Saez note that, "the top 0.01 percent of earners paid over 70 percent of their income in federal taxes in 1960, while they paid only about 35 percent of their income in 2005."[10] As noted above, Trump's tax plan proposes to reduce taxes on the rich even further. Meanwhile, at the time of writing the GOP-led Congress is proposing to make drastic cuts to Medicaid, reducing the number of poor people covered by health insurance. The winners of this health care proposal? The wealthiest Americans, who would benefit from a drastic tax cut. Even as the public tells government through their responses to polls and through their ballots on Election Day that the poor should have more and the rich should have less, government actions often have the opposite effect.[11] Below I consider a number of possible explanations for this democratic disconnect.

MAYBE IT'S NOBODY'S FAULT

Before blaming government for the widening gap between the haves and have-nots, we would do well to consider whether economic inequality has been increasing globally, not just in the United States. As economists Andrea Brandolini and Timothy Smeeding find, "the overall tendency in the last twenty years has been for an increase in both disposable and market income inequality in the large majority of rich nations."[12] Economists Salvatore Morelli, Timothy Smeeding, and Jeffrey Thompson concur: "Inequality increased (almost) everywhere over the 1970 to 2010 period."[13]

It is possible that national governments have less power to combat these global pressures than we often think. National governments face shared constraints and challenges in light of global trends over the past few decades, including technological changes and mismatches between the supply and demand for skilled workers.[14] In these global economic circumstances, national governments committed to downward redistribution find themselves playing catch-up.

That said, some national governments do more than others to address economic inequality. Indeed, in many countries downward redistribution has increased at about the same pace as inequality.[15] The United States, however, does relatively little to distribute wealth downward.[16] As discussed above, even as pretax income and wealth inequality have increased in the United States, the progressivity of federal taxes has fallen precipitously since the 1960s.[17] The government could also do more to redistribute wealth downward, not just through the welfare state programs that are the focus of this book, but also by shaping labor markets and bargaining, structuring corporate governance, and influencing the operation of financial markets.[18]

The power of government to combat rising inequality is limited, but it is far from negligible. The puzzle remains: Why does the United States not do more to redistribute wealth downward?

MAYBE THE PUBLIC IS UNWILLING TO ACT

One might explain the disconnect between class group attitudes and government action by arguing that sympathy for the poor and resentment of the rich are superficial – genuine attitudes, to be sure, but politically unimportant ones. If, for example, those individuals who are sympathetic to the poor and resentful of the rich were less likely than other Americans to participate in politics, it would be no surprise that their voices often go unheard.

We might expect those individuals who are sympathetic to the poor to be especially unlikely to participate in politics. For the vast majority of Americans who do not consider themselves to be poor, sympathy for the poor is an other-regarding emotion: concern for the welfare of others. And when it comes time to pay the cost of individual political participation, other-regarding emotions such as sympathy for the poor might fade into the background as individual cost-benefit calculations become more salient.

However, the hypothesis that sympathy for the poor depresses political action turns out to be unsustained by the data. Figure 7.1 shows associations between sympathy for the poor and a variety of participatory actions after holding constant related factors: strength of partisan identification, voter registration, church attendance, resentment of the rich, class self-identification, and demographics (drawing from the 2013 YouGov Study, regression coefficients in the Appendix). The results, which I had not anticipated, actually reveal *positive* and statistically significant associations between sympathy for the poor and political participation. After holding other relevant political variables constant, those at the high end of the sympathy for the poor scale were more than twice as likely as those at the low end to help a candidate in the 2012 election through such activities as volunteering, attending rallies, and canvassing on Election Day. They were more than ten times as likely to give money to a political party, and more than eighteen times as likely to give money to a nonpartisan group. Finally, those at the high end of the sympathy for the poor scale were more than seven times as likely as those at the low end to seek information while

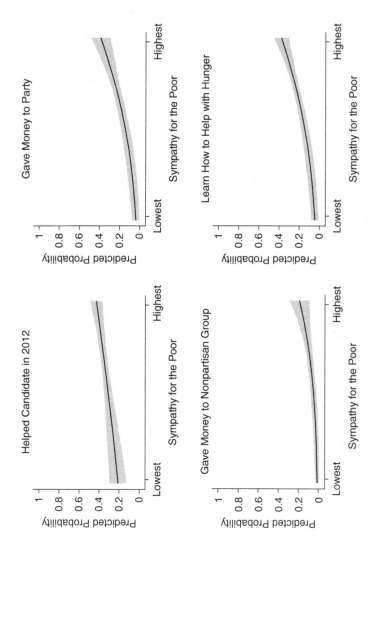

FIGURE 7.1 Positive associations between sympathy for the poor and political participation (2013 YouGov Study)

y-axis values indicate the predicted probability of engaging in the act of political participation named in the figure heading. x-axis values indicate sympathy for the poor. The figures are based on logistic regression analyses reported in Appendix 7a.

taking the survey via a website that provided avenues to help people dealing with hunger.

It also does not appear that resentment of the rich is demobilizing. I estimate the relationship between resentment of the rich and political participation in Figure 7.2, controlling for the same variables as in the previous analysis (regression coefficients in the Appendix). Unlike in the case of sympathy for the poor, there is no positive relationship between resentment of the rich and volunteering, attending rallies, canvassing, or donating money. But there is no negative relationship either. Those who resent the rich are no less likely than those who do not to participate in politics.

If anything, then, those who are sympathetic to the poor are more likely, not less likely, to participate in politics, while resentment of the rich is unrelated to participation patterns. It is also important to remember the findings from the previous chapter showing that sympathy for the poor and resentment of the rich can also influence action in the form of vote choice. Taken together, these findings lead us to reject the claim that class group attitudes are politically unimportant; we need to look elsewhere if we are to understand why the gap between the poor and the rich continues to increase in spite of public attitudes.

MAYBE POLITICIANS JUST DON'T UNDERSTAND

In order for elected officials to respond to public opinion, they must be aware of it. Officials' perceptions of public opinion are the central mechanism posited to link mass opinion to government policy.[19] If the public's attitudes toward class groups are to guide policymaking, therefore, politicians must perceive these attitudes accurately.

While there are currently no data that allow me to examine directly officials' perceptions of class group attitudes among the American public, groundbreaking research by David Broockman and Chris Skovron suggests that politicians systematically perceive the public to be more conservative on economic issues than it actually is.[20] In 2012, the scholars conducted a survey of 1,907 candidates for state legislative office in the United States. The survey asked the candidates to report their perceptions of their constituents' positions on universal health care and federal welfare programs[21] and then compared these perceptions to the authors' own estimates of actual opinion, district and national, on these issues.

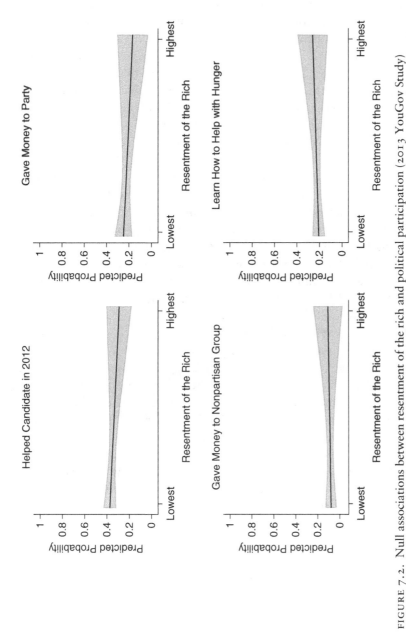

FIGURE 7.2. Null associations between resentment of the rich and political participation (2013 YouGov Study) *y-axis values indicate the predicted probability of engaging in the act of political participation named in the figure heading. x-axis values indicate resentment of the rich. The figures are based on logistic regression analyses reported in Appendix 7a.*

The results indicated that politicians had highly inaccurate perceptions about district opinion. Furthermore, the inaccuracies were systematic, skewed in a conservative direction; politicians underestimated public support for federal welfare programs and universal health care by more than ten percentage points on average. This pattern of misperceptions was evident among both liberal and conservative politicians, although conservative politicians' misperceptions were especially strong. Finally, the authors conducted a follow-up survey in late November of 2012 in order to determine whether politicians learned about public opinion over the course of election campaigns, and they found that politician accuracy did not increase over time. The scholars conclude that, "politicians can maintain strong collective misperceptions of public opinion even when a wealth of public opinion polling is readily available."

Perhaps, then, widespread sympathy for the poor and resentment of the rich coincide with government reluctance to pursue a downwardly redistributive agenda in part because politicians systematically underestimate public support for downwardly redistributive policies. It seems likely, in the context of Broockman and Skovron's findings, that politicians underestimate the extent and consequences of sympathy for the poor and resentment of the rich as well. Certainly they would do so if they listened to many social scientists who have made the same error.

Since representative polls at the state level are not all that common, it may not be all that surprising that state legislators are often ignorant of their constituents' opinions. But national polling about class-related issues is frequent.[22] And data from these polls routinely shows that majorities of Americans support higher taxes on the rich. It seems unlikely that the architects of the Trump tax plan, for example, are unaware of public opinion on this issue, since even a cursory Internet search would reveal a clear picture.[23] Similarly, the GOP proposal to repeal and replace the Affordable Care Act is widely disliked – "the most unpopular piece of major legislation Congress has considered in decades," as Christopher Warshaw and David Broockman observe.[24] It is so unpopular, in fact, that some GOP legislators are refusing to hold town meetings rather than confront their angry constituents.[25] But at the time of this writing, Senate Majority Leader Mitch McConnell and key Republicans in the Senate continue to push ahead.[26] In national politics, politicians' ignorance of public opinion may be part of the story, but it seems unlikely that it is the whole story.

CAUGHT BETWEEN A ROCK AND A SOFT PLACE

In order to get elected and remain in office, politicians need money – to get their campaign off the ground, to sponsor advertisements, to hire staff, and more.[27] Those in search of money would do well to seek out those who have it: the lion's share of political donations comes from multi-millionaires. Politicians trying to get the money they need often find themselves trying to appeal to rich people.

Politicians thus face competing incentives. On one hand, they must be voted in by the public, which prefers increased taxes on the rich. On the other, they also seek support from the rich themselves, who do not always share the preferences of the public. Rich donors are sophisticated and politically attentive. They are not easily deceived, and as might be expected they do not, as a rule, support the downward redistribution of wealth.[28] To run on a platform of government taking money from the rich, therefore, seems unpalatable – all the more so since many, perhaps most, politicians are well-off themselves[29] and since many will join corporate boardrooms after completing their government service.[30]

The public is more easily swayed. Ordinary individuals are politically unsophisticated[31] and inattentive[32] as a rule: rather like "a deaf spectator in the back row," as Walter Lippmann once put it.[33] In general, majorities of the public prefer that government give to the poor and take from the rich, but when it comes to a specific policy or candidate, politicians can find wiggle room. Indeed, in their book *Politicians Don't Pander*, Larry Jacobs and Robert Shapiro challenge what they call "perhaps the most widely accepted presumption about politics—that politicians slavishly follow public opinion."[34] The authors argue that elected officials spend much of their time attempting not to respond to public opinion but to *change* it, so that they can win support for the policies they favor.

One of the main ways elites attempt to shape public opinion is through framing. Any issue can be viewed from a range of perspectives, and policies appear more (or less) desirable from some perspectives than from others. Political elites therefore attempt to reorient public thinking by emphasizing certain considerations at the expense of others when talking about policies or when running campaigns for office.[35]

I argue, then, that politicians are caught between a rock (the rich) and a soft place (the public). The preferences of the rich and the public often run crossways – yet politicians can pacify the public by framing issues in ways that downplay class considerations. As the examples in the next two sections show, this can lead widespread sympathy for the poor and resentment of the rich to coincide with public support for policies and candidates that do little to redistribute wealth downward.

THE CASE OF THE "DEATH TAX" FRAME

In the early 1990s, James L. Martin began a crusade to end the federal estate tax on inheritances. He and others made the "death tax" label central to this effort, to the extent that in the office of Martin's anti-estate tax organization *60 Plus Association*, anyone caught describing the policy without the "death tax" appellation has to pay a one-dollar fine.[36] After pollster Frank Luntz claimed to Republicans in Congress that his poll results indicated that describing the estate tax as a death tax depressed its popularity, anti-estate tax activists increasingly coordinated around this messaging strategy.[37] Now the term "death tax" is a mainstay in the political lexicon, to the extent that even supporters of the tax often describe it using this wording.[38]

I have already discussed one reason why widespread resentment of the rich coincides with widespread opposition to the federal estate tax; many Americans are not aware that the tax is paid by only the affluent (Chapter 5). Now I consider an additional explanation. Perhaps, even though many Americans believe the rich to have more than they deserve, they are less likely to bring this consideration to bear on their opinion about the estate tax when it is described as a "death tax." The logic behind this "death tax" frame is simple; as law professor Edward McCaffrey observes, "To most people, death seems like the wrong time to tax."[39] Describing the policy as a death tax has the potential to elicit fears of mortality, or sympathy for the dying, distracting from other considerations that might lead one to support the policy, such as resentment of the rich.

This possibility is examined through a question wording experiment I conducted in the 2014 CCES Module.[40] Some respondents were randomly selected to the *Estate Tax Condition*. These respondents were asked: Do you favor, oppose, or neither favor nor oppose the federal "estate tax" on inheritances?[41] Others, meanwhile, were randomly assigned to the *Death Tax Condition*. These respondents were asked the exact same question except that the term "estate tax" was replaced with "death tax."[42] The results, presented in Figure 7.3, show that support for the policy is lower when it is described as a "death tax" than when it is

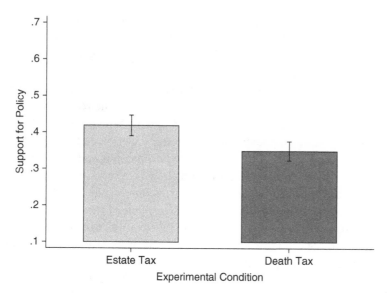

FIGURE 7.3 "Death Tax" frame decreases support for Estate Tax (2014 CCES Module)
The figure plots respondents' mean support for the estate tax, transformed onto a 0–1 scale, where 0 represents the lowest possible value and 1 represents the highest possible value of support (y-axis), broken out by experimental condition (x-axis).

described as an "estate tax." These findings suggest that the death tax frame is effective at depressing support for the policy.[43]

I have suggested not just that the "death tax" frame is effective but also that it succeeds in no small part *because* it crowds out the influence of resentment of the rich on opinion about the policy. When the estate tax is framed as a "death tax," Americans are less likely to think of it specifically as a tax on the wealthy. If this is correct, we should see that the relationship between resentment of the rich and opinion about the policy is weaker in the *Death Tax Condition* than in the *Estate Tax Condition*.

To test this hypothesis, I conduct an ordinary least-squares regression in which support for the federal estate tax is the dependent variable. The independent variable of interest is the interaction between resentment of the rich and assignment to experimental condition; this allows me to assess whether the relationship between resentment of the rich and support for the estate tax differs across the *Death Tax Condition* and the *Estate Tax Condition*. I also include theoretically relevant controls, identical to those in previous models presented in this book: sympathy for the poor, racial prejudice, partisanship, education, region, income, labor force participation, gender, age, and race.

Based on this regression analysis, I calculate the marginal effects of resentment of the rich on policy opinion and present the results in Figure 7.4 (regression coefficients in the Appendix). The figure shows that when the policy is described as an estate tax, the resentment of the rich is associated with opinion about the policy; those who score high on the resentment scale are more likely than those who score low on the scale to support the federal estate tax. This relationship is statistically significant (the confidence interval does not include zero) and large – more than half the scale of policy opinion. However, when the policy is described as a death tax, the relationship between resentment of the rich is negligible and not statistically distinct from zero. These results are as expected; the death tax frame crowds out resentment of the rich, reducing public support for the tax. Furthermore, the relationship between resentment of the rich and public opinion about the estate tax is statistically distinguishable across the experimental conditions, as indicated by a significance test on the coefficient on the interaction term. The impact of resentment of the

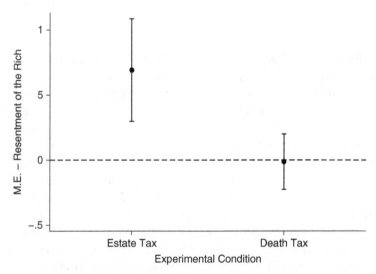

FIGURE 7.4 The Death Tax frame attenuates the relationship between resentment of the rich and opinion about the estate tax
The figure plots the marginal effect of resentment of the rich on predicted support for the estate tax (y-axis), by experimental condition (x-axis). The figure is based on the regression analysis presented in Appendix 7b.

rich on opinion about the estate tax is attenuated when the policy is described as a death tax.

Analyses earlier in this book showed that class group attitudes can be consequential for the beliefs and actions of the mass public; they shape policy opinion and electoral choice. But here we see that class group attitudes are not all-encompassing forces. Political elites can frame issues in ways that evoke alternative considerations, decreasing the salience of class group attitudes and thereby attenuating their influence on public opinion about policy. Due to these strategic actions of political elites, sympathy for the poor and resentment of the rich can coexist with public opposition to downwardly redistributive policy.

THE CASE OF DONALD TRUMP'S VICTORY IN 2016

If sympathy for the poor and resentment of the rich are so widespread in the American public, why did Americans elect Donald Trump? We should not forget that in the 2016 presidential election, the majority of ballots were cast for Hillary Clinton; Trump owes his victory in no small part to the Electoral College. Nonetheless, Trump won many votes – more votes, I argue, than he would have in an election where class considerations were more salient. While my previous analyses demonstrated that class group attitudes often affect voting in presidential elections, here I argue that the 2016 general presidential election was an exception. The public simply lacked clear cues about where the candidates stood with relation to the poor and the rich; in addition, other considerations dominated public thinking about Trump and Clinton, pushing attitudes toward the poor and the rich aside.

The first reason why widespread sympathy for the poor and resentment of the rich coexist with a Trump victory is that many other factors besides class group attitudes influence the voting decisions of Americans. First and foremost, partisanship exerts profound influence over the voting decisions of many Americans. That is, many Americans are either Democrats or Republicans, and most of those who turn out on Election Day vote their partisan affiliation, as scholars have known since the publication of *The American Voter*.[44] Indeed, these days, partisanship may matter even more than it did in the past, as negative sentiments toward the out-party are increasing.[45] In addition to partisanship, the outcomes of presidential elections are largely a function of what political scientists call "the fundamentals," including the level of economic growth,[46] presidential approval, and a tendency for the White House to change parties after two terms.[47] An analysis of the 2016 election by John Sides, Michael Tesler, and Lynn Vavreck concludes that "Fundamental predictors of election outcomes did not clearly favor either side."[48] Indeed, forecasts in early 2016 predicted a toss-up election.[49] It appears that Trump received many votes simply by virtue of being the Republican nominee during a period of modest economic growth and following two terms of Democratic control of the presidency.

Racism and sexism, endemic in the mass public, also tilted the balance toward Trump. Don Kinder and Allison Dale-Riddle[50] argue that the effect of social group attitudes on voting behavior hinges on "the prominence and clarity of cues." That is, in order for voters to bring their attitudes about social groups to bear on their evaluations of candidates, they need information "signaling that the candidates differ substantially in the social groups they favor and oppose." When it comes to race and gender, such information was readily available. The outgoing Democratic incumbent was the first black president in the nation's history, and the Democratic nominee was the first woman ever to capture a major party's nomination. Furthermore, as discussed by Brian Schaffner, Matthew MacWilliams, and Tatishe Nteta, the presidential candidates placed rhetoric about race and gender at the forefront of electoral discourse.[51] Cues about race and gender, then, were prominent and clear, which made it easier for members of the electorate to connect attitudes about race and gender to their evaluations of Trump and Clinton. Indeed, the available evidence suggests that Americans' racial prejudice and xenophobia,[52] as well as their sexism,[53] bolstered Trump's vote share.

What about attitudes toward the poor and the rich? These class group attitudes tend to be a source of Democratic advantage, as shown in Chapters 1 and 6. But we also saw that this Democratic advantage is not inevitable – it depends on clear cues that a Democratic candidate will attempt to help the poor or hurt the rich. Clinton did very little to emphasize class considerations in her campaign.[54] In fact, viewed in comparison to her Democratic primary opponent, Bernie Sanders, she was clearly an economic moderate. Clinton also took heat for delaying the release of transcripts to her speeches to Goldman Sachs, fueling the perception that she is beholden to the interests of the wealthy[55] – and the Clintons, of course, are known for being wealthy themselves.[56] Finally, rather than telling the American public that she hoped to use the power of the presidency to help the poor or take from the rich, Clinton chose to focus most of her messaging on personally attacking Donald Trump.[57]

Trump's unorthodox campaign complicated matters further. He was primarily known for being a wealthy businessman – but the Clinton campaign routinely attacked him on the grounds that he was not that wealthy after all.[58] While Trump's vague, often contradictory pronouncements made his economic policy positions difficult to pin down, many of them appeared not all that different from those of moderate Democrats such as Clinton.[59] Furthermore, his antiestablishment, outsider campaign may have activated populist sentiments and rural resentment.[60] When it came to issues related to class, in some cases Trump actually seemed to stake out progressive economic positions; for example, he suggested on numerous occasions that he would support raising taxes on the rich.[61] He also advocated for job-creation policies for coal miners, construction workers,[62] and members of similar occupational groups, which may have won him votes among working-class whites.[63]

The public, then, did not receive clear messages about where Clinton and Trump stood with respect to the poor and the rich. It should be no surprise, then, that sympathy for the poor and resentment of the rich appear to have had little influence on citizens' evaluations of these candidates. We already saw this was the case for Clinton from analyses presented in the previous chapter. We can now take a closer look at Trump's case by returning to the study examined there. Recall that the survey included two waves; in the first wave, respondents answered questions about their attitudes toward the poor and the rich, as well as questions measuring control variables. In the second wave, respondents evaluated Donald Trump on a feeling thermometer scale ranging from 0 (coldest) to 100 (highest). I regress warmth toward Trump on sympathy for the poor, resentment of the rich, and control variables plausibly related to class group attitudes and candidate evaluations: partisanship, racial stereotypes, and demographics. The results, presented in Figure 7.5 (regression coefficients in the Appendix), reveal no associations between class group attitudes and evaluations of Trump.

In the absence of clear cues about where the candidates stood with respect to the poor and the rich, the public had little to go on. Other forces organized the voting decisions of the American public: partisanship, the economy, and attitudes about race and gender, among others. Sympathy for the poor and resentment of the rich, it seems, were pushed aside.

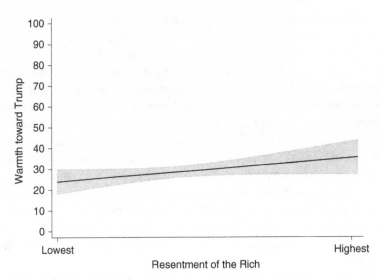

FIGURE 7.5 Null relationship between resentment of the rich and Trump support (2016 Qualtrics survey)
The y-axis indicates predicted warmth toward Trump; the x-axis indicates resentment of the rich. The figures are based on the regression analysis presented in Appendix 7c.

CONCLUSION

Politicians walk a fine line. In order to obtain and hold onto power, they need money from the rich and also votes from the public. But the preferences of the rich and the public can run against each other. rich people want to increase their wealth (or at least hold onto it), while the public, on balance, wants government to take it away.

One of the two masters that politicians serve is more pliable than the other. It is difficult to escape the wrath of rich donors, but there are strategies available to politicians who seek to mollify the public. First, as discussed in Chapter 5, much of the public is ignorant of the distributive consequences of many policies. By hiding who pays the costs and who reaps the benefits of such policies as the Home Mortgage Interest Deduction[64] and the so-called "Bush tax cuts,"[65] politicians can not only get away with failing to increase taxes on the rich but also can actually pass legislation that transfers wealth upwards. Second, the public is susceptible to framing effects. Here we have seen that when the federal estate tax on large inheritances is framed as a "death tax," this causes resentment of the rich to fade to the background, eroding public support for the tax. Critically, public ignorance of politics and framing effects can work in conjunction. For example, opponents of the estate tax seek to confuse and distract at the same time – to confuse by falsely claiming that "small family farms" are subject to the federal estate tax,[66] and to distract by framing the policy as a tax on the dying rather than as a tax on the rich.

As it is with policy, so it is with elections. It can be hard for voters – many of whom are not paying much attention – to tell where candidates stand in relation to the poor and the rich. If clear cues are not present, citizens cannot bring sympathy for the poor and resentment of the rich to bear on their voting decisions. This was the case in 2016. Had Trump made it clear that his policy proposals would distribute wealth away from the poor and toward the rich, he might have lost votes. Perhaps this is why he did not do so.

Caught between a rock and a soft place, politicians search for wiggle room by confusing and distracting the public. It is easier for government to do little about the growing gap between the richest and the rest when the public is kept in the dark.

Conclusion: The Path Behind and the Path Forward

In this final chapter, I review my findings and offer an assessment of the project as a whole. I begin with the questions at the heart of this book: What do Americans think about poor people and rich people? And how do these attitudes toward class groups influence public opinion and political behavior? The bulk of the chapter then explores the implications of the findings. In quick succession, I consider group-centered accounts of public opinion, the role of race and racial prejudice in American politics, public reactions to growing economic inequality, and unequal responsiveness to public preferences in the United States. Finally, I sketch out a path forward for academics and activists concerned with the importance of class to politics in the United States.

SUMMARY OF FINDINGS

I define sympathy for the poor as a durable outgroup attitude, consisting of the belief that poor people have less than they deserve coupled with a feeling of compassion for them. Resentment of the rich is also a durable outgroup attitude, consisting of the belief that rich people have more than they deserve and a feeling of anger toward them. These attitudes toward class groups are independent of standard political variables such as partisanship, ideology, core values, and principles (e.g., egalitarianism and humanitarianism), and demographic characteristics. They are also distinct from factors such as beliefs about economic outcomes: tolerance for economic inequality, attributions for economic success, and perceptions of economic mobility. Finally, they are independent from each other:

it is possible to sympathize with the poor without resenting the rich, and vice versa.

Sympathy for the poor and resentment of the rich are durable. People differ reliably from one another in the degree to which they view the poor with sympathy or the rich with resentment. This difference is likely to be rooted in geographic context, in interpersonal contacts, and in messages received about these class groups early in one's life, as well as fundamental processes of personality formation and genetic inheritance.

While these class group attitudes are not universal, they are pervasive. Majorities of the public believe that poor people have less than they deserve, and majorities also believe that rich people have more than they deserve. The evidence for this is consistent across multiple survey measures and across a variety of nationally representative samples of American citizens.

The impact of these class group attitudes on public opinion and political behavior depends on circumstances: while it is often profound, in other cases it is nonexistent. The connection between class group attitudes and opinion about a policy depends on whether it is clear to the public how the policy would affect the poor and the rich. It also depends on whether the issue is framed in terms that emphasize class considerations or in terms that downplay them.

The same is true for vote choice. In some elections, sympathy for the poor and resentment of the rich are likely to be relevant to candidate evaluations because the candidates have clear class reputations; that is, there is wide agreement about which class groups the candidates stand for (or against). In other elections, such as the 2016 presidential election, such messages are rare and murky. In these latter cases, sympathy for the poor or resentment of the rich are less likely to influence how voters cast their ballots.

While these findings about sympathy for the poor and resentment of the rich are important in their own right, they also enrich our understanding of a number of topics in the social sciences. First, the empirical results reported here help us understand why majorities of Americans support many downwardly redistributive policies. Sympathy for the poor and resentment of the rich often lead much of the public to favor government action to give to those at the bottom of the economic distribution and take from those at the top. Second, the findings yield new insights into voting behavior in the United States. When voters choose officials to represent them in public office, class group attitudes influence their decisions.

Finally, the results help us understand why government continues to do so little to combat economic inequality. While sympathy for the poor and resentment of the rich can powerfully shape policy opinion and voting behavior, the influence of these class group attitudes is not a foregone conclusion. Much of the public pays very little attention to politics and is susceptible to the persuasive effects of political communication. Elites can disrupt the connection between class group attitudes and political preferences by keeping the public confused and in the dark. In turn, this lets public officials off the hook – free to pursue policies that do little to diminish the growing gap between the richest and the rest.

GROUP-CENTERED POLITICS

Philip Converse's famous analysis of belief systems of mass publics is best known for its contention that ideological abstractions are beyond the reach of most citizens.[1] But Converse also presented an alternative account, which is that ordinary people often organize their political thinking around "visible social groupings." Decades later, and thanks in no small part to the scholarship of Don Kinder and his colleagues, we now know that Converse was right.[2] Much of the public forms its judgments about a proposed policy by considering which social groups would benefit – and which groups would suffer – if the policy were to pass. Candidate evaluations are also powerfully influenced by public attitudes toward groups that the candidates appear to stand for and against. The attitudes that people harbor toward a wide variety of groups, including groups related to race, religion, gender, and sexual orientation, lie at the heart of public opinion.

My account of the role of sympathy for the poor and resentment of the rich in American politics owes its greatest debt to this "group-centered"[3] tradition of scholarship on public opinion. Research in this line of inquiry has also found that the impact of group attitudes hinges on two factors. The first is public knowledge about which groups are affected; the public must have this knowledge in order to connect its group attitudes to its opinion about a policy or a candidate.[4] The second is the closeness of fit between group attitudes and the way the issue or election is framed.[5] The findings reported here reinforce this perspective. Class group attitudes carry more or less weight in public opinion depending on the information available to the public and whether political elites' framing of the issue or election emphasizes or downplays class considerations.

A skeptic might ask whether the findings reflect group attitudes at all – or whether, instead, economic self-interest is responsible for the patterns reported here. For example, a survey response that appears to show resentment of the rich might actually result from the desire to maximize one's own financial resources, by using government to take them from the wealthy. To be sure, a self-interested explanation of human behavior would have more difficulty accounting for the finding that many people also support increased government spending to aid poor people even when they are informed that their own taxes would be increased.[6] But it is possible that even what appears to be sympathy for the poor might reflect self-interested considerations; some individuals might express sympathetic-sounding sentiments only because they believe they will become poor someday (or believe themselves to be poor already, or believe their individual fate to be intertwined with the fate of the poor).

Possible, but not likely. First, my models of policy opinion and candidate choice control for a number of measures of self-interest: income, wealth, class group self-identification, and the individual's perceptions of her own economic mobility. Including these variables does little if anything to diminish the effects of sympathy for the poor and resentment of the rich; in any case, the measures of self-interest have little explanatory power. Second, in a series of supplementary tests, I replicate the analyses reported here but exclude those most likely to have skin in the game. These are the poorest respondents (those in the lowest third of the income distribution) in the case of opinion about policies that would transfer resources to the poor; they are the richest respondents (those in the highest third) in the case of opinion about policies that would increase taxes on the rich. When the respondents most likely to be directly affected by the policies are excluded, the results do not meaningfully change. Third, in a final set of ancillary analyses, I have found scant evidence that the effects of class group attitudes on public opinion interact with one's position in the economic distribution.

The failure of self-interest to contribute much to our understanding of the political preferences analyzed in this book might seem surprising. But these findings are consistent with previous research showing slim differences in public opinion across class groups.[7] Indeed, while it is nearly a truism in some quarters that self-interested considerations determine public opinion and political behavior, scholars have been hard-pressed to confirm this claim. As Don Kinder and Lynn Sanders put it, "[t]he presumption is strong, but the evidence is weak ... Public opinion resembles religion more than it does commerce."[8] The empirical results reported here corroborate the contention that group attitudes live at the center of public opinion, while economic self-interest resides at the periphery.

My findings also extend research on outgroup attitudes, which typically falls within a paradigm of prejudice against low-status groups. Scholars in this paradigm examine such topics as antipathy toward blacks,[9] sexism against women,[10] xenophobia,[11] intolerance of Muslims,[12] and homophobia.[13] They do so for good reason: prejudice against low-status outgroups is widespread and consequential. But less often considered is the possibility that negative attitudes toward *high-status* outgroups also organize political preferences. We have seen here that resentment of rich people is pervasive and often influences how the American public evaluates policies and candidates for public office. Other instances of this phenomenon are not well understood. We know much less than we might about blacks or Latinos who resent whites,[14] women with antipathy toward men,[15] or members of the LGBTQ community who dislike straight people.[16] We know less still about the effects of these attitudes on political preferences.

Scholars have also been slow to consider the possibility that Americans react to low-status outgroups not only with prejudice but also with sympathy. Yet sympathy for the poor is an important force shaping the political preferences of the American public. I suggest that social scientists would do well to consider other cases in which sympathy toward low-status outgroups is widespread and consequential. Happily, Jennifer Chudy has conducted pioneering research in this vein, theorizing and testing the role of white sympathy for black people in American politics.[17] When it comes to gender, however, social scientists have done little to build on Pamela Conover's account of sympathy toward women nearly three decades ago.[18] Our theories of intergroup attitudes would do well to wrestle with the questions: How pervasive are sympathetic orientations toward members of low-status groups? Who harbors these sympathetic attitudes, and why? How and when do such attitudes shape political preferences?

An additional contribution of this book to group-centered scholarship is to widen its focus to include class. With a few important exceptions, analyses of policy opinion and candidate choice rarely examine the influence of attitudes toward class groups. While a handful of important studies have explored class group attitudes and their effects, these studies tend to be primarily concerned with other factors. Here, I have built on the insights from existing scholarship, theorizing what class attitudes are and why and when they matter, developing and validating original measures of these attitudes, and testing their effects on political preferences. I hope the findings presented here convince scholars to pay attention to Jennifer Hochschild and Vesla Weaver's observation that "American politics and scholarship are impoverished by paying too little attention to class."[19]

RACE, SOCIAL WELFARE POLICY, AND RACIAL PREJUDICE

In the history of policymaking and political discourse in the United States, race has often been central to questions of deservingness.[20] Some have argued that racial heterogeneity in America stymies efforts to redistribute wealth downward.[21] Others point out that many of those government programs that do aid the poor or the middle class disproportionately privilege whites and often leave blacks behind.[22]

Consider, for example, the Freedmen's Bureau, which was created in 1865 to help free blacks (and, to a lesser extent, white refugees) in the aftermath of the Civil War. Linda Faye Williams shows that the Bureau was politically unpopular, and was often attacked by President Andrew Johnson, among others, as undermining the work ethic of its recipients.[23] Congress appropriated no funds to the Freedmen's Bureau, and it closed in 1872. Williams points out that in contrast, the Civil War veterans' pensions program (which primarily benefited white people) was politically secure; its benefits became more generous over time, and political discourse portrayed its beneficiaries as deserving.[24]

Many New Deal programs also reinforced a racial hierarchy. As Ira Katznelson shows, in order to win the support of key Southern legislators, these programs not only had to provide positive economic reinforcement for many white citizens but also had to restrict opportunities for black people. For example, for employment-based programs such as Social Security, employees in some sectors typically populated by black people – such as agricultural workers and domestic workers – were excluded entirely.[25]

Similarly, the early form of cash welfare, Aid for Dependent Children, almost exclusively benefited white people during the few decades following its inception. Over time, however, black people began to constitute an increasing proportion of welfare recipients. Media coverage of poverty began to disproportionately represent poor people as black – especially when discussing poor people in negative ways.[26] Political elites discussing welfare relied heavily on the image of the "welfare queen," a disparaging image of poor black single mothers, as the scholarship of Ange-Marie

Hancock demonstrates.[27] Welfare benefits were dramatically cut back in 1996 and remain low today.[28]

If race has been central to social policy throughout the history of the United States, it has also been central to public opinion about social policy as well. There is now a broad consensus among social scientists that in many instances, prejudice against blacks exerts a profound influence over the thinking of much of the American public.[29]

I seek no quarrel with this consensus; to the contrary, I have contributed to it. My colleagues and I have joined other scholars in making the case that prejudice against blacks is widespread,[30] durable,[31] and consequential for white opinion about policy.[32] We have also identified conditions under which prejudice influences white vote choice and turnout in elections with black candidates.[33]

But it is worth pointing out that research in this tradition, including my own scholarship, has often focused on instances in which racial prejudice is highly influential – and rightfully so, as there are many such instances and they are well worth studying. Of particular interest to this book, public opinion scholars have found that among whites, prejudice against blacks erodes support for a wide range of downwardly redistributive policies.[34]

Here I identify a case in which the power of prejudice is insufficient to reverse the dominant trend of sympathy for the poor in the American public. Certainly, white people are less sympathetic to the poor than are members of other racial and ethnic groups; furthermore, whites who are prejudiced against blacks are less sympathetic to the poor than whites who are not, perhaps in part because of the over-representation of black people in white perceptions of the poor. Prejudice against blacks, then, should be understood not to reverse the dominant trend of sympathy for the poor among the mass public but rather to place an upper bound upon it. As is so often the case, racial prejudice is an important part of the story; in this instance the story is not only about the potency of prejudice but also its limitations.

ECONOMIC INEQUALITY AND UNEQUAL DEMOCRACY

The past few decades have been characterized by stagnation at the bottom of the economic distribution coupled with rapid growth at the very top.[35] In this context, many have concluded that the American public tends to view the poor unfavorably and the rich favorably. It is understandable that observers might reach this conclusion, given that policy in

a democratic country is often thought to be driven by majoritarian preferences, given recent increases in economic inequality, and given that the
United States government does much less than it might – and less than
governments in many other Western industrialized countries – to redistribute wealth downward.

But we ought not assume that government does what the public wants.
In recent years, a number of studies in political science scholarship have
found that government responsiveness to public preferences is tilted
strongly toward economically better-off citizens. Furthermore, when the
preferences of well-off Americans and the rest of the public diverge, only
the preferences of well-off Americans appear to have consistent associations with government policy.[36] Government responsiveness to public
preferences, it appears, is highly unequal.

That said, scholars have yet to reach a consensus about the implications
of these findings for the health of American democracy. In response to the
claims of the unequal responsiveness researchers, other political scientists
point out that for many policies, the preferences of the well-off and the
preferences of the rest of the public do not differ all that much. Therefore,
these researchers argue, unequal responsiveness does not typically result
in substantially different policy outcomes.[37] Unequal responsiveness
scholars respond in turn by identifying a range of important policies on
which the preferences of well-off Americans differ from the preferences of
the public at large – and on which the preferences of well-off Americans
seem to dominate policymaking.[38]

I reposition this debate over unequal responsiveness by shifting the
focus from class *position* (socioeconomic status) to class *attitudes* (views
of the poor and the rich). Critics of unequal responsiveness scholarship are
correct that in many cases, public preferences are fairly consistent across
class backgrounds.[39] But if Americans are somewhat united across class
boundaries, they are also deeply divided in their attitudes toward class
groups. That is, while majorities of Americans believe the poor to have less
than they deserve and the rich to have more, there is also important
variation in these attitudes. Minorities of Americans appear to share the
Wall Street Journal's view of the poor as "lucky duckies"[40] or the view
that rich people are "job creators"[41] to be admired rather than resented.

Moreover, these divisions in attitudes toward class groups map onto
divisions in policy preferences. That is, those individuals who view the
poor without sympathy and the rich without resentment prefer a much
stingier welfare state, and it is the views of this minority segment of the
population that often carry the day. This book, then, draws attention to

a different form of unequal responsiveness, one tilted toward those few Americans who harbor antipoor and prorich sentiments.

Government reluctance to pursue a downwardly redistributive agenda can coexist with widespread public sympathy for the poor and resentment of the rich due to a number of factors. First, changes in the global economy leave national governments playing catch-up, a difficult proposition in a legislative system marked by numerous veto points. Second, politicians may have made the same error as academics, underestimating the extent of sympathy for the poor and resentment of the rich. Third, even if elected officials correctly perceive public opinion, they may discount majoritarian preferences in favor of the preferences of the superwealthy. In order to do so, political elites do not merely respond to public opinion but also endeavor to shape it – by hiding the distributive consequences of policy and by framing issues to emphasize alternative considerations so that attitudes toward class groups fade into the background.

LEAVING REIGNING MYTHS ABOUT CLASS BEHIND

I began this book by noting reigning myths that dominate our thinking about class. The first of these is that Americans do not think or talk about class very often. Journalist Dwight Garner, for example, claims that, "talking about social class is something that America has failed to do."[42] Another example can be seen in Kathy Cramer's landmark book about rural resentment in Wisconsin and its influence on political thinking. In an aside to her main argument, Cramer writes that, "people do not readily use the terminology of 'class.'"[43] While class terminology was not frequently used in Cramer's conversations with small groups of people in rural Wisconsin, the surveys analyzed here tell a different story. I find that when nationally representative samples of respondents are asked open-ended questions about what they like and dislike about presidential candidates and the two major political parties, they routinely and spontaneously mention poor people and rich people.[44] Furthermore, under predictable circumstances, attitudes toward the poor and the rich are tightly bound up with policy opinion and candidate evaluations. In important instances, class thinking is very much a part of political preferences in America.

Another reigning myth acknowledges that Americans think about class but the myth misinterprets the character of their thinking. Consider, for example, the following quotation from a recent book by journalist Matt Taibbi: "We have a profound hatred of the weak and the poor."[45] This myth is echoed by Andrea Campbell, in her groundbreaking book *Trapped in America's Safety Net*. Campbell argues compellingly that government policies often adopts a skeptical, begrudging, and punitive orientation toward the poor. But as a separate comment, at one point the book claims that government's hostile orientation toward the poor "reflects public attitudes."[46] This contention is based on no public opinion data aside from a personal conversation with a disability activist.

In a review of Campbell's book, Frances Fox Piven criticizes this assertion not for the lack of evidence behind it but because it does not go far enough: Piven argues that "this American antipathy to the poor itself has to be explained," suggesting that institutional practices and political theater are responsible for "American hostility toward the poor."[47] Before embarking on this research program, one might do well to consider the possibility that its animating premise is incorrect; the dominant pattern of American public opinion toward the poor is one of sympathy, not hostility.

The findings presented in this book also undermine what Leslie McCall notes, without endorsement, is a "common assumption that Americans do not resent the rich" among academics, political elites, and pundits.[48] For example, Benjamin Page and Larry Jacobs claim without direct evidence that "Americans do not envy or resent the rich."[49] In fact, substantial proportions of Americans do express resentment of the rich – and this resentment shapes their reactions to policies and candidates for public office.

ROADS NOT TAKEN

My primary focus has been to challenge reigning myths about how the American public thinks about class, and to develop an alternative account that focuses on mass attitudes toward poor people and rich people. This effort, by necessity, has left a number of important areas unexplored. Additional inquiry is required for scholars to reach a better understanding of class attitudes in the United States and their importance to American politics.

One area ripe for exploration is public attitudes toward *subgroups* of the class groups examined here. We might expect that the working poor, or poor children, are subgroups of the poor that are especially likely to be viewed as deserving of government aid.[50] We might also consider subgroups of the rich; debates over Mitt Romney's wealth in the 2012 presidential election are telling in this regard. When Obama told an Ohio crowd "I wasn't born with a silver spoon in my mouth," this was widely interpreted as a criticism of Romney for having inherited his wealth.[51] Romney denied this claim, saying in a private fundraiser that he "inherited nothing ... Everything that Ann and I have we earned the old-fashioned way."[52] These competing claims garnered substantial attention: at issue was not whether Romney was rich, but what kind of rich person he was.[53] Subgroup attitudes are certainly worth examining further, although the results presented here show that class subgroups are rarely mentioned by Americans who are asked what they like and dislike about presidential candidates and political parties. It is attitudes toward superordinate class groups – poor people and rich people *writ* large – that appear to dominate political thinking.

Social scientists could also do more to analyze a wider range of class group attitudes than has been possible here. Perhaps the chief omission of the project presented here has been public attitudes toward class *ingroups*. Researchers might address questions such as: Who identifies as working class, and who identifies as middle class, and why?[54] Which of those individuals who identify as working class or middle class also embrace group consciousness: the belief that one's class group is getting a raw deal and needs to work together in order to further its interests?[55] What are the consequences of these psychological attachments to class groups for mass political thinking, vote choice, and participation? Under what conditions does elite rhetoric include references to the working class and the middle class, and what effects does such rhetoric have on the mass public?

An exploration of the relationship between class attitudes and partisanship might also prove fruitful. The findings reported here appear to uncover a durable Democratic advantage when it comes to perceptions of the poor and the rich. The open-ended responses referenced above reveal that many claim they prefer the Democratic Party (and its candidates) because they perceive it to be more likely than the Republican Party to help the poor and less likely to help the rich.

But this Democratic advantage appears to be contingent rather than inevitable. Recall the findings from the survey experiment in Chapter 6: a candidate whose record indicates that he would help the poor is more popular – especially among those respondents sympathetic to the poor – regardless of whether the candidate is a Democrat, Republican, or nonpartisan. Indeed, it is possible that class attitudes, like racial attitudes, actually affect how people sort themselves into the two major parties.[56]

Finally, I recommend closer attention to the interactions between attitudes about class groups and public tolerance for economic inequality. Extant scholarship sometimes treats these two as interchangeable, but they have different properties. For one thing, it appears that for most people class group attitudes come to mind more readily than attitudes about inequality, as individuals rarely use inequality terminology when discussing what they like and dislike about political entities. For another, some people who express tolerance for income inequality in principle also report that poor people have less than they deserve, or that rich people have more. Class attitudes are also more tightly bound up with support for downwardly redistributive policy than are attitudes about economic inequality.[57] We need to know more about the juxtaposition of these attitudes. Why do class attitudes exert a more powerful influence on political preference formation than beliefs about inequality? Who uses class attitudes rather than (or in addition to) beliefs about economic inequality to make sense of politics, and why?

THE PATH FORWARD FOR ACTIVISTS

Academics are not the only ones who should let go of the myth that Americans hate the poor and love the rich; political activists who seek a more equitable distribution of wealth should do the same. The findings in this book demonstrate that all else equal, revealing that a policy or a candidate is propoor or antirich is likely to increase its appeal – not for all Americans, of course, but on balance. Participants in political efforts to distribute wealth more fairly would do well to view the American public not as an inevitable enemy but as a potential ally.

For an example of how political rhetoric about class can facilitate efforts to mitigate economic inequality, consider the debate over the "fiscal cliff" of January 2013.[58] At that time a group of laws that had been enacted previously were scheduled to take effect simultaneously, increasing taxes for a wide range of citizens and businesses while also cutting spending in a number of government programs. The Congressional Budget Office predicted that this fiscal cliff would lead to a mild recession.[59]

In the midst of this looming crisis, President Obama saw an opportunity to garner public support for his reelection bid. In an interview on July 9, 2012, he vowed to veto any bill that would extend Bush-era tax cuts on the richest Americans, claiming that, "to extend tax breaks for that top 2 percent of wealthiest Americans would cost us $1 trillion over the next decade."[60] Obama repeated this message throughout the summer and the fall of 2012.[61] This was good strategy: his promises to raise taxes on the rich likely won him votes.

Just two days after Obama's reelection victory, the GOP pushed back. On November 8, 2012, GOP House Speaker John Boehner was asked by "World News" anchor Diane Sawyer, "[Obama] campaigned on specific increases in tax rates from 35% to 39%. So, is that on the table right now?" Boehner's response was telling. He did not criticize Obama for "class warfare" or defend the rich as job creators. Instead, he sought to reframe the issue: "Raising taxes on small business people is the wrong prescription given where our economy is." Sawyer followed up, referencing poll results indicating that majorities of Americans supported increased taxes. Boehner again downplayed class, framing the issue as about increased taxes generally and about political infeasibility: "Raising tax rates is unacceptable. And frankly, it couldn't even pass the House. I'm not sure it could pass the Senate. So the votes aren't there."[62] On November 14, Obama responded, emphasizing class considerations once more to argue that his plan to extend tax cuts for all but the wealthiest Americans would eliminate half of the fiscal cliff.[63]

This dynamic continued for the remainder of 2012. President Obama, House Democratic Leader Nancy Pelosi, Senate Majority Leader Harry Reid, and other prominent Democrats coordinated on a simple message: the nation was headed for a fiscal cliff because of Republican unwillingness to increase taxes on the rich.[64] On December 30, Obama went onto political talk shows to make a final pitch: "They say that their biggest priority is making sure that we deal with the deficit in a serious way, but the way they're behaving is that their only priority is making sure that tax breaks for the wealthiest Americans are protected. That seems to be their only overriding, unifying theme."[65] The Democratic talking point appeared to pay off: December polls suggested that voters were substantially more likely to blame Republicans than Democrats for lack of progress toward a fiscal cliff resolution.[66]

It was a close call, but eventually Republicans caved. On January 1, 2013, the American Taxpayer Relief Act of 2012[67] was passed by Congress and signed into law the next day by President Obama. The legislation amounted to a large downward redistribution of wealth. Unemployment benefits were extended, at a cost of about $30 billion, and college tuition credits for poorer families were extended as well. The Earned Income Tax Credit, which transfers resources to working poor people, was expanded. Meanwhile, the federal estate tax rate on large inheritances increased from 35% to 40%, the capital gains rate increased from 15% to 20%, and income taxes on high-income earners[68] increased from 35% to 39.6%. In this instance, it appears that a clear, consistent focus on class considerations mobilized public opinion, changing politician incentives by increasing the rewards to those who supported a bundle of policies that aid the poor and take from the rich.

This success story suggests that activists seeking to decrease economic inequality would do well to make the distributive consequences of policy clear if they want the public to rally to their side. Of course, the public is not the only political actor that matters. Fighting inequality requires a multipronged effort that involves social movements, think tanks, candidates, the media, both major political parties, and more. If activists want the public to be an ally in this struggle, they will do well to place class considerations front and center.

Appendices

APPENDIX TO CHAPTER I

Open-ended Responses to Questions about the Two Major Parties

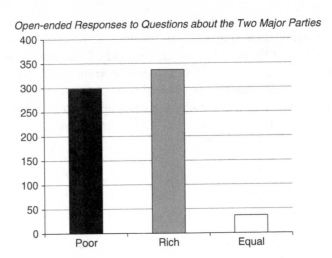

Open-ended Responses to Questions about Presidential Candidates

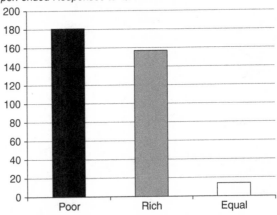

APPENDIX 1A 1992 ANES survey.
y-axis values indicate the number of responses including the relevant term. All of the following qualify as including the term "equal": equality, inequality, equal, unequal, and equivalent.

Open-ended Responses to Questions about the Two Major Parties

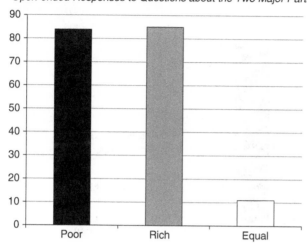

Open-ended Responses to Questions about Presidential Candidates

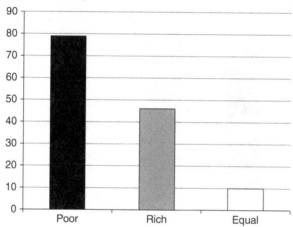

APPENDIX 1B 1996 ANES survey.
y-axis values indicate the number of responses including the relevant term. All of the following qualify as including the term "equal": equality, inequality, equal, unequal, and equivalent.

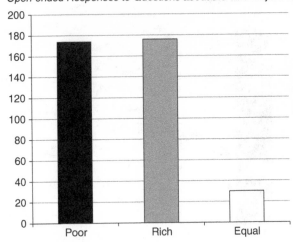

Open-ended Responses to Questions about the Two Major Parties

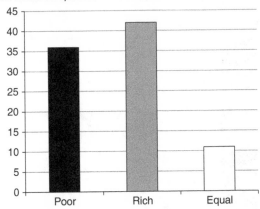

Open-ended Responses to Questions about Presidential Candidates

APPENDIX 1C 2000 ANES survey.
y-axis values indicate the number of responses including the relevant term. All of the following qualify as including the term "equal": equality, inequality, equal, unequal, and equivalent.

APPENDIX TO CHAPTER 4. COEFFICIENT TABLES
CORRESPONDING TO FIGURES 4.1 AND 4.2 (ORGANIZED BY
DATASET)

APPENDIX 4A *2013 YouGov Study*

	Eliminate Poverty Line	Reduce Rich/Poor Gap
Sympathy for the Poor	0.55***	0.30***
	(0.12)	(0.06)
Resentment of the Rich	0.15	0.23***
	(0.13)	(0.07)
Party ID (Rep.)	−0.36***	−0.35***
	(0.09)	(0.04)
Ideology (Cons.)	−0.33***	−0.45***
	(0.10)	(0.06)
Prejudice against Blacks	−0.02	0.18
	(0.15)	(0.11)
Age	−0.05	−0.13**
	(0.11)	(0.05)
Female	0.07	0.03
	(0.05)	(0.02)
Married	0.01	−0.05*
	(0.04)	(0.02)
South	−0.04	−0.04
	(0.04)	(0.02)
Some College	−0.02	−0.06*
	(0.05)	(0.03)
College Grad	−0.08	0.01
	(0.06)	(0.03)
Black	0.06	0.06*
	(0.08)	(0.03)
Latino	0.08	0.03
	(0.06)	(0.05)
Other Race	−0.01	−0.00
	(0.11)	(0.05)
Rich	−0.10	0.08
	(0.10)	(0.11)
Working Class	0.02	0.00
	(0.05)	(0.03)
Poor	0.17**	−0.00
	(0.06)	(0.03)

(continued)

APPENDIX 4A *(continued)*

	Eliminate Poverty Line	Reduce Rich/Poor Gap
Other Class/Ref.	−0.01	−0.00
	(0.11)	(0.05)
Constant	0.43**	0.62***
	(0.16)	(0.09)
N	179	760
R-squared	0.57	0.50

*** $p < 0.001$; ** $p < 0.01$; * $p < 0.05$; cell entries are ordinary least squares regression coefficients (standard errors in parentheses). All variables are coded from 0 to 1. The column headings indicate dependent variables. The sample size is smaller for the analysis of beliefs about whether government should eliminate the poverty line because an embedded experiment was conducted on this question and only the control condition is analyzed here; additional experimental conditions are analyzed in Chapter 7. Analysis weighted for national representativeness.

APPENDIX 4B *2014 CCES Module*

	Assistance to Unemployed	Aid to Poor	Housing for Homeless	Aid to Homeless	Tax Break on Low Incomes
Sympathy for the Poor	0.29**	0.69***	0.40***	0.40***	0.40***
	(0.10)	(0.09)	(0.06)	(0.06)	(0.08)
Resentment of the Rich	0.30*	−0.14	0.09	0.27*	0.09
	(0.15)	(0.13)	(0.05)	(0.10)	(0.12)
Racial Resentment	−0.21**	−0.06	−0.06	−0.09*	−0.14*
	(0.08)	(0.07)	(0.05)	(0.04)	(0.06)
Prejudice against Blacks	−0.01	−0.19	−0.18*	−0.14	−0.04
	(0.13)	(0.12)	(0.08)	(0.09)	(0.12)
Party ID (Rep.)	0.00	−0.21***	−0.04	−0.08*	−0.10*
	(0.07)	(0.06)	(0.04)	(0.04)	(0.05)
Ideology (Cons.)	−0.19**	−0.18**	−0.19***	−0.18***	−0.06
	(0.08)	(0.07)	(0.05)	(0.05)	(0.07)
Humanitarianism	−0.07	−0.03	0.11*	0.06	0.19**
	(0.09)	(0.09)	(0.06)	(0.06)	(0.07)
Egalitarianism	0.25***	0.25***	0.01	0.02	0.08
	(0.06)	(0.07)	(0.04)	(0.04)	(0.05)
Likely to Become Rich	0.04	−0.04	0.12**	0.13**	0.11*
	(0.08)	(0.07)	(0.04)	(0.04)	(0.05)

(continued)

APPENDIX 4B *(continued)*

	Assistance to Unemployed	Aid to Poor	Housing for Homeless	Aid to Homeless	Tax Break on Low Incomes
Likely to Become Poor	0.02	0.01	0.02	0.01	0.04
	(0.07)	(0.07)	(0.04)	(0.04)	(0.06)
Success Result of Work	−0.12***	−0.01	−0.04	−0.03	−0.06*
	(0.04)	(0.04)	(0.02)	(0.03)	(0.03)
Education	−0.20***	−0.10*	−0.07*	−0.12***	−0.08
	(0.06)	(0.05)	(0.04)	(0.04)	(0.05)
South	0.02	−0.02	0.02	0.04	−0.02
	(0.03)	(0.03)	(0.02)	(0.02)	(0.03)
Income	−0.15*	−0.08	−0.19***	−0.18**	−0.16*
	(0.09)	(0.09)	(0.06)	(0.06)	(0.08)
Income – Missing	−0.11*	−0.00	−0.11**	−0.09**	−0.11**
	(0.06)	(0.07)	(0.04)	(0.04)	(0.05)
Unemployed	−0.13*	−0.04	−0.04	−0.02	0.12*
	(0.07)	(0.06)	(0.05)	(0.05)	(0.06)
Male	−0.03	−0.02	−0.05*	−0.00	0.03
	(0.03)	(0.03)	(0.02)	(0.02)	(0.03)
Age	0.03	−0.07	0.04	0.04	−0.07
	(0.07)	(0.07)	(0.05)	(0.05)	(0.06)
Hispanic	−0.01	0.14*	0.03	0.04	0.13*
	(0.11)	(0.06)	(0.04)	(0.04)	(0.06)
Black	0.12*	0.08	0.03	0.07	0.01
	(0.06)	(0.07)	(0.04)	(0.04)	(0.05)
Other Race	−0.06	−0.01	−0.01	−0.03	−0.09*
	(0.07)	(0.06)	(0.03)	(0.04)	(0.05)
Constant	0.73***	0.47***	0.63***	0.62***	0.43***
	(0.13)	(0.14)	(0.09)	(0.09)	(0.12)
N	691	693	689	686	687
R-squared	0.39	0.48	0.43	0.45	0.41

*** $p < 0.001$; ** $p < 0.01$; * $p < 0.05$; cell entries are ordinary least squares regression coefficients (standard errors in parentheses). All variables are coded from 0 to 1. The column headings indicate dependent variables. Analyses weighted for national representativeness.

APPENDIX 4C *2013 ANES Recontact Survey*

	Govt. Aid to Unemployed	Govt. Ensure All Have Jobs	Increase Taxes on $250k+	Increase Taxes on Millionaires
Sympathy for the Poor	0.16***	0.18***	−0.08	0.03
	(0.04)	(0.05)	(0.06)	(0.05)
Resentment of the Rich	0.09*	0.25***	0.37***	0.31***
	(0.05)	(0.05)	(0.06)	(0.05)
Income Inequality Is Bad	−0.03	0.04	0.26***	0.18***
	(0.03)	(0.03)	(0.04)	(0.04)
Prejudice against Blacks	−0.02	0.07	0.10**	0.05
	(0.04)	(0.04)	(0.05)	(0.04)
Party ID (Rep.)	0.02	−0.00	−0.12**	−0.06
	(0.03)	(0.04)	(0.05)	(0.04)
Ideo. Self-ID (Cons.)	−0.10**	−0.13***	−0.16**	−0.17***
	(0.05)	(0.05)	(0.07)	(0.06)
Egalitarianism	0.28***	0.24***	0.19**	0.21***
	(0.05)	(0.06)	(0.08)	(0.07)
Limited Government	−0.12***	−0.20***	−0.14***	−0.10***
	(0.02)	(0.03)	(0.04)	(0.03)
Age	−0.00	−0.08**	0.11**	0.15***
	(0.03)	(0.03)	(0.05)	(0.04)
Education	−0.10***	−0.02	−0.02	−0.02
	(0.03)	(0.03)	(0.05)	(0.04)
Male	0.01	0.02	−0.00	−0.03
	(0.02)	(0.02)	(0.02)	(0.02)
South	0.03*	0.02	0.01	0.01
	(0.02)	(0.02)	(0.02)	(0.02)
Income	−0.08***	−0.06*	−0.00	0.04
	(0.03)	(0.03)	(0.05)	(0.04)
Own Home	−0.02	−0.03	−0.01	−0.04*
	(0.02)	(0.02)	(0.03)	(0.02)
Constant	0.41***	0.30***	0.47***	0.48***
	(0.08)	(0.08)	(0.10)	(0.08)
N	1,426	1,426	1,425	1,424
R-squared	0.33	0.39	0.30	0.35

*** $p < 0.001$; ** $p < 0.01$; * $p < 0.05$; cell entries are ordinary least squares regression coefficients (standard errors in parentheses). All variables are coded from 0 to 1. The column headings indicate dependent variables. Analyses weighted for national representativeness.

APPENDIX TO CHAPTER 5

APPENDIX 5A *Coefficient Table Corresponding to Figure 5.1 (2013 ANES Recontact Survey)*

	Govt. Services	Affordable Care Act	Govt. Spending on Education	Limit Corporate Contributions
Sympathy for the Poor	0.05	−0.14	0.01	−0.03
	(0.08)	(0.08)	(0.09)	(0.06)
Knowledge Index	−0.15*	−0.13	−0.11	−0.08
	(0.07)	(0.09)	(0.10)	(0.09)
Sympathy for the Poor * Knowledge Index	0.13	0.33*	0.18	−
	(0.12)	(0.14)	(0.15)	−
Resentment of the Rich	0.09*	0.04	0.10	−0.01
	(0.04)	(0.06)	(0.05)	(0.12)
Resentment of the Rich * Knowledge Index	−	−	−	0.48*
	−	−	−	(0.19)
Income Inequality Is Bad	−0.04	0.04	−0.00	0.12**
	(0.03)	(0.03)	(0.03)	(0.04)
Prejudice against Blacks	−0.05	−0.04	0.07	0.03
	(0.03)	(0.04)	(0.04)	(0.05)
Party ID (Republican)	−0.10**	−0.30***	0.02	−0.05
	(0.04)	(0.04)	(0.04)	(0.05)
Ideological Self-ID (Cons.)	−0.12*	−0.27***	−0.20***	−0.13
	(0.05)	(0.06)	(0.06)	(0.07)
Egalitarianism	0.29***	0.28***	0.29***	0.00
	(0.04)	(0.06)	(0.06)	(0.08)
Limited Government	−0.16***	−0.19***	−0.07**	0.04
	(0.03)	(0.03)	(0.03)	(0.04)
Age	0.04	−0.02	−0.06	0.16**
	(0.03)	(0.04)	(0.03)	(0.05)
Education	−0.02	0.09*	0.01	0.10
	(0.03)	(0.04)	(0.03)	(0.05)
Male	0.01	−0.02	−0.01	−0.06*
	(0.01)	(0.02)	(0.02)	(0.02)
South	0.00	0.02	0.01	0.00
	(0.01)	(0.02)	(0.02)	(0.02)
Income	−0.08**	−0.01	0.08*	0.06
	(0.03)	(0.04)	(0.03)	(0.05)
Own Home	0.01	−0.01	0.01	−0.02
	(0.02)	(0.02)	(0.02)	(0.03)

(continued)

APPENDIX 5A *(continued)*

	Govt. Services	Affordable Care Act	Govt. Spending on Education	Limit Corporate Contributions
Constant	0.53***	0.70***	0.51***	0.57***
	(0.08)	(0.09)	(0.09)	(0.11)
N	1,344	1,425	1,426	1,425
R-squared	0.51	0.54	0.23	0.11

*** $p < 0.001$; ** $p < 0.01$; * $p < 0.05$; cell entries are ordinary least squares regression coefficients (standard errors in parentheses). All variables are coded from 0 to 1. The column headings indicate dependent variables.

APPENDIX 5B *Coefficient Table Corresponding to Figure 5.5 (2014 CCES Module)*

	Support for Estate Tax
Resentment of the Rich	0.25
	(0.14)
Tell Condition	0.01
	(0.11)
Resentment of the Rich * Tell Condition	0.22
	(0.17)
Sympathy for the Poor	0.14*
	(0.07)
Prejudice against Blacks	0.02
	(0.09)
Party ID (Rep.)	−0.32***
	(0.04)
Education	0.09
	(0.05)
South	−0.04
	(0.03)
Income	−0.04
	(0.07)
Income – Missing	−0.03
	(0.05)
Unemployed	−0.01
	(0.05)
Male	0.03
	(0.03)

(continued)

APPENDIX 5B *(continued)*

	Support for Estate Tax
Age	−0.21***
	(0.06)
Hispanic	−0.07
	(0.06)
Black	−0.10*
	(0.05)
Other Race	0.01
	(0.07)
Constant	0.32*
	(0.13)
N	840
R-squared	0.30

*** $p < 0.001$; ** $p < 0.01$; * $p < 0.05$; cell entries are ordinary least squares regression coefficients (standard errors in parentheses). All variables are coded from 0 to 1. The column heading indicates the dependent variable; higher values indicate greater support for the estate tax.

APPENDIX 5C *Coefficient Table Corresponding to Figure 5.8 (2014 CCES Module)*

	Support for HMID
Sympathy for the Poor	−0.01
	(0.08)
HMID Information Condition	0.18
	(0.12)
Resentment of the Rich	0.23
	(0.12)
Resentment of the Rich * HMID Information Condition	−0.53**
	(0.17)
Racial Resentment	0.10
	(0.05)
Prejudice against Blacks	0.00
	(0.08)
Party ID (Rep.)	0.05
	(0.05)
Ideology (Cons.)	0.01
	(0.06)

(continued)

APPENDIX 5C *(continued)*

	Support for HMID
Humanitarianism	0.07
	(0.07)
Egalitarianism	−0.05
	(0.04)
Likely to Become Rich	0.05
	(0.05)
Likely to Become Poor	0.03
	(0.05)
Work, not Luck, Causes Success	0.01
	(0.03)
Education	0.09*
	(0.04)
South	0.03
	(0.02)
Income	0.08
	(0.06)
Income – Missing	0.08
	(0.04)
Unemployed	−0.13*
	(0.06)
Male	0.06*
	(0.02)
Age	−0.03
	(0.05)
Hispanic	−0.06
	(0.06)
Black	0.02
	(0.04)
Other Race	−0.04
	(0.05)
Support for HMID in wave 1	0.60***
	(0.05)
Constant	−0.14
	(0.14)
N	690
R-squared	0.43

*** $p < 0.001$; ** $p < 0.01$; * $p < 0.05$; cell entries are ordinary least squares regression coefficients (standard errors in parentheses). All variables are coded from 0 to 1. The column heading indicates the dependent variable; higher values indicate greater support for the home mortgage interest deduction (HMID).

APPENDIX TO CHAPTER 6

APPENDIX 6A *Coefficient Table Corresponding to Figure 6.3 (2013 YouGov Study)*

	Candidate Is Nonpartisan	Candidate Is Democrat	Candidate Is Republican
Help Poor Condition	0.39**	0.46**	−0.04
	(0.15)	(0.16)	(0.17)
Sympathy for the Poor	−0.15	−0.12	−0.36**
	(0.11)	(0.11)	(0.12)
Help Poor Condition * Sympathy for the Poor	0.38*	0.36*	0.55**
	(0.16)	(0.17)	(0.18)
Party ID (Republican)	0.15	0.16	0.33**
	(0.09)	(0.08)	(0.11)
Help Poor Condition * Party ID (Republican)	−0.48***	−0.59***	−0.11
	(0.12)	(0.00)	(0.15)
Ideology (Conservative)	0.44***	0.13	0.33**
	(0.10)	(0.10)	(0.12)
Help Poor Condition * Ideology (Conservative)	−0.59***	−0.62***	−0.46**
	(0.15)	(0.15)	(0.16)
Constant	0.24*	0.37***	0.39**
	(0.10)	(0.10)	(0.12)
N	204	204	199
R-squared	0.38	0.51	0.37

*** $p < 0.001$; ** $p < 0.01$; * $p < 0.05$; cell entries are ordinary least squares regression coefficients (standard errors in parentheses). All variables are coded from 0 to 1. The column headings indicate dependent variables.

APPENDIX 6B *Coefficient Table Corresponding to Figure 6.4 (2013 YouGov Study)*

	Democratic Respondents	Republican Respondents
Help Poor Condition	−0.03	−0.27
	(0.20)	(0.15)
Sympathy for the Poor	−0.45*	−0.54***
	(0.19)	(0.14)
Help Poor Condition * Sympathy for the Poor	0.61*	0.83***
	(0.26)	(0.21)

(continued)

APPENDIX 6B *(continued)*

	Democratic Respondents	Republican Respondents
Constant	0.65***	0.74***
	(0.15)	(0.10)
N	91	121
R-squared	0.48	0.33

*** p < 0.001; ** p < 0.01; * p < 0.05; cell entries are logistic regression coefficients (standard errors in parentheses). All variables are coded from 0 to 1. The column headings indicate dependent variables.

APPENDIX 6C *Coefficient Table Corresponding to Figure 6.5 (2013 YouGov Study)*

	Candidate Helping District
Help District Condition	−0.00
	(0.09)
Sympathy for the Poor	−0.03
	(0.07)
Help District Condition * Sympathy for the Poor	−0.03
	(0.10)
Party ID (Republican)	−0.09
	(0.05)
Help District Condition * Party ID (Republican)	0.06
	(0.08)
Ideology (Conservative)	0.08
	(0.06)
Help District Condition * Ideology (Conservative)	−0.01
	(0.08)
Constant	0.55***
	(0.07)
N	184
R-squared	0.03

*** p < 0.001; ** p < 0.01; * p < 0.05; cell entries are logistic regression coefficients (standard errors in parentheses). All variables are coded from 0 to 1. The column headings indicate dependent variables.

APPENDIX 6D *Coefficient Table Corresponding to Figure 6.6 (2013 YouGov Study)*

	Respondents High on Impression Management	Respondents Low on Impression Management
Help Poor Treatment Condition	0.35	0.43*
	(0.19)	(0.18)
Sympathy for the Poor	−0.15	−0.15
	(0.11)	(0.11)
Help Poor Treatment * Sympathy for the Poor	0.43*	0.35
	(0.22)	(0.19)
Party ID (Rep.)	0.15	0.15
	(0.09)	(0.09)
Help Poor Treatment * Party ID (Rep.)	−0.64***	−0.38**
	(0.17)	(0.14)
Ideology (Cons.)	0.44***	0.44***
	(0.11)	(0.10)
Help Poor Treatment * Ideology (Cons.)	−0.45*	−0.71***
	(0.20)	(0.18)
Constant	0.24*	0.24*
	(0.11)	(0.10)
N	149	159
R-squared	0.37	0.39

*** $p < 0.001$; ** $p < 0.01$; * $p < 0.05$; cell entries are logistic regression coefficients (standard errors in parentheses). All variables are coded from 0 to 1. The column headings indicate dependent variables.

APPENDIX 6E *Coefficient Table Corresponding to Figure 6.8 (2013 YouGov Study)*

	Vote Choice for Obama in 2012
Sympathy for the Poor	1.43*
	(0.76)
Resentment of the Rich	1.75*
	(0.85)
Income Inequality Is Bad	0.29
	(0.59)
Prejudice against Blacks	−2.02**
	(0.66)
Party ID (Rep.)	−6.44***
	(0.64)

(continued)

APPENDIX 6E *(continued)*

	Vote Choice for Obama in 2012
Ideology (Cons.)	−5.34***
	(0.80)
Age	0.74
	(0.76)
Education	0.60
	(0.72)
Male	−0.45
	(0.32)
South	-0.61*
	(0.31)
Income	0.05
	(0.64)
Own Home	−0.90
	(0.51)
Constant	6.05***
	(1.10)
Observations	1,181

*** $p < 0.001$; ** $p < 0.01$; * $p < 0.05$; cell entries are logistic regression coefficients (standard errors in parentheses). All variables are coded from 0 to 1. The column headings indicate dependent variables.

APPENDIX 6F *Coefficient Table Corresponding to Figure 6.9 (2016 Qualtrics Survey)*

	Warmth toward Sanders	Warmth toward Clinton
Resentment for the Rich	0.12*	0.04
	(0.05)	(0.05)
Black-White Stereotype Index	−0.15	−0.05
	(0.11)	(0.09)
Party ID (Rep.)	−0.48***	−0.65***
	(0.03)	(0.03)
Female	0.02	−0.00
	(0.02)	(0.02)
Age	−0.17**	0.14**
	(0.05)	(0.05)
Income	0.04	0.02
	(0.05)	(0.04)

(continued)

APPENDIX 6F *(continued)*

	Warmth toward Sanders	Warmth toward Clinton
Education	0.05	0.07
	(0.10)	(0.09)
South	−0.01	0.02
	(0.02)	(0.02)
Black	−0.08*	0.17***
	(0.03)	(0.03)
Constant	0.73***	0.55***
	(0.10)	(0.09)
Observations	772	774
R-squared	0.26	0.46

Standard errors in parentheses. *** $p < 0.001$; ** $p < 0.01$; * $p < 0.05$

APPENDIX TO CHAPTER 7

APPENDIX 7A *Coefficient Table Corresponding to Figures 7.1 and 7.2 (2013 YouGov Study)*

	Helped Candidate 2012	Gave Money to Party	Gave Money to Nonpartisan	Learn How to Help Hunger
Sympathy for the Poor	1.21**	3.25***	3.43**	2.64***
	(0.47)	(0.83)	(1.32)	(0.60)
Resentment of the Rich	−0.45	−0.65	0.39	0.32
	(0.51)	(0.96)	(1.29)	(0.62)
Party ID (Rep.)	1.03***	1.66***	−0.77	−0.08
	(0.24)	(0.50)	(0.64)	(0.29)
Registered to Vote	1.09*	–	–	1.01*
	(0.45)	–	–	(0.42)
Church Attendance	0.03	0.48	1.07	0.54
	(0.26)	(0.49)	(0.66)	(0.29)
Age	0.02***	0.02*	0.01	−0.02**
	(0.006)	(0.01)	(0.01)	(0.006)
Female	−0.31	−0.42	−1.53***	−0.10
	(0.18)	(0.32)	(0.45)	(0.20)
Married	−0.15	0.33	−0.18	0.08
	(0.19)	(0.35)	(0.54)	(0.21)

(continued)

APPENDIX 7A *(continued)*

	Helped Candidate 2012	Gave Money to Party	Gave Money to Nonpartisan	Learn How to Help Hunger
South	−0.01	0.32	−0.98	−0.39
	(0.21)	(0.34)	(0.63)	(0.24)
Some College	0.71**	1.17**	1.00	−0.08
	(0.22)	(0.41)	(0.61)	(0.23)
College Grad	1.05***	1.68***	1.58*	0.13
	(0.24)	(0.46)	(0.68)	(0.26)
Black	0.11	−0.06	−0.16	0.17
	(0.29)	(0.54)	(0.82)	(0.34)
Latino	−0.66	0.10	0.66	0.03
	(0.35)	(0.63)	(0.82)	(0.34)
Other Race	0.40	0.47	1.61	0.62
	(0.37)	(1.03)	(1.10)	(0.34)
Middle Class	0.78**	0.41	0.26	0.37
	(0.26)	(0.42)	(0.82)	(0.28)
Working Class	0.35	0.28	0.65	0.29
	(0.25)	(0.42)	(0.72)	(0.27)
Constant	−4.62***	−6.89***	−6.15***	−3.72***
	(0.68)	(0.42)	(1.74)	(0.69)
N	761	343	343	791
Prob. > F	0.0000	0.0001	0.0001	0.0004

*** $p < 0.001$; ** $p < 0.01$; * $p < 0.05$; cell entries are logistic regression coefficients (standard errors in parentheses). All variables are coded from 0 to 1. The column headings indicate dependent variables.

APPENDIX 7B *Coefficient Table Corresponding to Figure 7.4 (2014 CCES Module)*

	Support for Estate Tax
Resentment of the Rich	0.69**
	(0.24)
Death Tax Condition	0.37*
	(0.16)
Resentment of the Rich * Death Tax Condition	−0.70**
	(0.26)

(continued)

APPENDIX 7B *(continued)*

	Support for Estate Tax
Sympathy for the Poor	0.15
	(0.09)
Racial Prejudice	-0.13
	(0.10)
Party ID	-0.28***
	(0.05)
Education	0.15**
	(0.06)
South	-0.01
	(0.03)
Income	-0.12
	(0.08)
Income Missing	-0.03
	(0.07)
Unemployed	0.09
	(0.05)
Male	-0.0003
	(0.03)
Age	-0.24***
	(0.07)
Latino	0.07
	(0.05)
Black	-0.14**
	(0.05)
Other Race	0.14
	(0.08)
Constant	0.12
	(0.20)
N	984
R-squared	0.322

*** $p < 0.001$; ** $p < 0.01$; * $p < 0.05$; cell entries are ordinary least squares regression coefficients (standard errors in parentheses). All variables are coded from 0 to 1. The column headings indicate dependent variables.

APPENDIX 7C *Coefficient Table Corresponding to Figure 7.5 (2016 Qualtrics Survey)*

	Warmth toward Trump
Resentment of the Rich	0.06
	(0.05)
Racial Prejudice	0.62***
	(0.10)
Republican	0.42***
	(0.03)
Female	0.04
	(0.02)
Age	0.22***
	(0.05)
Income	0.04
	(0.04)
Education	−0.14
	(0.10)
South	0.05*
	(0.02)
Black	−0.02
	(0.03)
Constant	−0.26**
	(0.09)
N	765
R-squared	0.303

*** p < 0.001; ** p < 0.01; * p < 0.05; cell entries are ordinary least squares regression coefficients (standard errors in parentheses). All variables are coded from 0 to 1. The column headings indicate dependent variables.

Endnotes

INTRODUCTION: REIGNING MYTHS ABOUT CLASS ATTITUDES

1. For example, in *Esquire*, Dwight Garner writes, "[T]alking about social class is something that America has failed to do." And, "We've long preferred to believe that class doesn't exist here." From "We Admire Americans Who Don't Forget Their Roots." February 2, 2017. Accessed online: www.esquire.com/lifestyle/a51761/class-in-america/. Similarly, Rich Lowry writes in *The National Review* that "In contemporary America, "the conversation about race" never ends ... We don't talk about class nearly as often ..." From "Class, Not Race." March 17, 2015. Accessed online: www.nationalreview.com/article/415480/class-not-race-rich-lowry. Richard Reeves of the Brookings Institution contends that, "The United States imagines itself as a classless society." From "Classless America, Still?" August 27, 2014. Accessed online: www.brookings.edu/blog/social-mobility-memos/2014/08/27/classless-america-still/.

2. In "Why America Hates Its Poor" in *Salon*, Nico Lang claims that the following sentiment "sums up our feelings nicely: 'I HATE POOR PEOPLE.'" April 11, 2015. Accessed online: www.salon.com/2015/04/11/why_we_hate_poor_people_partner/. An article by Suzanne Moore in *The Guardian*, meanwhile, argues that in both the United States and the United Kingdom, "Instead of Being Disgusted by Poverty, We Are Disgusted by Poor People Themselves." February 15, 2012. Accessed online: www.theguardian.com/commentisfree/2012/feb/16/suzanne-moore-disgusted-by-poor. See also *The Huffington Post*'s "Why Do We Hate the Poor?" by Alden Loury, December 5, 2008. Accessed online: www.huffingtonpost.com/alden-loury/why-do-we-hate-the-poor_b_140586.html. Finally, see *The Stranger*'s "Why It Is Easy to Hate the Poor." In this article, Charles Mudede argues, without survey evidence, that "the middle class may even hate the poor more than the rich do."

3. In his article "Why Americans Don't Hate the Rich," Jerry Adler in *Newsweek* claims without evidence that "What Americans lack is what the European working classes gleefully exhibit: resentment of the rich personally." The article does

note, however, that many Americans support increased taxes on the rich.
February 6, 2009. Accessed online: www.newsweek.com/why-americans-dont
-hate-rich-82585. Paul Krugman, meanwhile, writing for *The New York Times*,
speaks of a "destructive ... myth of the deserving rich ... an obvious desire to
believe that rising incomes at the top are kind of the obverse of the alleged social
problems at the bottom. According to this view, the affluent are affluent because
they have done the right things: they've gotten college educations, they've gotten
and stayed married, avoiding illegitimate births, they have a good work ethic, etc.
And implied in all this is that wealth is the reward for virtue, which makes it hard
to argue for redistribution." January 18, 2014. Accessed online: https://krugman
.blogs.nytimes.com/2014/01/18/the-myth-of-the-deserving-rich/. Finally, in *The
National Review*, Victor Davis Hanson argues that "Americans neither hate nor
envy meritocratic elites ... what drives proverbially average Americans crazy is
not the success and money of others ..." "It's the Hypocrisy, Stupid." June 6,
2017. Accessed online: www.nationalreview.com/article/448320/hypocrite-demo
crats-lecture-country-exempt-themselves-resemble-jimmy-swaggart.

4. Paul Krugman argues in *The New York Times* that ordinary Americans have
   been hoodwinked by political elites, and therefore have become unable to
   recognize how they would benefit from higher taxes on the wealthy and
   government programs that would help the poor and the middle class.
   "[I]magine yourself as a hired gun for the right tail of the income distribution.
   What would you do in an effort to stop the median voter from realizing that she
   would benefit from a more European-style system? Well, you'd do everything
   you can to exaggerate the disincentive effects of higher taxes, while trying to
   convince middle-income voters that the benefits of government programs go to
   other people ... So far, efforts along these lines have been remarkably successful." From "Notes on the Political Economy of Redistribution," September 21,
   2012. Accessed online: krugman.blogs.nytimes.com/2012/09/21/notes-on-the
   -political-economy-of-redistribution/.

5. See *The Washington Post*, "Why the White Working Class Votes against Itself"
   by Catherine Rampell. December 22, 2016. Accessed online: www.washington
   post.com/opinions/why-the-white-working-class-votes-against-itself/2016/12/
   22/3aa65c04-c88b-11e6-8bee-54e800ef2a63_story.html?utm
   _term=.3b77cb430d45. Also see "Why Obamacare Enrollees Voted for
   Trump" by Sarah Kliff. December 13, 2016. *Vox.com*. Accessed online: ww
   w.vox.com/science-and-health/2016/12/13/13848794/kentucky-obamacare-tr
   ump. Similarly, sociologist Steve Viscelli reports on his interviews with truckers
   in *The Atlantic*: "In the course of 10 years of research on the trucking industry,
   I met many drivers who had tried their hand at contracting and been wiped out
   by it, financially and personally. Yet, I continually met new drivers eager to give
   it a shot. One driver I met was convinced that he could become a millionaire if
   he bought a truck from his company and kept racking up miles at the same
   incredible pace as he had during his first nine months on the job. But the fact is,
   a typical truck driver won't become a millionaire—far from it." From: "Truck
   Stop: How One of America's Steadiest Jobs Turned into One of Its Most
   Grueling." May 10, 2016. Accessed online: www.theatlantic.com/business/ar
   chive/2016/05/truck-stop/481926/.

6. Eduardo Porter in *The New York Times*, for example, claims without survey evidence that "Trump Budget Proposal Reflects Working-Class Resentment of the Poor." March 7, 2017. Accessed online: www.nytimes.com/2017/03/07/business/economy/trump-budget-entitlements-working-class.html. See also "The New Resentment of the Poor," written by the editorial board of *The New York Times* on August 30, 2011. Accessed online: www.nytimes.com/2011/08/31/opinion/the-new-resentment-of-the-poor.html.

7. For an example of this claim, see historian Thomas Frank's (2012) book *Pity the Billionaire*.

8. That said, many journalists do an excellent job engaging with survey research. See, for example, Cassidy, John. 2015. "Is Support for Income Redistribution Really Falling?" *The New Yorker*. April 17, 2015. Accessed online: www.newyorker.com/news/john-cassidy/is-support-for-income-redistribution-really-falling.

9. In this book I leave to the side the important question of how Americans view other class groups such as the working class and the middle class. See Chapter 1 and Conclusion.

10. Cillizza, Chris. "Is Barack Obama 'Black'? A Majority of Americans Say No." *Washington Post*. April 14, 2014. Accessed online: www.washingtonpost.com/news/the-fix/wp/2014/04/14/is-barack-obama-black/?utm_term=.adfc160eb715.

11. In a recent article in *The New York Times*, Matthew Shaer referred to Chelsea Manning by her preferred pronoun, "she," as has been standard practice in many journalistic accounts of her release. See Shaer, Matthew. "The Long, Lonely Road of Chelsea Manning." *The New York Times*. June 12, 2017. Accessed online: https://www.nytimes.com/2017/06/12/magazine/the-long-lonely-road-of-chelsea-manning.html. In contrast, David French of *The National Review* described Manning with the pronoun "he." See French, David. "Chelsea Manning's Release is Nothing to Celebrate." *The National Review*. May 18, 2017. Accessed online: www.nationalreview.com/corner/447758/chelsea-mannings-release-nothing-celebrate. After being criticized, French stood by his original description: "I identified a man as a man … When I use a male pronoun to describe Chelsea Manning, I'm not trolling. I'm not being a jerk. I'm not trying to make anyone angry. I'm simply telling the truth. I'm reflecting biological reality, and I'm referring to the created order as outlined in Genesis 1 – 'So God created man in his own image, in the image of God he created him; male and female he created them.'" See French, David. "Chelsea Manning and the Problem of Pronouns." *The National Review*. May 19, 2017. Accessed online: www.nationalreview.com/article/447798/chelsea-manning-man-masculine-pronouns-should-not-be-illegal.

12. For an important exception, see Grossman and Hopkins (2016).

13. Bartels (2008) examines the possibility of connections between attitudes toward class groups and political opinions in a handful of important cases. For example, Bartels finds scant evidence of associations between attitudes toward class groups and public opinion about the so-called "Bush tax cuts" (e.g., the Economic Growth and Tax Relief Reconciliation Act of 2001 and the Jobs and Growth Tax Relief Reconciliation Act of 2003). This finding is

consistent with the argument I make here: the influence of sympathy for the poor and resentment of the rich on policy opinion hinges on political information. In the case of the Bush tax cuts, widespread public ignorance about the distributive consequences of these policies precluded Americans from bringing their attitudes about class groups to bear on their opinions.

14. This is discussed further in Chapter 2.

15. This well-known theory of the policymaking process appeared in the flagship journal of the American Political Science Association, *The American Political Science Review* (Schneider and Ingram 1993). It is a standard fixture in undergraduate and graduate courses in public policy, and has been cited 1,777 times (according to Google Scholar) at the time of writing.

16. The coding procedure was as follows. (1) Read the table of contents of each issue of each journal; (2) Download any article that appears to be related to class; (3) At the end of each journal-decade, open all of the downloaded articles and read the abstracts; (4) Discard any articles that are obviously not related based on the abstract; (5) Examine remaining articles to see if the analysis incorporates class attitudes. Thanks to Logan Strother for invaluable research assistance with the coding analysis.

17. There is substantial research on whether economic considerations affect voting. But this scholarship examines whether these considerations are pocketbook or sociotropic, and whether they are retrospective or prospective. This is a far cry from analyzing the impact of attitudes toward specific class groups on vote choice.

18. Examples include: *Why Is There No Socialism in the United States?* (Sombart 1976), and *It Didn't Happen Here: Why Socialism Failed in the United States* (Lipset and Marks 2001), and "Why Is There No Socialism in the United States?" (Foner 1984). See also Hartz (1955).

19. For a discussion and critique of research that characterizes the U.S. welfare state as a "laggard" in comparative context, see Howard (2007).

20. For examples of scholars promulgating this explanation, see the first chapter of Hochschild (1981) and Bonica et al. (2013).

21. Page and Jacobs (2009). Also see Cook and Barrett (1992) and Free and Cantril (1967). As Martin Gilens (1999) notes, "Americans show surprisingly strong support for government social responsibility ... In fact, Americans not only support most of the welfare-state programs that currently exist, but they also think that in most areas the government is not doing enough to help its citizens." Gilens' book is often taken to mean that majorities of Americans oppose government aid to poor people. As discussed later, this is a misinterpretation.

22. For example, Jennifer Hochschild (1981, pp. 1–2) argues as follows: "more people would benefit than would lose from downward redistribution. And yet never has the poorer majority of the population, not to speak of the poorest minority, voted itself out of its economic disadvantage." Hochschild makes this argument in support of her contention that one reason that there is not more socialism in the United States is that "the American poor apparently do not support the downward redistribution of wealth." I criticize this line of argument on a number of fronts as the book proceeds.

23. For a summary of public opinion on these issues, see Bobo and Licari (1989) Clement and Guskin (2017) Dugan (2015), Geiger (2016), Pew Center (2014), Saad (2013), Sniderman et al. (1989), Somin (2015), Strother (2016), and Swift (2016).

24. Moreover, the electorate itself was limited to white, male landowners in most states when the United States Constitution was ratified.

25. Quotation taken from Rossiter (1961), p. 72.

26. See Neustadt (1991).

27. From Hacker and Pierson (2014).

28. Downs (1957) actually suggests a number of circumstances in which the policy positions of the major parties in a two-party system might not converge to the preferences of the median voter. These include: (1) when the distribution of voters has a high variance and is not clustered around the mode; (2) when there is substantial government uncertainty about the real policy positions of voters (this is especially likely when interest groups exert substantial effort attempting to persuade government officials that voters harbor different preferences than they actually do); (3) when voters at the extremes feel more strongly about their policy preferences than voters in the middle; and, relatedly, (4) when parties fear losing extremist voters.

29. See especially Hacker and Pierson (2014). They characterize most interpretations of Downs as suggesting that there are no durable winners in politics, as this cycle's winners are next cycle's losers (see Mayhew 2000). On this account, elections offer only temporary advantages to one party. Hacker and Pierson argue, in contrast, that winning elections can have long-run effects, as the winning party is able to make policy (and impose that policy on the losers) – and these policies "can create facts on the ground, durably altering resources and incentives" which can weaken or even eliminate the losers. In other words, each election can fundamentally alter future politics, moving policymaking far from the preferences of the median voter (Hacker and Pierson 2014: 641; see also Moe 2005; Patashnik 2008; Strother 2017).

30. See Drezner (2015), Fiorina and Abrams (2010), McCarty, Poole, and Rosenthal (2008), and Poole (2012).

31. See Baumgartner and Leech (1998), Becker (1985), Boydstun (2013), Fenno (1978), Romer and Rosenthal (1978), Schlozman, Verba, and Brady (2012), and Wright (1990).

32. Another reason for this is "status quo bias," as Gilens (2012) puts it. Policy change is hard to come by, as there are so many veto players in the American political system. Therefore, many proposed policies are never passed even if they are favored by vast majorities of Americans.

33. From Gilens (2012); see also Gilens and Page (2014). The claim that the majoritarian public has little to no influence on policy change is not accepted by all scholars, however, as discussed in the Conclusion.

34. For example, Schlozman and Verba (1979) find that Americans' beliefs about economic opportunity are not much affected by labor market participation: the employed and the unemployed exhibit similar (though not identical) attitudes toward a range of economic policies and attitudes about economic mobility.

35. Moderate, but not trivial. Hout, Brooks, and Manza's (1995) analysis reveals discernible differences in class voting for much of the mid-twentieth century. Their over-time analysis shows that professionals and nonmanagerial white-collar workers moved into the Democratic party and managers and the self-employed sorted into the Republican party in the postwar era. These shifts clarified the class structure of the parties; Republicans became more managerial, and Democrats increasingly consisted of semi-skilled and low-skill workers. Partisan voting differences among these occupational groups rose to about 12 percentage points.

36. See Kinder and Sanders (1996) and Kinder and Winter (2001).

37. See, for example, Enns and Wlezien (2011) and Evans (1999).

38. This "cash-like" designation is added to include food stamps (see Gilens 1999).

39. See Gilens (1999) on the role of white racial prejudice and media coverage of welfare recipients. Also see Hancock (2004) on the effects of the image of the "welfare queen" on policymaking debates.

40. See Gilens (1999), Henderson (2014), Howard (2007), Jacobs and Shapiro (1999), and Pew Center (2013).

41. None of this is intended to deny the importance of racial attitudes to attitudes about class groups. For example, as will be seen, prejudice against black people erodes' whites sympathy for the poor.

42. These open-ended responses were obtained through a restricted data request from the American National Election Studies. Ideally, I would analyze data from additional years, such as 2004, 2012, and 2016, but these were not available at the time my research was conducted.

43. As McCall (2013) observes, for a long time it was uncommon for survey researchers to ask respondents their views about economic inequality. Social scientists have become more focused on survey responses to questions about economic inequality in recent years, however. Some assess the extent to which Americans are comfortable with increasing economic inequality, others examine whether Americans are even aware that economic inequality is increasing in the first place, and still others examine whether increases in inequality affect American tolerance for inequality and support for government-led efforts to combat inequality (Bartels 2008; Bonica et al. 2013; Johnston and Newman forthcoming; Kelly and Enns 2010; Luttig 2013; McCall 2013; McCall and Kenworthy 2009; Norton and Ariely 2011; Page and Jacobs 2009; Schlozman, Verba, and Brady 2012).

44. Kim, Pedersen, and Mutz (2016).

45. See Feldman and Steenbergen (2001) for an analytical treatment of this puzzle.

46. This section of the book replicates and extends a series of important experiments conducted by Suzanne Mettler and Matt Guardino (Mettler 2011). My key addition is the inclusion of class group attitudes into the design. In brief, I argue that ignorance about the distributive consequences of some policies precludes ordinary Americans from bringing their attitudes about the poor and the rich to bear on their policy opinions. This explains why in some important cases, downward redistribution is less popular than it would be otherwise.

47. I borrow this metaphor from Kinder and Sanders (1996).
48. There is one important exception: candidates for political office often tell rags-to-riches stories about themselves (Carnes and Sadin 2015).
49. See Carnes and Lupu (2017)

I IN THEIR OWN WORDS

1. Four undergraduate students blind to the hypotheses of the study independently coded all of the responses and then met to resolve discrepancies. A graduate student and I also independently reviewed their coding for accuracy.
2. For example, in the pre-election wave of the 2008 ANES, respondents were asked, "Is there anything in particular about BARACK OBAMA that might make you want to vote FOR him?" If the respondent said yes, the interviewer asked the respondent a follow-up question: "What is that?" Respondents are also asked, "Is there anything in particular about BARACK OBAMA that might make you want to vote AGAINST him?" If the respondent said yes, the interviewer asked the respondent a follow-up question: "What is that?" Interviewers asked respondents the same questions about John McCain. Later in the survey, respondents were asked, "Is there anything in particular that you LIKE about the Democratic Party?" If the respondent said yes, the interviewer asked the respondent a follow-up question: "What is that?" Respondents were also asked, "Is there anything in particular that you DISLIKE about the Democratic Party?" If the respondent said yes, the interviewer asked the respondent a follow-up question: "What is that?" Interviewers asked respondents the same questions about the Republican Party. The wording is similar in the 1992, 1996, and 2000 ANES surveys as well, except that of course the names of the presidential candidates from the two major parties are different.
3. See, for example, McCall (2013) and Page and Jacobs (2009).
4. See Conover (1988), Converse (1964), and Nelson and Kinder (1996).
5. Quotations are not always exact, because interviewers do not always replicate the respondents' wording perfectly; indeed, it appears that they do not always try to do so. For example, the exact text of one response to the question of whether there is anything the respondent dislikes about the Republican Party is as follows: "they seem to help the rich people and that is why she do not like it." It seems likely that the respondent did not refer to herself in the third person but rather that the interviewer was attempting to capture the gist of the respondent's remarks rather than to reproduce them exactly. I also did light editing to remove typographical errors and any potentially identifying information.
6. The coding process is as follows. Recall that in the ANES, interviewers ask respondents what they like and dislike about each of the two major parties and each of the candidates for the presidency from these two parties. Here the answers to these questions are collapsed, for ease of presentation and because the patterns are the same for each of the individual questions. The analyses code all mentions of the poor or the rich (only this exact term "poor" or "rich" counts as a mention of this group) as favorable, unfavorable, or ambiguous. If a candidate or party is praised for helping the poor (or the rich), this counts as a

favorable mention of this class group. If a candidate or party is disparaged for helping the poor (or the rich), this counts as an unfavorable mention of this class group. In some cases it is unclear whether the respondent desires the class group to be helped; these cases are coded as ambiguous. For example, in answer to whether there is anything the respondent disliked about the Democratic Party, one response is as follows: "The Dem. party has a tendency to not have the right attitude toward the poor. I don't mean they're not compassionate but I don't agree with the way they go about helping poor people." It does appear that the respondent wants to help poor people in some way, but it is not clear whether this respondent views the poor favorably or not. Thus the response is coded as ambiguous.

7. In 1992, the poor were mentioned favorably 430 times, and unfavorably 8 times; 41 mentions were ambiguous. In 1996, the poor were mentioned favorably 142 times, and unfavorably 2 times; 17 mentions were ambiguous. In 2000, the poor were mentioned favorably 180 times and unfavorably 7 times; 22 mentions were ambiguous. Turning to the rich: in 1992, the rich were mentioned favorably 24 times and unfavorably 439 times; 32 mentions were ambiguous. In 1996, the rich were mentioned favorably 4 times and unfavorably 114 times; 13 mentions were ambiguous. In 2000, the rich were mentioned favorably 8 times and unfavorably 182 times; 27 mentions were ambiguous. Again, these analyses collapse across all of the open-ended questions for each survey year, although the same patterns hold for each individual question.

8. See Grossmann and Hopkins (2016) on class issues and partisan favorability specifically, and Petrocik (1996) on issue ownership generally.

9. These may not actually be subgroups, if the adjectives "very" and "ultra" are not intended as qualifiers but as (redundant) descriptors.

10. This is coded as a subgroup because only working people get paid.

11. It is possible, however, that respondents refer to subgroups of the poor indirectly. Praising the Democratic Party for helping "working people" or "the little guy" might refer to a perception of the working poor.

12. For example, when locally governed parishes in England took over responsibility for the poor from the centralized church in the fourteenth century, this distinction was applied regularly, and discussions surrounding the 1834 Poor Law used the terms "deserving" and "undeserving" to apply to subgroups of the poor (Webb and Webb 1927). This deserving/undeserving distinction has endured; indeed it has become a foundational element of welfare state policy in the United States. As Skocpol (1992) observes: "institutional and cultural oppositions between morally 'deserving' and the less 'deserving' run like fault lines through the entire history of American social provision."

13. See Gordon (1994), Skocpol (1992), and Williams (2010).

14. For example, historian Michael B. Katz (1989) argues that, "Before the middle of the nineteenth century, the unworthy poor had become a fixture in 'the popular mind.'" But Katz only analyzes elite discourse, not mass opinion. Additional examples from Campbell (2014) and Piven (2015) are discussed in Conclusion.

15. See Converse (1964).

16. This represents the 2015 poverty line for families of four. Last accessed October 28, 2015, at: http://aspe.hhs.gov/2015-poverty-guidelines.
17. See Huddy and Feldman (2009), Hutchings (2009), Kinder and Sanders (1996), and Tesler (2012).
18. See Luttig (2013), Piston (2010), Piston, Krupnikov, Milita, and Ryan (forthcoming), and Tesler and Sears (2010).
19. See Krupnikov and Piston (2015), Pasek et al. (2009), and Pasek et al. (2014).
20. See Hutchings et al. (2014) and Sinyangwe (2012).
21. Only white respondents were included in this survey because the primary purpose of this survey was to examine another topic: white attitudes about race.
22. See the Appendix for the (very similar) results for a pilot study on this topic I conducted through Amazon's Mechanical Turk platform.

2 A THEORY OF ATTITUDES TOWARD CLASS GROUPS AND THEIR POLITICAL CONSEQUENCES

1. See Kinder and Dale-Riddle (2012).
2. See Eagly and Chaiken (1993).
3. See Converse (1964) and Nelson and Kinder (1996).
4. See Kinder and Dale-Riddle (2012).
5. See Huddy and Feldman (2009).
6. See Burns and Gallagher (2010).
7. See Sides and Gross (2013).
8. See Sniderman, Brody, and Tetlock (1991).
9. See Chong (1993).
10. See Weeks and Lupfer (2004).
11. See Johnson, Richeson, and Finkel (2011).
12. See Franko, Tolbert and Witko (2013).
13. See Hout, Brooks, and Manza (1995).
14. See Kinder and Dale-Riddle (2012).
15. See Bowles, Gintis, and Groves (2008).
16. See Feldman (1983), Feldman and Zaller (1992), and Gilens (1996).
17. See Cuddy, Fiske and Glick (2008), and Fiske et al. (2002).
18. Bartels (2008).
19. Bartels also examines perceptions of class groups' tax burdens.
20. Bartels (2008, 143).
21. "The *political* significance of economic inequality is mostly lost on many Americans. Although they may express genuine allegiance to egalitarian values, they are not sufficiently attuned to the political debate to see how those values are implicated in major policy choices" (Bartels 2008).
22. These include the effects of partisan control of government on economic inequality, the level of government responsiveness to citizens, and in-depth case studies of specific policies.
23. McCall (2013).
24. Much of McCall's analysis uses the following three survey questions in agree-or-disagree format: 1. "Differences in income in America are too large."

2. "Inequality continues to exist because it benefits the rich and powerful." 3. "Large disparities in income are necessary for America's prosperity." McCall carefully identifies conditions under which Americans care (or do not care) about economic inequality; she also thoroughly examines relationships between beliefs about inequality and beliefs about economic opportunity over time. To that end, these questions have a number of virtues, not least of which is that they are repeated over decades in nationally representative survey data. For my purposes, however, it is important to note that only one of these questions mentions the rich, and survey respondents might interpret this question as a question about attributions for inequality or a question about "powerful" people rather than, or in addition to, a question about rich people. That said, McCall does analyze additional survey questions measuring attitudes toward rich people, including opinions about executive pay and beliefs about economic opportunity.

25. See Kluegel and Smith (1986, 112). The full question wording is: "Some people say that incomes should be completely equal, with every family making roughly the same amount of money; others say that things should stay about the same as they are now; and still others think incomes should be less equal than they are now. Ideally do you think there should be . . ." Response options include: "Complete equality of income," "More equality than there is now," "About the present level of income equality," and "Less equality of incomes than there is now."

26. The full question wording is: "It would be a good thing if all people received the same amount of money no matter what jobs they do. Do you . . . " Response options include: "Strongly Agree," "Agree," "Disagree," or "Strongly Disagree."

27. Schlozman, Verba, and Brady (2012, 60).

28. Rasmussen (2016).

29. Hanley (2009).

30. "Empathic concern" is defined as an "affective outcome" consisting of "feelings of sympathy and compassion for unfortunate others" (Davis 1994, pp. 17–19, 57). Some definitions of "empathy" are also consistent with this perspective (e.g., Hoffman 1984, 1987).

31. See Nussbaum (2001). Nussbaum often uses the term "compassion," but argues that the difference between the two is minimal.

32. See Davis (1994).

33. See Batson (2011).

34. See, Batson (1991; 2011), Hoffman (1984; 1987), Toi and Batson (1982), and Vaish, Carpenter, and Tomisello (2009).

35. See Chudy (2016); also see Tesler and Sears (2010) and Tesler (2012).

36. See Conover (1988).

37. See Feldman and Zaller (1992).

38. Feldman and Zaller (1992, 282).

39. See Bartels (2008).

40. See Henry et al. (2004) and Rose and Baumgartner (2013).

41. Gilens (1999).

42. Kinder (1998)

43. Gilens (1999). Gilens also included a question about whether "most people who don't succeed in life are just plain lazy," but it is unclear whether this question reflects beliefs about success generally or poverty in particular, especially since responses to this question did not correlate highly with responses to the question that was explicitly about poor people. Gilens reports that the Cronbach's alpha of the index of these two questions is only 0.38.
44. Feather and Sherman (2002, p. 954).
45. See also Ben-Ze'ev (2000), Parrott (1991), Rawls (1971), and Smith et al. (1996). Note that some social psychologists restrict resentment to public, sanctioned feelings that another person or group has undeserved advantage, referring to privately held feelings of this kind as "hostile envy" (e.g., Smith et al. 1996).
46. See Feather and Nairn (2005) and Leach and Spears (2008).
47. See Cikara and Fiske (2012) and Feather and Sherman (2002).
48. From "Protestors Target NY's Richest in Millionaires March," Andrew Siff, October 13, 2011. www.nbcnewyork.com/news/local/Millionaires-March-1 -Percent-99-Percent-Occupy-Wall-Street-131528853.html.
49. See Bartels (2008).
50. From Kluegel and Smith (1986): 29 percent said this was a "Very Important" reason and 39 percent said it was "Important."
51. From Kluegel and Smith (1986): 27 percent said this was a "Very Important" reason and 40 percent said it was "Important."
52. See Fiske (2011), although she attributes these findings to envy rather than resentment.
53. See Conover (1988).
54. See Kinder and Dale-Riddle (2012).
55. See Jackman and Jackman (1983).
56. Merton and Rossi (1950).
57. See Conover (1988) and Nelson and Kinder (1996).
58. See Sears (2001).
59. See Conover (1988).
60. On the relationship between disgust sensitivity and opinion about homelessness policy, see Clifford and Piston (2016).
61. See Cuddy, Fiske, and Glick (2008).
62. See Conover (1988).
63. See especially Kinder and Dale-Riddle (2012) on this point.
64. See Bandura (1969).
65. See Kinder and Kam (2009).
66. See Jennings and Markus (1984) and Sears (2001).
67. See Mendelberg, McCabe, and Thal (2017).
68. See Knecht and Martinez (2009), Lee, Farrell, and Link (2004), and Wilson (1996) on the positive effects of intergroup contact on attitudes toward the poor; but also see Sands (2017).
69. See Hopkins (2009).
70. See Hopkins (2009).
71. See Feldman and Steenbergen (2001).
72. See Feldman (1988b).
73. See Kinder and Kam (2009).

74. See Sidanius and Pratto (1999).
75. See Kinder and Dale-Riddle (2012) and Nelson and Kinder (1996).
76. See, for example, social identity theory (Hogg and Abrams 1988; Tajfel 1981; Tajfel and Turner 1979), social dominance (Sidanius and Pratto 1999), system justification theory (Jost, Banaji, and Nosek 2004), ethnocentrism (Kinder and Kam 2009; Sumner 1906), and reference group theory (Hyman 1960; Hyman 1968; Merton 1968).
77. See Converse (1975), Delli Carpini and Keeter (1996), and Lippmann (1920).
78. See Simon (1956).
79. See Nelson and Kinder (1996) and Sniderman, Brody, and Tetlock (1991).
80. From Kinder and Dale-Riddle (2012).
81. See Huddy and Feldman (2009), Kinder and McConnaughy (2006), and Hurwitz and Peffley (2005).
82. See Chong (1993), Kuklinski et al. (1991), and Sullivan, Piereson, and Marcus (1982).
83. Nelson and Kinder (1996). See also Sniderman, Brody, and Tetlock (1991).
84. Kinder and Dale-Riddle (2012).
85. See Nelson and Kinder (1996).
86. See Tesler (2012).
87. See Kinder and Kam (2009).
88. Furthermore, partisanship may inflect the relationship between class group attitudes and candidate evaluations. Since Democrats are viewed to more likely than Republicans to help the poor (Petrocik 1996), reactions to Democratic candidates may be in part a function of whether one likes or dislikes the poor. Similarly, to the extent that the actions of the Republican Party are perceived to benefit the rich, reactions to Republican candidates may be in part a function of whether one likes or dislikes the rich. See, for example, a Bloomberg News Poll finding that 60% of Americans report that, "Republicans have put too much emphasis on protecting the wealthy." Last accessed at: www.bloomberg.com/news/2012–12-13/republicans-deemed -too-pro-rich-57-in-poll-want-change.html. The relationship between partisanship, attitudes toward class groups, and candidate evaluations is examined further in Chapter 6.
89. The full name is the ANES 2013 Internet Recontact Study, an additional study of individuals recontacted from the 2012 ANES Time Series, including weights for national representativeness. I submitted questions that I designed to the ANES through the Online Commons proposal process, and the ANES agreed to administer these questions in 2013. For details, see: http://election studies.org/studypages/anes_panel_2013_inetrecontact/anes_panel_2013_ inetrecontact.htm.
90. YouGov uses a matching algorithm with respect to gender, age, race, education, party identification, ideology, and political interest to produce an Internet sample that closely approximates the demographic makeup of known marginals for the general population of the United States from the U.S. Census Bureau's 2008 American Community Survey. For more information on CCES modules (which also use YouGov to administer the survey) see http://projects.iq.harvard.edu/cces/home.

91. Political science faculty at Syracuse University purchased a module (N = 1000) on the 2014 CCES. As with the 2013 YouGov Study referenced above, the CCES is administered by YouGov, using YouGov's sampling frame.
92. See Kinder and Palfrey (1993).
93. A proponent of this view is not required to believe that Americans are indifferent to class – just that class is a social distinction rather than a political one. Given that "politics is a sideshow in the great circus of life" (Dahl 2006 [1956]) and that citizens generally "morselize" (Lane 1962), leaving thoughts about politics disconnected from each other and from their private lives (see also Hochschild 1981), this argument would hold that class may often be salient in social life, but it is not in political life.

3 ATTITUDES TOWARD THE POOR AND THE RICH IN THE UNITED STATES

1. See Brady (1988) as well as Pasek and Krosnick (2010).
2. Conover (1988).
3. In an earlier version of this project, I included a wider range of survey questions, including those measuring perceptions of competence of the poor and the rich (Cuddy, Fiske, and Glick 2008) and those asking about additional potential emotions such as admiration for the rich. As discussed in Chapter 1, these questions are not used here, as they did not typically reflect the vernacular used by respondents in open-ended responses. Furthermore, including them in pilot analyses did not improve the explanatory power of my models of policy opinion and electoral choice.
4. Conover (1988).
5. Conover (1988).
6. Kluegel and Smith (1986).
7. From *Wall Street Journal*, Editorial, "The Non-Taxpaying Class: Those Lucky Duckies!" November 20, 2002.
8. See Sidanius and Pratto (1999).
9. See Lerner (1981).
10. See Jost, Banaji, and Nosek (2004).
11. Kluegel and Smith (1986).
12. See especially Meertens and Pettigrew (1997).
13. Bartels (2008).
14. I might have constructed the indices somewhat differently, including the exact same questions for both attitudes toward the poor and attitudes toward the rich in order to maintain balance. I do not do so because the distributions indicate that the dominant perspective of the poor is one of sympathy, while the dominant perspective of the rich is one of resentment, and I construct the indices to reflect this finding. But it is important to note that neither the results presented here nor the results in subsequent chapters change meaningfully if the alternative approach is adopted; across both measurement strategies, the influence of class group attitudes is both powerful and conditional.

15. See Markus (2001) for discussion and validation testing of this measure of the value of limited government.
16. See Batson (2011) and Davis (1994).
17. See especially Kalmoe (2014).
18. See Kinder and Kam (2009) for an analytical treatment of ethnocentrism.
19. See Feldman and Steenbergen (2001).

4 WHY SO MANY AMERICANS SUPPORT DOWNWARD REDISTRIBUTION

1. Sociologists Newman and Jacobs (2010), for example, misrepresent Gilens' scholarship as follows: "Gilens finds that as the image of the poor got blacker, willingness to support expenditures for the poor fell through the floorboards."
2. Briefly, Gilens demonstrates that many white Americans' stereotypes about the work ethic of black people, in combination with media portrayals of welfare recipients as disproportionately black, result in widespread public opposition to welfare.
3. The Great Recession lasted from 2008 to 2012; Occupy Wall Street began in 2011.
4. It would be possible for self-interest to lead majorities of Americans to support policies intended to aid the poor if majorities perceived themselves as poor, or if they perceived themselves to benefit from such programs. In fact, few Americans identify as poor, but many do receive benefits from means-tested programs – or, at least, they or their close relatives will receive benefits at some point over the course of their lifetime (Campbell 2014). But individuals are frequently unaware that they benefit from social welfare programs (Mettler 2011), making it unlikely that considerations of self-interest are relevant for them. Further discussion of the role of self-interest can be found in Chapter 1.
5. See Tesler (2016).
6. An important question outside the scope of this book is whether the poor actually do benefit from such programs on balance, even if they receive some material aid from them. Scholarship has revealed evidence that public assistance programs have a wide range of deleterious effects (Campbell 2014; Soss, Fording, and Schram 2011).
7. See, for example, Gilens (1999) and Page and Jacobs (2009).
8. See Feldman and Zaller (1992) and Free and Cantril (1967).
9. See especially Gilens (1999).
10. Page and Jacobs (2009).
11. See, for example, Gilens (1999).
12. See Bartels (2008).
13. See Williamson (2017).
14. See Howard (1997) and Mettler (2011).
15. See, for example, Hochschild (1981).

16. See Feldman (1982), Fong (2001), Kinder (1986), Kinder and Kiewet (1979; 1981), Kinder and Sanders (1996), Mansbridge (1990), and Sears et al. (1980).
17. See Bergan (2009) and Doherty, Gerber, and Green (2006).
18. See Alesina and Ferrara (2005).
19. See Chong et al. (2001), Hunt et al. (2010), and Sears and Funk (1991).
20. Taken from the ANES cumulative data file. See: http://electionstudies.org/st udypages/anes_timeseries_cdf/anes_timeseries_cdf.htm.
21. See Cook and Barrett (1992), Gilens (1999), and Page and Jacobs (2009).
22. Page and Jacobs (2009).
23. Kluegel and Smith (1986, p. 5). See also Converse (1964).
24. See Arieli (1964), Bellah et al. (1985), Hofstader (1948), Huntington (1981), and Weber (1930).
25. See Feldman and Zaller (1992), Kluegel and Smith (1986), Kinder and Sanders (1996), Markus (2001), McClosky and Zaller (1984), Shen and Edwards (2005).
26. Kluegel and Smith (1986, p. 289).
27. See, for example, de Tocqueville (1835) and Lipset (1979).
28. See Rae et al. (1981).
29. See Feldman (1988b) and Kinder and Sanders (1996).
30. Feldman and Zaller (1992, p. 285).
31. Feldman and Steenbergen (2001, p. 659).
32. Kinder and Sanders (1996, p. 159).
33. Wong (2010, p. 197).
34. Kinder and Sanders (1996, p. 159).
35. Wong (2010, p. xviii).
36. Some scholars use ordered logistic regressions for dependent variables with a small number of categories (five or fewer). I have done so in supplementary analyses, and in no case does the pattern of findings meaningfully change.
37. Converse (1964) was referring, of course, to his argument rather than mine.
38. See Nelson and Kinder (1996) and Sniderman, Brody and Tetlock (1991).
39. See Huddy and Feldman (2009).
40. See Burns and Gallagher (2010).
41. See, for example, Achen (2002).
42. See also McCall (2013).
43. See Gilens (1999).
44. See Page and Jacobs (2009).
45. See Feldman and Steenbergen (2001).
46. See Feldman (1988b).
47. The question reads, "There are many homeless people in the United States today. How much would you say each of the following causes people to become homeless?" Among the factors listed was "greedy rich people," and the breakdown of responses was as follows: A great deal – 19%; Some – 19%; A little – 22%; None – 40%. I summed across the "A great deal," "Some," and "A little" categories to reach the percentage of people who listed greedy rich people as a cause of homelessness.

48. The analyses presented so far, in using the 2013 YouGov Study and the 2014 CCES Module, have relied on opt-in samples. Some scholars argue that weighting these for national representativeness is sufficient (Rivers 2006; Vavreck and Rivers 2008), but others argue that only address-based samples such as those used by the ANES are sufficient for claims of national representativeness to be credible (Baker et al. 2010). The pattern of findings I present here is consistent across both the opt-in and the address-based samples.

49. See McCall (2013).

50. Of course, this simulation is unrealistic insofar as it assumes that sympathy for the poor and resentment of the rich change without affecting any of the control variables. Still, it is illustrative of the potential of class group attitudes to explain the popularity of downwardly redistributive policy.

51. This is at least in part because sympathy for the poor is not strongly associated with opinion about these policies that would tax those at the top of the economic distribution, whereas both sympathy for the poor and resentment of the rich are associated with opinion about the other policies. The effect of reducing both sympathy for the poor and resentment of the rich to zero is therefore greater for the other policies.

52. See Markus (2001).

53. That said, some political scientists (e.g., Feldman and Steenbergen 2001) make valuable progress toward this goal, as discussed above.

54. See Bartels (2008), Feldman (1983), Feldman and Zaller (1992), Gilens (1999), Hacker and Pierson (2005), Hochschild (1981), Kluegel and Smith (1986), Lane (1962), McCall and Kenworthy (2009), Page and Jacobs (2009).

5 THE ROLE OF POLITICAL KNOWLEDGE

1. Converse (1964).

2. Converse (1964).

3. Similarly, others were asked, before answering the government services question, to tell the interviewer "what kinds of things come to mind when you think about fewer government services." Respondents were asked follow-up questions as well, such as "Do you see any problems with reducing government services?" or "Any other reasons that you favor reducing government services?"

4. I lack direct measures of knowledge about the distributive consequences of these policies, but remedy this problem in the analyses of the estate tax and the home mortgage interest deduction later in this chapter. At this point, I measure knowledge through responses to standard recall questions about visible political figures. Respondents were asked what office each of the following people hold: John Boehner, Joe Biden, David Cameron, and John Roberts. A recall scale was generated on the basis of responses to these questions, ranging from 0 correct to 4 correct. (For a critique of this measure, see Lupia 2015; for a defense, see Kinder and Kalmoe 2017.) In the Appendix, I present regression models that are identical to those in Table 5.1, except that an interactive term between the relevant class group attitude and the recall scale score is added: the

figure displays marginal effects of class group attitudes at the lowest and highest scores on this scale. The coefficient on this interaction term is statistically significant in some, but not all, cases. In other words, in only some cases is the association between class group attitudes and policy opinion statistically distinct across knowledge levels. That said, Figure 5.1 shows that the politically knowledgeable are driving the relationships between class group attitudes and policy opinion displayed in Table 5.1.

5. The modern version of this tax was enacted in 1906, phased out gradually in 2001, reinstated in 2010 due to impermanence in the 2001 legislation, and then made permanent in 2013.

6. See Bartels (2008), Krupnikov et al. (2006), and Slemrod (2006).

7. Bartels (2008, pp. 207–208). See also Slemrod (2006).

8. Graetz and Shapiro (2005, p. 254).

9. Bartels (2008, p. 208).

10. Bartels (2008, p. 213).

11. Levendusky and Jackman (2003, pp. 25–26), for example, argue that, "scholars should accept, once and for all, that the interviewer rating is a flawed measure of political knowledge. There is considerable cross-interviewer heterogeneity, and using this measure risks contaminating the entire model with large amounts of measurement error." Lupia (2015), meanwhile, finds several problems with the measure: "the actual means by which the interviewer assessments were produced, what we know about the lack of training and quality control associated with the measure, and the fact that the assessments occurred after the respondent completes the survey means that the interviewer assessments are unlikely to be consistent across interviewers, independent of respondent answers, or consistent across election "years." Based on these critiques, Lupia concludes, "I recommend that this variable not be used to draw general judgments about the effect of information or knowledge."

12. Here I describe one manipulation; the results of an additional manipulation, whether the estate tax is described as a "death tax," are presented in Chapter 7.

13. This ask/tell design replicates and extends the analysis in an unpublished manuscript by John Sides (2010). The critical difference between Sides' analysis and my own is the central role of resentment of the rich evident here. I also borrowed elements of this ask/tell design from a survey experiment on a very different topic reported in Stoker and Hochschild (2004).

14. This finding is consistent with results from some scholarship, however, including both Slemrod (2006) and Sides (2010). Bartels (2008) also notes that the 2003 NPR/Kaiser Foundation/Kennedy School survey asked respondents who favored eliminating the estate tax why they responded this way, and 62 percent of respondents gave the reason that "It affects too many people."

15. The marginal effects plotted in this figure are based on an ordinary least-squares regression of estate tax opinion on resentment of the rich, the percentage of people thought to be affected by the tax, and the interaction of the two. The interaction term is marginally significant (p < 0.10).

16. See Howard (1997) and Mettler (2011).

17. The design and analysis extend Mettler and Guardino's (Mettler 2011) experiment in two key ways. First, the key hypothesis investigated here is whether resentment of the rich is activated by information, whereas Mettler and Guardino's focus is on the main effect of information. Second, while Mettler and Guardino's experiment, like the experiment presented here, has a control group in which no information about the distributive consequences are provided, the results for this group are not presented in their analysis, whereas in the analysis presented here the comparison between the control group and the information group is central.

18. As in the case of Mettler and Guardino's experiment, the information about distributive benefits comes from the Joint Committee on Taxation, "Estimates of Federal Tax Expenditures for Fiscal Years 2006–2010."

19. These predicted values are calculated based on an ordinary least squares regression in which the dependent variable is HMID opinion and the independent variables are a dummy variable for the experimental condition, the resentment of the rich index, the interaction of the experimental condition and resentment of the rich, lagged HMID opinion (wave 1), and control variables from previous analyses (see appendix). The interaction term is statistically significant (p 0.001).

20. Mettler (2011).

6 EFFECTS OF CLASS GROUP ATTITUDES ON VOTE CHOICE

1. See Kinder and Palfrey (1993).

2. As with any experiment in which attitude questions are asked after the manipulation, it is important to assess whether the experimental stimuli affected responses to the questions: regression analyses of class group attitudes on experimental conditions revealed no evidence that this was the case. Also, in order to address this concern further, I replicated the experiment on a separate sample from Mechanical Turk, using a two-wave panel design in which sympathy for the poor was measured in the first wave and candidate preference in the second. The results are consistent with the results reported here.

3. From "The New Resentment of the Poor." *The New York Times*, August 30, 2011. Last accessed at: www.nytimes.com/2011/08/31/opinion/the-new-resentment-of-the-poor.html?_r=0.

4. See Hochschild (1981) and Newman and Jacobs (2010) for examples of this account.

5. See Markus (2001).

6. In separate models I include the interaction between respondent ideology and experimental condition. The pattern of findings described here remains unchanged.

7. The marginal effects plots presented in this chapter are based on regression models (see Appendix) in which all control variables are set to their means.

8. See especially Petrocik (1996).

9. Additional analyses break out the results by respondent ideology; the results indicate that the effects of sympathy for the poor extend to both liberal and conservative respondents.

10. The authors use the term "self-monitoring," but I stick with "impression management" terminology, consistent with some research in psychology, in order to convey how important it is to these respondents to give off a favorable impression.

11. See Berinsky and Lavine (2012).

12. See Berinsky (2004) and Berinsky and Lavine (2012).

13. As an alternative approach, I also include an interaction with the impression management scale, which takes advantage of variation in the scale obscured by a median split. The results are similar to those presented here: the relationship between sympathy for the poor and support for the candidate endures across the impression management scale.

14. See Berinsky and Lavine (2012).

15. See Kinder and Dale-Riddle (2012), Piston (2010), and Tesler and Sears (2010).

16. See Kenski, et al. (2010).

17. See Grossmann and Hopkins (2016) and Petrocik (1996), as well as recent polling data that indicate that the public perceives Republicans to be more likely to favor the rich, and Democrats to be more likely to assist the poor. The results of a Pew Research Center survey conducted December 8–13, 2015, are available at www.pewsocialtrends.org/2016/02/04/most-americans-say-gov ernment-doesnt-do-enough-to-help-middle-class/. See also the results of a Pew survey conducted July 16–26, 2012, at www.pewsocialtrends.org/2012/ 08/27/yes-the-rich-are-different/.

18. For example, see "Obama: 'Help Main Street' As Well As Wall Street," CNN, September 19, 2008. Last accessed at: www.cnn.com/2008/POLITICS/09/19/c ampaign.wrap/index.html?eref=onion. See also "Obama and McCain Plans for Income Taxes," Anthony Mason, CBS News, September 9, 2008. Last accessed at: www.cbsnews.com/news/obama-and-mccain-plans-for-income-taxes/.

19. "For Incomes Below $100,000, a Better Tax Break in Obama's Plan." Steven Greenhouse, October 30, 2008.

20. "Obama Ad Attacks McCain for Owning Seven Houses," *CBS News*, Brian Montopoli, August 21, 2008. Last accessed at: www.cbsnews.com/news/ob ama-ad-attacks-mccain-for-owning-seven-houses/.

21. See also: "A housing issue: John McCain not sure how many he and wife Cindy own." *New York Daily News*, Richard Sisk, August 21, 2008.

22. "Obama vs. McCain: It's about Your Money," Shelly Banjo, October 26, 2008. Last accessed at: www.wsj.com/articles/SB122497140074869661.

23. Schneider and Ingram (1993).

24. Of course, Schneider and Ingram were writing in the early 1990s, while this election occurred in 2008. Yet evidence presented in Chapter 3 suggests that sympathy for the poor was dominant in the American public during the time that Schneider and Ingram wrote as well.

25. Kenski, Hardy, and Jamieson (2010).

26. Bartels (2013).

27. See Vavreck and Sides (2014).
28. Tesler (2016). See also Pasek et al. (2014) and Yadon and Piston (forthcoming).
29. See Smith (2014) and Smith (2016).
30. See Abramowitz (2014).
31. Vavreck and Sides (2014) do briefly consider this possibility, as discussed in the next paragraph.
32. Last accessed March 16, 2013, at: http://cnnpressroom.blogs.cnn.com/2012/02/01/mitt-romney-middle-income-americans-are-focus-not-very-poor/.
33. See Vavreck and Sides (2014).
34. "After Iowa, Obama Campaign Sharpens 2 Negative Portrayals of Romney," Helene Cooper and Mark Landler, January 4, 2012.
35. Here too it is possible that these perceptions of Romney and Obama were driven by long-standing reputations of the two major parties (Green, Palmquist, and Schickler 2002).
36. See Vavreck and Sides (2014).
37. The article also noted, however, that this title "did not work out well last time." "Clinton's Countless Choices Hinge on One: 2016." Jodi Kantor, December 8, 2012.
38. "Run Hillary Run!: Majority Want a Clinton 2016 Candidacy." Jon Cohen, December 5, 2012.
39. "Bernie Sanders, Long-Serving Independent, Enters Presidential Race as a Democrat," Alan Rappeport, April 29, 2015.
40. "Is Bernie Sanders too Radical for America?" Peter Dreier, June 30, 2015.
41. "Bernie Sanders, the surprise story of the year," John Wagner, October 13, 2015.
42. "Sanders draws more than 20,000 in Boston, building on a strong week." *The Washington Post*, John Wagner, October 3, 2015.
43. "New poll shows that black voters really aren't 'Feeling the Bern,'" Mackenzie Israel-Trummel and Ariela Schachter, blog post on *The Monkey Cage* hosted at *The Washington Post*, February 18, 2016. See also "Bernie Sanders' surge doesn't mean the Democratic race is wide open. Here's why," Michael Tesler, blog post on *The Monkey Cage* hosted at *The Washington Post*, September 17, 2015.
44. This moniker came from an article in *The New York Times* titled "The Socialist Senator," by Mark Leibovich, January 21, 2007.
45. Shapiro criticizes "a number of dubious assumptions about human psychology" including the assumption "that the poor and middle classes compare themselves to the wealthy when thinking about what is feasible or just" (119). Shapiro contends further that, "Workers do not compare themselves to their bosses in assessing their circumstances. They do not compare themselves to the rich, but rather to workers like themselves" (121).
46. "People will be more likely to blame others who are close to themselves in the social order for their plight rather than the wealthy, who seem unimaginably far away" (120).

47. People who "internalize ideologies" that are "inward-looking" will not demand redistribution through public institutions. Instead, they will "blame themselves for their circumstances and accept that they should look inward when trying to improve them" (pp. 121–122).
48. Shapiro (2002, pp. 120–121).
49. See also Bartels (2008) and McCall (2013).
50. From Dahl (1956, 125). It is far from certain whether elections actually deliver the goods, however, as discussed in the next chapter. See also Achen and Bartels (2016).
51. For example, Campbell et al. (1960).
52. See Fiorina (1981).

7 WHY DON'T POLITICIANS LISTEN?

1. Edelman (1985, p. 12).
2. See Davis and Rappeport (2017), Pew Center (2017), Amadeo (2017), Irwin (2017), Rappeport (2017), Rubin (2017), and Walters (2017).
3. For evidence of the disconnect between public preferences and government actions when it comes to the specific issue of the redistribution of wealth, see Page and Jacobs (2009).
4. Social Security also has downwardly redistributive effects (Howard 2007)., as
5. Especially since the Earned Income Tax Credit and Medicaid have actually been expanding in recent years. See Howard (2007), and for more recent data see MACPAC (2016) and de Rugby (2014).
6. Income tax rates in the United States are among the most progressive in the world – yet the effects of the income tax are less progressive in the United States than in many other nations, because the marginal rate applied to the highest earners is considerably lower than in those other nations. See Crook (2012) and Matthews (2013).
7. Government efforts are especially meager in states with high percentages of black people. Howard (2007) notes that about 25% of people in Alabama are black, and the average welfare benefit for a family of three is $164 a month as of the year 2000. But in New Hampshire, where less than 1% of people are black, the average welfare benefit for a family of three is $575 per month. The same is true of Medicaid. New Hampshire spends about three times as much money on each of its Medicaid children as Alabama does. These are not isolated examples: Howard finds that after holding constant other relevant political factors, benefit levels of TANF are negatively associated with the percentage of black people in that state.
8. This is because the lion's share of the benefits of economic growth during this time period went to the top 1 percent of income earners. See Campbell (2014).
9. See Campbell's (2014) description of her brother's harrowing experience with Medi-Cal: Medicaid as implemented in California. Also see Soss, Fording, and Schram (2011).

10. As Piketty and Saez (2007) put it, "the progressivity of the U.S. federal tax system at the top of the income distribution has declined dramatically since the 1960s." See also Leonhardt (2010).

11. The CBO estimates that fifteen million people would lose their health insurance under Senate Republicans' June 26th plan – a number that could rise to twenty-six million by 2026 (CBO 2017). Additionally, the bill would cut taxes by about $765 billion over the next decade, and the benefits of those cuts would be concentrated among the wealthy. The Tax Policy Center estimates that the top one percent of earners would receive about 40 percent of the tax savings, while the top 20 percent of earners would receive about two-thirds of the total tax savings (Tax Policy Center 2017). See also Horsley (2017) and Sanger-Katz (2017).

12. Brandolini and Smeeding (2008).

13. Morelli, Smeeding, and Thompson (2014).

14. See Jacobs and Soss (2010), but see Mishel, Shierholz, and Schmitt (2013).

15. See Mahler and Jesuit (2006).

16. See Enns et al. (2014).

17. See Piketty and Saez (2007).

18. See Kelly (2009) and Hacker and Pierson (2010).

19. See Warren and Stokes (1963).

20. See Broockman and Skovron (2013).

21. The survey asked about same-sex marriage as well; here I focus on the results for economic issues.

22. See Druckman and Jacobs (2015), Jacobs and Shapiro (2000), and Karpowitz (2009).

23. A simple Google search with the terms "public opinion taxes rich" yielded the following, among others: Clemente (2017), Newport (2017), Newport (2016), Weissmann (2015), Weldon (2015), and Dutton (2012).

24. Still, it is possible that even on this issue, for which data are readily available, Republican legislators are unaware of their constituents' preferences. Warshaw and Broockman (2017) write, "[P]oliticians are surprisingly poor at estimating public opinion in their districts and states, Republicans in particular. G.O.P. politicians tend to overestimate support for conservative health care views by about 20 percentage points – meaning Senate Republicans might see their states as just barely supporting the A.H.C.A." See also Taylor (2017), Savransky (2017), Williams (2017), Shephard (2017), and Jacobs (2017).

25. See Przybyla (2017) and Marcos (2017).

26. See Kaplan and Pear (2017).

27. See Gilens (2012) for a discussion of evidence that money influences election outcomes.

28. Data on the preferences of the richest Americans are hard to come by, but see Page, Bartels, and Seawright's (2013) pioneering study in Chicago.

29. See Carnes (2013) for an analysis of the skewed class background of politicians and its effects on policymaking.

30. Max Palmer and Benjamin Schneer (2016) find that about half of former governors and senators serve on a corporate board after leaving office.

31. See Converse (1964) and Kinder and Kalmoe (2017) for evidence that the bulk of the mass public is "innocent" of ideology.
32. Compared to political elites, that is. See Delli Carpini and Keeter (1996), and see Hutchings and Piston (2011b) for a review.
33. See Lippmann (1920).
34. See Jacobs and Shapiro (2000).
35. For an excellent overview of scholarship on framing, see Chong and Druckman (2007).
36. "Meet Mr. Death," by Joshua Green, *The American Prospect*, December 19, 2001.
37. "Linking Tax to Death May Have Brought Its Doom," USA Today, May 20, 2001.
38. See, for example, "The Case for Death Duties," The Economist, October 25, 2007.
39. Quoted in "Meet Mr. Death," by Joshua Green, *The American Prospect*, December 19, 2001.
40. This is the same experiment reported in Chapter 5, but I analyze some conditions there, and others here, for presentational purposes.
41. Response options are "Strongly favor", "Somewhat favor", "Slightly favor", "Neither favor nor oppose", "Slightly oppose", "Somewhat oppose", and "Strongly oppose". This seven-point scale is transformed onto a 0–1 interval in the figure.
42. In neither of these conditions were respondents informed that only the affluent are affected by the tax.
43. However, a similar analysis finds little evidence that the "death tax" frame is effective (Bartels 2008).
44. Campbell, Converse, Miller, and Stokes (1960). Also see Green, Palmquist, and Schickler (2002).
45. See Abramowitz and Webster (2016), Iyengar and Westwood (2015), Mason (2015), and Roush (2016).
46. Also, high levels of unemployment under a Democratic incumbent may have favored the Republican Party. While official unemployment in 2015–2016 was slightly below the median for the last 50 years, labor force participation is actually at its lowest rate since the "stagflation" days of the 1970s (Thompson 2016; Mathur and McCloskey 2016). This is because the official unemployment rate of the Bureau of Labor Statistics only counts those who are not working but are actively seeking work as unemployed – but increasingly, many people are either underemployed or not seeking work (Casselman 2014).
47. See for example, Campbell (2017), Lewis-Beck and Tien (2016), Erikson and Wlezein (2014), and Norpoth (2004).
48. From Sides, Tesler, and Vavreck (2016, p. 52).
49. See for example Campbell (2016), Norpoth (2016), Abramowitz (2016), and Lewis-Beck and Tien (2016), among many others.
50. Kinder and Dale-Riddle (2012, p. 20).
51. Trump's Democratic and Republican opponents criticized his racism and sexism throughout the 2016 presidential campaign. *The Telegraph* published

a list of sexist comments Trump has made in public life (Cohen 2017). *The Huffington Post* has published a comparable list documenting a number of Trump's racist comments and actions (O'Connor and Marans 2017). See also Jardina, McElwee, and Piston (2016).

52. Analyses of the available survey evidence suggest that people who hold prejudiced views toward immigrants (especially Hispanic/Latino/a immigrants), Muslims, and blacks were disproportionately likely to vote for Trump. Indeed, the effects of these prejudicial attitudes on vote choice were stronger than they had been in recent presidential elections (Sides 2017; Sides, Tesler, and Vavreck 2016; Tesler 2016).

53. Carly Wayne, Nick Valentino, and Marzia Oceno (2016) find that sexism is strongly correlated with support for Trump, after holding constant relevant variables including partisanship, ideology, authoritarianism, and ethnocentrism. They also demonstrate that experimentally manipulating anger heightens the association between sexism and support for Trump.

54. That said, the challenge from Bernie Sanders in the Democratic primary did appear to force Clinton to give more attention to income inequality and build her left-wing populist credentials. See *Al Jazeera America* (2015).

55. See Chozick, Confessore, and Barbaro (2016).

56. See Overby (2016).

57. See Rahn and Oliver (2016).

58. See Chozick (2016) and White (2016).

59. See Starr (2016), Frank (2016), and Latimer (2017). See also Gallup (2016).

60. Kathy Cramer (2016a) finds in her interviews with groups of Wisconsin citizens that many rural residents feel that urban areas receive an undeservedly large share of power, resources, and respect. Cramer (2016b) also argues that Trump's campaign tapped into this rural resentment.

61. See Long (2015), Wolfgang (2016), and Hains (2016).

62. See Keizer (2016), Chideya (2016), and Solman (2016).

63. It is not clear that this is the case, however. Sides (2017) shows that whites without a college education were shifting to the Republican Party prior to the presidential election in 2016. Furthermore, Brian Schaffner, Matthew MacWilliams, and Tatishe Nteta (2017, p. 3) find that variation in public attitudes about race and gender "explain about two-thirds of the education gap among whites in the presidential vote."

64. Faricy (2015) finds that when the Republican Party has control of the government, tax expenditures that disproportionately benefit the wealthy are especially likely to pass. For additional scholarly treatments of the hidden, often upwardly redistributive effects of tax expenditures, see Hacker (2002, 2004), Howard (1997, 2007), Mettler (2011).

65. Bartels (2008) finds that the Bush tax cuts of 2001 and 2003 would have been markedly less popular had the public been more knowledgeable about them. Hacker and Pierson (2014) argue that public ignorance about these tax cuts was no accident: political elites intentionally disguised their upwardly redistributive effects.

66. See Bartels (2008) for an example.

CONCLUSION: THE PATH BEHIND AND THE PATH FORWARD

1. Converse (1964).
2. Kinder and Dale-Riddle (2012), Kinder and Kalmoe (2017), Kinder and Kam (2009), and Nelson and Kinder (1996).
3. The term "group-centered" comes from Kinder and Kalmoe (2017, 136).
4. See especially Kinder and Dale-Riddle (2012).
5. See especially Nelson and Kinder (1996).
6. See, for example, Page and Jacobs (2009).
7. See Kinder and Winter (2001), Page and Jacobs (2009), Schlozman and Verba (1979).
8. Kinder and Sanders (1996, pp. 261–262).
9. Recent reviews include Huddy and Feldman (2009) and Hutchings and Piston (2011a).
10. For an overview of scholarship on attitudes about gender and the effects of these attitudes on public opinion, see Burns and Gallagher (2010).
11. In turn, white opposition to immigrants is often driven by prejudice against Latinos (e.g., Brader, Valentino, and Suhay 2008; Hajnal and Rivera 2014).
12. For important recent examples, see Lajevardi (2016) and Tesler (2016).
13. See, for example, Ayoub and Garretson (2017) as well as Lupia et al. (2010).
14. In their analysis of perceptions of competition among whites, blacks, Latinos, and Asians, Bobo and Hutchings (1996, p. 968) write: "coverage of the items tapping perceived threat should be expanded to assess whether and why racial minorities perceive White Americans as competitive threats. In hindsight, this was a serious omission in our survey design and should be a high priority in future research."
15. Suzanne Moore (2016) of *The New Statesman* argues, "I think that any intelligent women hates men." Elsewhere in the essay, she ties this emotion to politics: "As a class, I hate men ... I want to see this class broken. There can't be even basic equality for women without taking away the power of men – and by that I don't mean feeling sorry for them because they have no friends or suggesting that they have small genitals. I mean the removal of their power." Similarly, in an article titled "Why I Hate Men," Julie Bindel (2006) of *The Guardian* ties anger toward men, or a subgroup of men, to gender consciousness: "I will say loud and proud, yes, today I hate men, and will tomorrow and the day after. But only the men who perpetrate these crimes against my sisters, and those who do nothing to stop it. Are you in either one of those categories? If so, then I despise you."
16. While I know of no research in political science on this topic, the following news account is suggestive: in Provincetown, Massachusetts, straight people have complained of being taunted with the term "breeders," and one woman claimed that dog feces was put next to her car as an act of harassment. Antipathy to straight people may arise as a reaction to heterosexism; much of the conflict reported in the news account appears to be based in gay people's anger over Provincetown residents signing a petition to pass a state-wide constitutional amendment banning gay marriage. This became public

knowledge when the names of 43 Provincetown residents who signed this amendment were published on knowthyneighbor.org. See Liu (2006).

17. Chudy (2016).
18. Conover (1988). For an important review of the importance of attitudes about gender to American politics, see Burns and Gallagher (2010).
19. Hochschild and Weaver (2007).
20. Along with other social characteristics such as gender, age, ablebodiedness, and history of military service (Gordon 1994; Skocpol 1992).
21. See Alesina and Glaeser (2004).
22. This section draws heavily on the scholarship of Linda Faye Williams (2010) and, to a lesser extent, Ira Katznelson (2005).
23. All this despite the fact that Bureau programs were structured to ensure that recipients were working in some way. As Williams (2010, p. 52) notes, in several Southern states, black women who received aid but did not have jobs (even if there were no jobs available) were gathered into a central location and forced to do "community service" as a condition of receiving aid, such as washing the clothes of any white people who wanted it done without payment. Williams writes: "It was as if slavery had been a 250-year holiday from work."
24. Some black people benefited from the Civil War veterans' pensions program as well. But as Williams observes, the vast majority of black veterans came from and returned to slaveholding states. These veterans had a very hard time proving their identity (they had often been designated by their masters' last name), and their widows had an even harder time doing so. The procedures to prove eligibility were often prohibitively costly and time-consuming; black veterans were disproportionately unlikely to receive benefits from the program.
25. That said, even as these programs reinforced racial inequality they also provided resources to black people (Williams 2010).
26. Gilens (1999).
27. Hancock (2003, 2004).
28. "Welfare reform" legislation in 1996 replaced Aid for Families with Dependent Children (AFDC) with Temporary Assistance for Needy Families (TANF). Under the AFDC, the federal government had committed to pay for welfare for all those people who met the states' eligibility criteria. These criteria varied tremendously from state to state, but prior to 1996 all of those who were deemed to be eligible under the criteria could enroll. Under TANF, this was replaced with the following: the federal government allocates a fixed sum of money to the state, and the state decides how to spend it. In addition, the new program – TANF, or temporary assistance for needy families – made it much more difficult to be eligible to receive benefits. States can exclude teenage mothers, for example, or they can impose a family cap, where if a mother on welfare has another child, the state can deny the mother benefits. All in all, these changes have resulted in government becoming significantly less responsive to financial need. See Howard (2007, chapter 5) and Soss, Fording, and Schram (2011, chapter 11).

29. That said, debates about the meaning and measurement of racial prejudice continue (see Huddy and Feldman 2009 for a review).
30. Among both whites and Latinos: see Krupnikov and Piston (2016), Piston (2010), and Yadon and Piston (forthcoming).
31. See Lupia et al. (2015).
32. See Hutchings and Piston (2011a) and Kalmoe and Piston (2013) as well as Strother, Piston, and Ogorzalek (2017).
33. See Krupnikov and Piston (2015a), Krupnikov and Piston (2015b), and Krupnikov, Piston, and Bauer (2016).
34. See Hutchings (2009) and Kinder and Sanders (1996).
35. See Saez and Zucman (2016).
36. See especially Bartels (2008), Gilens (2012), and Gilens and Page (2014).
37. See Enns (2015), Soroka and Wleizen (2008), and Ura and Ellis (2008).
38. See, for example, Gilens (2015).
39. See also Page and Jacobs (2009).
40. "The Non-Taxpaying Class: Those Lucky Duckies!" November 20, 2002.
41. "Who Are the Real Job Creators?" Martin Fridson, *Forbes*, June 17, 2013.
42. Garner (2017).
43. From Cramer (2016a).
44. It is unclear why this method resulted in discussions of class while Cramer's did not. One possibility is that class is more salient to national politics than local or state politics; another is that the people in the small groups in Wisconsin differ in substantial ways from people across the country who participate in surveys.
45. Taibbi (2014). The entire quotation is: "Unquestionably, however, something else is at work, something that cuts deeper into the American psyche. We have a profound hatred of the weak and the poor, and a corresponding groveling terror before the rich and successful, and we're building a bureaucracy to match those feelings."
46. See Campbell (2014).
47. See Piven (2015, p. 1115).
48. See McCall (2013, p. 181). Again, McCall does not endorse this claim; rather, she subjects it to critical scrutiny.
49. From Page and Jacobs (2009, p. 31)
50. As discussed previously, previous research has already shown that one subgroup of the poor – comprised of welfare recipients – is viewed quite negatively (e.g., Bartels 2008; Gilens 1999). Negative views of this subgroup turn on intersections among class, race, and gender, as scholarship about the public identity of the "welfare queen" has revealed (Hancock 2003, 2004).
51. See Parnes (2012).
52. See Mother Jones (2012).
53. As *The Wall Street Journal* put it: "[T]he Obama comment strikes at the heart of a sensitive issue for the wealthy: How much of their success is truly self-made or how much was inherited?" (Frank 2012). See also Bauman (2012), Barbaro, Applebaum, and Gabriel (2012), and Horowitz (2012).
54. See Jackman and Jackman's (1983) pioneering research in this regard.
55. See Miller et al. (1981).

56. See Carmines and Stimson (1989), Valentino and Sears (2005), and Tesler (2016).
57. On this point see McCall's (2013) findings of weak to moderate relationships between beliefs about economic inequality and support for downwardly redistributive policies.
58. Calmes (2012).
59. Congressional Budget Office (2012).
60. Dwyer (2012).
61. Montgomery (2012).
62. Video of the exchange is available at this website (Bell 2012): http://abcnews .go.com/blogs/politics/2012/11/nancy-pelosi-no-fiscal-cliff-deal-without-tax -rate-hike-for-wealthy/.
63. See CNBC.com (2012).
64. See Bell (2012) and Wong (2012). See www.c-span.org/video/?309792–1/se nate-session for video of Michigan Democratic Senator Debbie Stabenow emphasizing the desirability of tax increases on the rich: "Those wealthiest few being at the table to do their part to make sure we can solve the biggest deficit crisis we have had as a country."
65. See Williams and Carroll (2012).
66. See Clement (2012).
67. Media coverage of the act can be found here: Montgomery and Kane (2013), Smith (2013), and PBS Newshour (2013). Information about the distributive consequences of the act can be found here: Huang (2013).
68. However, the threshold for "high-income earners" was not $250,000 ($300,000 for couples) as Obama had proposed, but rather $400,000 ($450,000 for couples). This victory was a partial one.

References

Abramowitz, Alan I. 2014. "Long-Term Trends and Short-Term Forecasts: The Transformation of U.S. Presidential Elections in an Age of Polarization." *PS: Political Science and Politics* 47: 289–292.

Abramowitz, Alan I. 2016. "Will Time for a Change Mean Time for Trump?" *PS: Political Science and Politics* 49(4): 659–660.

Abramowitz, Alan I. and Steven Webster. 2016. "The Rise of Negative Partisanship and the Nationalization of U.S. Elections in the 21st Century." *Electoral Studies* 41(1): 12–22.

Abrams, Dominic and Michael A. Hogg. 1988. "Comments on the Motivational Status of Self-Esteem in Social Identity and Intergroup Discrimination." *European Journal of Social Psychology* 18(4): 317–334.

Achen, Christopher H. 2002. "Toward a New Political Methodology: Microfoundations and ART." *Annual Review of Political Science* 5: 423–450.

Achen, Christopher H. and Larry M. Bartels. 2016. *Democracy for Realists: Why Elections Do Not Produce Responsive Government*. Princeton, NJ: Princeton University Press.

Adler, Jerry. 2009. "Why Americans Don't Hate the Rich." *Newsweek*. Accessed online: www.newsweek.com/why-americans-dont-hate-rich-82585.

Alesina, Alberto and Edward L. Glaeser. 2004. *Fighting Poverty in the U.S. and Europe: A World of Difference*. New York, NY: Oxford University Press.

Alesina, Alberto and Eliana La Ferrara. 2005. "Preferences for Redistribution in the Land of Opportunities." *Journal of Public Economics*, 89(5–6): 897–931.

Al Jazeera America. 2015. "Hillary Clinton Targets Income Inequality in Major Economic Policy Speech." *Al Jazeera America*, July 13, 2015.

Amadeo, Kimberly. 2017. "Trump's Tax Plan and How It Would Affect You." *The Balance*. June 24, 2017. Accessed online: www.thebalance.com/trump-s-tax-plan-how-it-affects-you-4113968.

Arieli, Yehoshua. 1964. *Individualism and Nationalism in American Ideology*. Cambridge, MA: Harvard University Press.

Ayoub, Phillip M. and Jeremiah Garretson. 2017. "Getting the Message Out: Media Context and Global Changes in Attitudes toward Homosexuality." *Comparative Political Studies* 50(8): 1055–1085.

Baker, R., S. Blumberg, J. Brick, M. Couper, M. Courtright, J. Dennis, D. Dillman, M. Frankel, P. Garland, R. Grovers, C. Kennedy, J. Krosnick, and P. Lavrakas. 2010. "Research Synthesis: AAPOR Report on Online Panels." *Public Opinion Quarterly* 74: 711–781.

Bandura, Albert. 1969. " Social-Learning Theory of Identificatory Processes," in *Handbook of Socialization Theory and Research*. David Goslin, ed. Chicago, IL: Rand McNally, 213–262.

Banjo, Shelly. 2008. "Obama vs. McCain: It's about Your Money." *wsj.com*. www.wsj.com/articles/SB122497140074869661.

Bartels, Larry M. 2008. *Unequal Democracy*. Princeton, NJ: Princeton University Press.

Bartels, Larry M. 2013. "Political Effects of the Great Recession." *Annals of the American Academy of Political and Social Science* 650:1, 47–75.

Barbaro, Michael, Benyamin Applebaum, and Trip Gabriel. 2012. "Romney and His Money." *The New York Times*, January 20, 2012. Accessed online: www.nytimes.com/2012/01/20/us/politics/fact-check-romney-and-his-fathers-money.html.

Batson, C. Daniel. 1991. *The Altruism Question: Toward a Social-Psychological Answer*. Hillsdale, NJ: Erlbaum.

Batson, C. Daniel. 2011. *Altruism in Humans*. New York, NY: Oxford University Press.

Baumann, Nick. 2012. "Romney Says 'I Didn't Inherit Money from My Parents.' Really?" *Mother Jones*, January 20, 2012. Accessed online: www.motherjones.com/politics/2012/01/romney-says-i-didnt-inherit-money-my-parents-its-complicated/.

Baumgartner, Frank R. and Beth L. Leech. 1998. *Basic Interests: The Importance of Groups in Politics and Political Science*. Princeton, NJ: Princeton University Press.

Becker, Gary S. 1985. "Public Policies, Pressure Groups, and Dead-Weight Costs." *Journal of Public Economics* 28(3): 329–347.

Bell, Benjamin. 2012. "Nancy Pelosi: No Fiscal Cliff Deal without Tax Rate Hike For Wealthy." *ABC News*, November 16, 2012. Accessed online: http://abcnews.go.com/blogs/politics/2012/11/nancy-pelosi-no-fiscal-cliff-deal-without-tax-rate-hike-for-wealthy/.

Bellah, Robert N., Richard Madsen, William M. Sullivan, Ann Swidler, and Steven M. Tipton. 1985. *Habits of the Heart: Individualism and Commitment in American Life*. Berkeley: University of California Press.

Ben-Ze'ev, A. 2000. *The Subtlety of Emotions*. Cambridge, MA: Massachusetts Institute of Technology Press.

Bergan, Daniel E. 2009. "The Draft Lottery and Attitudes towards the Vietnam War." *Public Opinion Quarterly* 73(2): 379–384.

Berinsky, Adam J. 2004. "Can We Talk? Self-Presentation and the Survey Response." *Political Psychology* 25: 643–659.

Berinsky, Adam J., Gregory A. Huber, and Gabriel S. Lenz. 2012. "Evaluating Online Labor Markets for Experimental Research: Amazon.com's Mechanical Turk." *Political Analysis* 20(3): 351–68.

Berinsky, Adam J. and Howard Lavine. 2012. "Self-Monitoring and Political Attitudes," in *Improving Public Opinion Surveys: Interdisciplinary Innovation and the American National Election Studies.* John H. Alrich and Kathleen M. McGraw, eds. Princeton, NJ: Princeton University Press.

Bindel, Julie. 2006. "Why I Hate Men." *The Guardian,* November 2, 2006. Accessed online: www.theguardian.com/commentisfree/2006/nov/02/whyihatemen.

Bloomberg. "Republicans Deemed Too Pro-Rich, 57% in Poll Want Change." Last accessed online: www.bloomberg.com/news/2012-12-13/republicans-deemed-too-pro-rich-57-in-poll-want-change.html.

Bobo, Lawrence and Vincent L. Hutchings. 1996. "Perceptions of Racial Group Competition: Extending Blumer's Theory of Group Position to a Multiracial Social Context." *American Sociological Review* 61(6): 951–972.

Bobo, Lawrence and Frederick C. Licari. 1989. "Education and Political Tolerance: Testing the Effects of Cognitive Sophistication and Target Group Affect." *Public Opinion Quarterly* 53(3): 285–308.

Bonica, Adam, Nolan McCarty, Keith T. Poole, and Howard Rosenthal. 2013. "Why Hasn't Democracy Slowed Rising Inequality?" *The Journal of Economic Perspectives* 27(3): 103–123.

Bowles, Samuel, Herbert Gintis, and Melissa Osborne Groves, eds. 2008. *Unequal Chances: Family Background and Economic Success.* Princeton, NJ: Princeton University Press.

Boydstun, Amber E. 2013. *Making the News: Politics, The Media, and Agenda Setting.* Chicago, IL: University of Chicago Press.

Brader, Ted, Nicholas A. Valentino, and Elizabeth Suhay. 2008. "What triggers public opposition to immigration? Anxiety, group cues, and immigration threat." *American Journal of Political Science* 52(4): 959–978.

Brady, Henry. 1988. "The Perils of Survey Research: Interpersonally Incomparable Responses." *Political Methodology* 11: 269–291.

Brandolini, Andrea and Timothy M. Smeeding. 2008. "Inequality Patterns in Western Democracies: Cross-Country Differences and Changes over Time," in *Democracy, Inequality, and Representation in Comparative Perspective.* Pablo Beramendi and Christopher J. Anderson, eds. New York, NY: Russell Sage Foundation.

Broockman, David E. and Christopher Skovron. 2013. "What Politicians Believe about Their Constituents: Asymmetric Misperceptions and Prospects for Constituency Control." Working paper (February 14, 2013).

Burns, Nancy and Katherine Gallagher. 2010. "Public Opinion on Gender Issues: The Politics of Equity and Roles." *Annual Review of Political Science* 13: 425–443.

Calmes, Jackie. 2012. "Demystifying the Fiscal Impasse That Is Vexing Washington." *The New York Times,* November 15, 2012. Accessed online: www.nytimes.com/2012/11/16/us/politics/the-fiscal-cliff-explained.html

Campbell, Andrea Louise. 2014. *Trapped in America's Safety Net.* Chicago, IL: University of Chicago Press.

Campbell, Angus, Phillip E. Converse, Warren E. Miller, and Donald E. Stokes. 1960. *The American Voter.* Chicago, IL: University of Chicago Press.

Campbell, James E. 2016. "Introduction." *PS: Political Science & Politics* 49(4): 649–654.

Campbell, James E. 2017. "A Recap of the 2016 Election Forecasts." *PS: Political Science & Politics* 50(2): 331–338.

Carmines, Edward G. and James A. Stimson. 1989. *Issue Evolution: Race and the Transformation of American Politics.* Princeton, NJ: Princeton University Press.

Carnes, Nicholas. 2013. *White-Collar Government: The Hidden Role of Class in Economic Policy Making.* Chicago, IL: University of Chicago Press.

Carnes, Nicholas and Noam Lupu. "It's Time to Bust the Myth: Most Trump Voters Were Not Working Class." *Washington Post*, June 5, 2017. Accessed online: www.washingtonpost.com/news/monkey-cage/wp/2017/06/05/its-time-to-bust-the-myth-most-trump-voters-were-not-working-class/?utm_term=.5d6bc47c5cae.

Carnes, Nicholas and Meredith L. Sadin. 2015. "The 'Mill Worker's Son' Heuristic: How Voters Perceive Politicians from Working-Class Families—and How They Really Behave in Office." *Journal of Politics* 77: 285–298.

Carpini, Michael X. Delli and Scott Keeter. 1996. *What Americans Know about Politics and Why It Matters.* New Haven, CT: Yale University Press.

Casselman, Ben. 2014. "Missing: Up to 4 Million Workers." *FiveThirtyEight*, March 26, 2014. Accessed online: https://fivethirtyeight.com/features/missing-up-to-4-million-workers/.

Cassidy, John. 2015. "Is Support for Income Redistribution Really Falling?" *The New Yorker.* April 17, 2015. Accessed online: www.newyorker.com/news/john-cassidy/is-support-for-income-redistribution-really-falling.

Chideya, Farai. 2016. "Trump's Blue Collar Base Wants More Jobs and an American Like the Past." *FiveThirtyEight*, September 13, 2016. Accessed online: https://fivethirtyeight.com/features/trumps-base-is-blue-collar-his-voters-looking-for-a-return-to-better-times/.

Chong, Dennis. 1993. "How People Think, Reason, and Feel about Rights and Liberties." *American Journal of Political Science* 37: 867–899.

Chong, Dennis, Jack Citrin, and Patricia Conley. 2001. "When Self-Interest Matters." *Political Psychology* 22(3): 541–570.

Chong, Dennis and Jamie Druckman. 2007. "Framing Public Opinion in Competitive Democracies." *American Political Science Review* 101: 637–655.

Chozick, Amy. 2016. "Hillary Clinton Wars against Treating Donald Trump as 'Normal' Candidate." *The New York Times*, May 22, 2016. Accessed online: www.nytimes.com/2016/05/23/us/politics/hillary-clinton-donald-trump-campaign.html

Chozick, Amy, Nicholas Confessore, and Michael Barbaro. 2016. "Leaked Speech Excerpts Show a Hillary Clinton at Ease With Wall Street." *The New York*

Times October 7, 2016. Accessed online: www.nytimes.com/2016/10/08/us/politics/hillary-clinton-speeches-wikileaks.html.

Chudy, Jennifer. "Racial Sympathy in American Politics." Doctoral Dissertation, University of Michigan.

Cikara, Mina and Susan T. Fiske. 2011. "Stereotypes and Schadenfreude: Affective and Physiological Markers of Pleasure at Outgroup Misfortunes." *Social Psychological and Personality Science* 3(1): 63–71.

Cillizza, Chris. 2014. "Is Barack Obama 'black'? A majority of Americans say no." *Washington Post*. April 14, 2014. Accessed online: www.washingtonpost.com/news/the-fix/wp/2014/04/14/is-barack-obama-black/?utm_term=.adfc160eb715.

Clawson, Dan and Mary Ann Clawson. 1999. "What Has Happened to the U.S. Labor Movement? Union Decline and Renewal." *Annual Review of Sociology* 25: 95–119.

Clawson, Rosalee A. and Rakuya Trice. 2000. "Poverty As We Know It: Media Portrayals of the Poor. *The Public Opinion Quarterly* 64(1): 53–64.

Clement, Scott. 2012. "Poll: Fiscal Cliff Blame Would Fall Heaviest on GOP." *Washington Post*, December 4, 2012. Accessed online: www.washingtonpost.com/politics/poll-fiscal-cliff-blame-would-fall-heaviest-on-gop/2012/12/04/e917cd38-3e3b-11e2-a2d9-822f58ac9fd5_story.html.

Clement, Scott and Emily Guskin. 2017. "Polls Show Mixed Support for Military Action against North Korea, but Suggest It Should Rise." Washington Post, August 10, 2017. Accessed online: www.washingtonpost.com/news/the-fix/wp/2017/08/10/polls-show-mixed-support-for-military-against-action-north-korea-but-suggest-it-could-rise/?utm_term=.ded48c4a6fdf

Clemente, Frank. 2017. "The Tax Debate: Post-Election Polling Shows the Public Opposes Tax Cuts for Corporations and the Wealthy." Americans for Tax Fairness Memorandum, February 27, 2017.

Clifford, Scott and Spencer Piston. 2017. "Explaining Public Support for Counterproductive Homeless Policy: The Role of Disgust. *Political Behavior* 39: 503–525.

CNBC.com. 2012. "Obama: Ending Tax Cuts for Rich Resolves Half of 'Cliff'." *CNBC*, November 14, 2012. Accessed online: www.cnbc.com/id/49821777.

Cohen, Claire. 2017. "Donald Trump Sexism Tracker: Every Offensive Comment in One Place." *The Telegraph*, July 14, 2017. Accessed online: www.telegraph.co.uk/women/politics/donald-trump-sexism-tracker-every-offensive-comment-in-one-place/.

Cohen, Jon. 2012. "Run Hillary Run! Majority Want a Clinton 2016 Candidacy." *Washington Post*. www.washingtonpost.com/news/the-fix/wp/2012/12/05/run-hillary-run-majority-want-a-clinton-2016-candidacy/?utm_term=.c99b69a6202e.

Congressional Budget Office (CBO). 2012. *Economic Effects of Policies Contributing to Fiscal Tightening in 2013*.

Congressional Budget Office (CBO). 2017. *Cost Estimate for H.R. 1628: Better Care Reconciliation Act of 2017*. June 26, 2017.

Conover, Pamela J. 1988. "The Role of Social Groups in Political Thinking." *British Journal of Political Science* 18: 51–76.

Converse, Philip E. 1964. "The Nature of Belief Systems in Mass Publics," in *Ideology and Discontent*, David Apter, ed. New York, NY: The Free Press, 206–261.

Cook, Fay Lomax and Edith J. Barrett. 1992. *Support for the American Welfare State: The Views of Congress and the Public*. New York, NY: Columbia University Press.

Cooper, Helene and Mark Landler. 2012. "Obama Campaign Focuses Its Attacks On Romney." *nytimes.com*. www.nytimes.com/2012/01/05/us/politics/dem ocrats-target-romney-after-iowa-win.html.

CNN. 2008. "Obama: 'Help Main Street' As Well As Wall Street." *CNN.com*. www.cnn.com/2008/POLITICS/09/19/campaign.wrap/index.html? eref=onion.

———. 2012. "Mitt Romney: Middle Income Americans Are Focus, Not Very Poor." *cnnpressroom.blogs.cnn.com*. http://cnnpressroom.blogs.cnn.com/2012/02/01/mitt-romney-middle-income-americans-are-focus-not-very-poor/.

Cramer, Kathy. 2016. "How rural resentment helps explain the surprising victory of Donald Trump." *Washington Post*, November 13, 2016. Accessed online: w ww.washingtonpost.com/news/monkey-cage/wp/2016/11/13/how-rural-resen tment-helps-explain-the-surprising-victory-of-donald-trump/?utm_term =.ef41528bda81.

Cramer, Kathy. 2016a. *The Politics of Resentment*. University of Chicago Press.

Crook, Clive. 2012. "U.S. Taxes Really Are Unusually Progressive." *The Atlantic*, February 10, 2012. Accessed online: www.theatlantic.com/business/archive/2012/02/us-taxes-really-are-unusually-progressive/252917/.

Cuddy, Amy C., Susan T. Fiske, and Peter Glick. 2008. "Warmth and Competence as Universal Dimensions of Social Perception: The Stereotype Content Model and the BIAS Map." *Advances in Experimental Social Psychology* 40: 62–149.

Dahl, Robert. 2006 [1956]. *A Preface to Democratic Theory*. Chicago, IL: University of Chicago Press.

Davis, Julie Hirschfeld and Alan Rappeport. 2017. "White House Proposes Slashing Tax Rates, Significantly Aiding Wealthy." *The New York Times*, April 26, 2017. Accessed online: www.nytimes.com/2017/04/26/us/politics/trump-tax-cut-plan.html?action=click&contentCollection=The%20Upshot&module=RelatedCoverage&region=Marginalia&pgtype=article.

Davis, Mark H. 1994. *Empathy: A Social Psychological Approach*. Boulder, CO: Westview Press, Inc.

de Rugby, Veronique. 2014. "Trends in EITC Spending and Numbers of Beneficiaries." *Mercatus Center*, April 15, 2014. Accessed online: www.mer catus.org/publication/trends-eitc-spending-and-numbers-beneficiaries.

deTocqueville, Alexis [J.P. Mayer, ed; George Lawrence, trans.]. 2006 [1835]. *Democracy in America*. New York, NY: Harper Perennial Modern Classics.

Doherty, Daniel, Alan S. Gerber, and Donald P. Green. 2006. "Personal Income and Attitudes toward Redistribution: A Study of Lottery Winners." *Political Psychology* 27(3): 441–458.

Downs, Anthony. 1957. *An Economic Theory of Democracy*. New York, NY: Harper & Row.

Dreier, Peter. 2015. "Is Bernie Sanders too Radical for America?" *prospect.org*. http://prospect.org/article/bernie-sanders-too-radical-america.

Drezner, Daniel W. 2015. "The end of the median voter theorem in presidential politics?" *Washington Post*, May 29, 2015. Accessed online: www.washing tonpost.com/posteverything/wp/2015/05/29/the-end-of-the-median-voter-th eorem-in-presidential-politics/?utm_term=.a017bcf59dc4.

Druckman, James N. and Lawrence R. Jacobs. 2015. *Who Governs?: Presidents, Public Opinion, and Manipulation*. Chicago, IL: University of Chicago Press.

Dugan, Andrew. 2015. "In U.S., Support Up for Doctor-Assisted Suicide." Gallup. May 27, 2015. Accessed online: www.gallup.com/poll/183425/sup port-doctor-assisted-suicide.aspx

Dutton, Sarah. 2012. "Polls show longtime support for tax hikes on rich." *CBS News*, December 14, 2012. Accessed online: www.cbsnews.com/news/polls-show-longtime-support-for-tax-hikes-on-rich/.

Dwyer, Devin. 2012. "Obama Vows Veto for Full Extension of Bush Tax Cuts." *ABC News*, July 9, 2012. Accessed online: http://abcnews.go.com/blogs/pol itics/2012/07/obama-vows-veto-for-full-extension-of-bush-tax-cuts/.

Eagly, Alice Hendrikson, and Shelly Chaiken. 1993. *The Psychology of Attitudes*. San Diego: Harcourt Brace Jovanovich College Publishers.

Economist, The. 2007. "The Case for Death Duties." *economist.com*. www.econ omist.com/node/10024733.

Economist, The. 2015. "Outlaw Economics: Policies to Shift Income from Rich to Poor May Prove Less Effective than Imagined." Accessed online: www.econ omist.com/news/finance-and-economics/21648044-policies-shift-income-ric h-poor-may-prove-less-effective.

Edelman, Murray. 1985. *The Symbolic Uses of Politics, with a New Afterword* (2nd edition). Chicago, IL: University of Illinois Press.

Enns, Peter K. 2015. "Relative Policy Support and Coincidental Representation." *Perspectives on Politics* 13(4): 1053–1064.

Enns, Peter K., Nathan J. Kelly, Jana Morgan, Thomas Volscho, and Christopher Wiito. 2014. "Conditional Status Quo Bias and Top Income Shares: How U.S. Political Institutions Have Benefited the Rich." *Journal of Politics* 76(2): 289–303.

Enns, Peter K. and Christopher Wlezien, eds. 2011. *Who Gets Represented?* New York, NY: Russell Sage Foundation.

Erikson, Robert S. and Christopher Wlezein. 2014. "Forecasting US Presidential Elections Using Economic and Noneconomic Fundamentals." *PS: Political Science & Politics* 47(2): 313–316.

Evans, Geoffrey. 1999. *The End of Class Politics? Class Voting in Comparative Context*. New York, NY: Oxford University Press.

Faricy, Christopher. 2015. *Welfare for the Wealthy: Parties, Social Spending, and Inequality in the United States*. Cambridge University Press.

Feather, N.T., and Katherine Nairn. 2005. "Resentment, Envy, Schadenfreude, and Sympathy: Effects of Own and Other's Deserved and Undeserved Status." *Australian Journal of Psychology* 57: 87–102.

Feather, N.T., and Rebecca Sherman. 2002. "Envy, Resentment, Schadenfreude, and Sympathy: Reactions to Deserved and Undeserved Achievement and Subsequent Failure." *Personality and Social Psychology Bulletin* 7: 953–961.

Feldman, Stanley. 1982. "Economic Self-Interest and Political Behavior." *American Journal of Political Science* 26(3): 446–466.

 1988a. "Economic Individualism and American Public Opinion." *American Politics Research* 11(1): 3–29.

 1988b. "Structure and Consistency in Public Opinion: The Role of Core Beliefs and Values." *American Journal of Political Science* 31: 416–440.

Feldman, Stanley and Leonie Huddy. 2005. "Racial Resentment and White Oppression to Race-Conscious Programs: Principles or Prejudice?" *American Journal of Political Science,* 49(1): 168–183.

Feldman, Stanley and Marco R. Steenbergen. 2001. "The Humanitarian Foundation of Support for Social Welfare." *American Journal of Political Science* 45: 658–677.

Feldman, Stanley and John Zaller. 1992. "The Political Culture of Ambivalence: Ideological Responses to the Welfare State." *American Journal of Political Science* 36: 268–307.

Fenno, Richard F. 1978. *Home Style: House Members in Their Districts.* New York, NY: Pearson.

Fiorina, Morris. 1981. *Retrospective Voting in American National Elections.* New Haven: Yale University Press.

Fiorina, Morris P., Samuel J. Abrams, and Jeremy C. Pope. 2016. *Culture War? The Myth of a Polarized America,* 3rd edition. New York, NY: Longman.

Fiske, Susan T. 2011. *Envy Up, Scorn Down: How Status Divides Us.* New York, NY: Russell Sage Foundation.

Fiske, Susan T., Amy C. Cuddy, Peter Glick, and Jun Xu. 2002. "A Model of (Often Mixed) Stereotype Content: Competence and Warmth Respectively Follow from Perceived Status and Competition." *Journal of Personality and Social Psychology* 82: 878–902.

Foner, Eric. 1984. "Why Is There No Socialism in the United States?" *History Workshop Journal* 17(1): 57–80.

Fong, Christina. 2001. "Social Preferences, Self-Interest, and the Demand for Redistribution." *Journal of Public Economics* 82(2): 225–246.

Frank, Robert. 2012. "Is It Fair to Call Romney a 'Silver Spoon?'" *The Wall Street Journal,* April 19, 2012. Accessed online: https://blogs.wsj.com/wealth/2012/04/19/is-it-fair-to-call-romney-a-silver-spoon/.

Frank, T.A. 2016. "What If Trump Had Run as a Democrat?" *Vanity Fair,* March 18, 2016. Accessed online: www.vanityfair.com/news/2016/03/what-if-don ald-trump-had-run-as-a-democrat.

Frank, Thomas. 2012. *Pity the Billionaire: The Hard-Times Swindle and the Unlikely Comeback of the Right.* New York, NY: Metropolitan Books.

Franko, William, Caroline J. Tolbert, and Christopher Witko. 2013. "Inequality, Self-Interest, and Public Support for 'Robin Hood' Tax Policies." *Political Research Quarterly* 66: 923–937.

Free, Lloyd A. and Hadley Cantril. 1967. *The Political Beliefs of Americans: A Study of Public Opinion.* New Brunswick, NJ: Rutgers University Press.

Fridson, Martin. 2013. "Who Are the Real Job Creators?" *forbes.com*. www.for
bes.com/sites/investor/2013/06/17/who-are-the-real-job-creators/
#7ba116a5399a.

Gallup. 2015. "Fewer Americans Identify as Middle Class in Recent Years."
gallup.com. www.gallup.com/poll/182918/fewer-americans-identify-mid
dle-class-recent-years.aspx.

Gallup. 2016. "Trump Seen as Less Conservative than Prior GOP Candidates."
Gallup.com. www.gallup.com/poll/196064/trump-seen-less-conservative-pr
ior-gop-candidates.aspx.

Gans, Herbert J. 1995. *The War against the Poor: The Underclass and
Antipoverty Policy*. New York, NY: Basic Books.

Garner, Dwight. 2017. "We Admire Americans Who Don't Forget Their Roots."
Esquire, February 2, 2017. Accessed online: www.esquire.com/lifestyle/a51
761/class-in-america/.

Geiger, Abigail. 2016. "Support for marijuana legalization continues to rise." Pew
Research Center. October 12, 2016. Accessed online: www.pewresearch.org/
fact-tank/2016/10/12/support-for-marijuana-legalization-continues-to-rise/

Gilens, Martin. 1999. *Why Americans Hate Welfare*. Chicago, IL: University of
Chicago Press.

2012. *Affluence and Influence: Economic Inequality and Political Power in
America*. Princeton, NJ: Princeton University Press.

2015. "The Insufficiency of 'Democracy by Coincidence': A Response to Peter
K. Enns." *Perspectives on Politics* 13(4): 1065–1071.

Gilens, Martin and Benjamin I. Page. 2014. "Testing Theories of American
Politics: Elites, Interest Groups, and Average Citizens." *Perspectives on
Politics* 12(3): 564–581.

Gordon, Linda. 1994. *Pitied but Not Entitled: Single Mothers and the History of
Welfare, 1890–1935*. New York, NY: Free Press.

Graetz, Michael J. and Ian Shapiro. 2005. *Death by a Thousand Cuts: The Fight
Over Taxing Inherited Wealth*. Princeton, NJ: Princeton University Press.

Green, Donald, Bradley Palmquist, and Eric Schickler. 2002. *Partisan Hearts and
Minds: Political Parties and the Social Identities of Voters*. New Haven, CT:
Yale University Press.

Green, Joshua. 2016. "Meet Mr. Death." *prospect.org*. http://prospect.org/article/
meet-mr-death.

Greenhouse, Steven. 2008. "For Incomes below $100,000, a Better Tax Break in
Obama's Plan." *The New York Times*. www.nytimes.com/2008/10/31/us/p
olitics/31taxes.html.

Grossmann, Matt, and David Hopkins. 2016. *Asymmetric Politics: Ideological
Republicans and Group Interest Democrats*. New York, NY: Oxford
University Press.

Hacker, Jacob S. 2002. *The Divided Welfare State: The Battle over Public and
Private Benefits in the United States*. New York: Cambridge University Press.

Hacker, Jacob S. 2004. "Privatizing Risk without Privatizing the Welfare State:
The Hidden Politics of Social Policy Retrenchment in the United States."
American Political Science Review 98: 243–260.

Hacker, Jacob S. and Paul Pierson. 2010. *Winner-Take-All Politics: How Washington Made the Rich Richer—and Turned Its Back on the Middle Class*. New York, NY: Simon and Schuster.

Hacker, Jacon S. and Paul Pierson. 2014. "After the 'Master Theory': Downs, Schattschneider, and the Rebirth of Policy-Focused Analysis." *Perspectives on Politics* 12(3): 643–662.

Hains, Tim. 2016. "Trump: I Believe in Raising Taxes on the Wealthy, 'Including Myself.'" *RealClearPolitics*, April 21, 2016. Accessed online: www.realclear politics.com/video/2016/04/21/trump_i_believe_in_raising_taxes_on_the _wealthy_including_myself.html.

Hajnal, Zoltan and Michael U. Rivera. 2014. "Immigration, Latinos, and White Partisan Politics." *American Journal of Political Science* 58(4): 773–789.

Hancock, Ange-Marie. 2003. "Contemporary Welfare Reform and the Public Identity of the 'Welfare Queen'." *Race, Gender & Class*: 31–59.

Hancock, Ange-Marie. 2004. *The Politics of Disgust and the Public Identity of the Welfare Queen*. New York, NY: New York University Press.

Hanley, Ryan Patrick. 2009. *Adam Smith and the Character of Virtue*. Cambridge, England: Cambridge University Press.

Hanson, Victor Davis. 2017. "It's the Hypocrisy, Stupid." *The National Review*. Accessed online: www.nationalreview.com/article/448320/hypocrite-demo crats-lecture-country-exempt-themselves-resemble-jimmy-swaggart.

Hartz, Louis. 1955. *The Liberal Tradition in America*. New York, NY: Harcourt, Brace & Co.

Henderson, Michael B. 2014. "The 2013 Education Next Survey: Americans React to Common Core and Other Education Policies." *Education Next* 14(1): 8–13.

Henry, P. J., Christine Reyna, and Bernard Weiner. 2004. "Hate Welfare but Help the Poor: How the Attributional Content of Stereotypes Explains the Paradox of Reactions to the Destitute in America." *Journal of Applied Social Psychology* 34(1): 34–58.

Hochschild, Jennifer L. 1981. *What's Fair? American Beliefs about Distributive Justice*. Cambridge: Harvard University Press.

Hochschild, Jennifer L. and Vesla Weaver. 2007. "Policies of Racial Classification and the Politics of Racial Inequality," in: *Remaking America: Democracy and Public Policy in an Age of Inequality*. Joe Soss, Jacob Hacker, and Suzanne Mettler, eds., New York, NY: Russell Sage Foundation, 159–182.

Hoffman, M.L. 1984. " Interaction of Affect and Cognition in Empathy," in *Emotions, Cognition, and Behavior*. C.E. Izard, J. Kagan, and R. B. Zajonc, eds. New York, NY: Cambridge University Press, 103–131.

1987. "The Contribution of Empathy to Justice and Moral Judgment," in *Empathy and Its Development*. N. Eisenberg and J. Strayer, eds. New York, NY: Cambridge University Press, 47–80.

Hofstader, Richard. [2011] 1948. *The American Political Tradition and the Men Who Made It*. Knopf Doubleday Publishing Group.

Hopkins, Daniel. 2009. "Partisan Reinforcement and the Poor: The Impact of Context on Explanations for Poverty." *Social Science Quarterly* 90: 744–764.

Horowitz, Jason. 2012. "A Brief History of Mitt Romney, Total Cheapskate." *GQ*, September 30, 2012. Accessed online: www.gq.com/story/gordon-clay -a-teenager-looking.

Horsley, Scott. 2017. "GOP Health Care Bill Would Cut about $765 Billion in Taxes over the Next 10 Years." *NPR*, May 4, 2017. Accessed online: www .npr.org/2017/05/04/526923181/gop-health-care-bill-would-cut-about-765 -billion-in-taxes-over-10-years.

Hout, Michael, Clem Brooks, and Jeff Manza. 1995. "The Democratic Class Struggle in the United States, 1948–1992." *American Sociological Review* 60(6): 805–828.

Howard, Christopher. 1997. *The Hidden Welfare State*. Princeton, NJ: Princeton University Press.

Howard, Christopher. 2007. *The Welfare State Nobody Knows*. Princeton, NJ: Princeton University Press.

Huddy, Leonie and Stanley Feldman. 2009. "On Assessing the Political Effects of Racial Prejudice." *Annual Review of Political Science* 12: 423–447.

Huang, Chye-Ching. 2013. *Budget Deal Makes Permanent 82 Percent of President Bush's Tax Cuts*. Report by Center on Budget and Policy Priorities, January 3, 2013.

Hunt, Corrie V., Anita Kim, Eugene Borgida, and Shelly Chaiken. 2010. "Revisiting the Self-Interest versus Values Debate: The Role of Temporal Perspective." *Journal of Experimental Social Psychology* 46 (6): 1155–1158.

Huntington, Samuel P. 1981. *American Politics: The Promise of Disharmony*. Cambridge: Harvard University Press.

Hurwitz, Jon and Mark Peffley. 2005. "Explaining the Great Racial Divide." *Journal of Politics* 67(3): 762–783.

Hutchings, Vincent L. 2009. "Change or More of the Same? Evaluating Racial Attitudes in the Obama Era." *Public Opinion Quarterly* 73(5): 917–942.

Hutchings, Vincent L., Vanessa Cruz Nichols, LaGina Gause, and Spencer Piston. 2014. "Whitewashing: How Obama Used Implicit Racial Cues as a Defense against Political Rumors." Presented at the Annual Meeting of the Midwest Political Science Association.

Hutchings, Vincent L. and Spencer Piston. 2011a. "The Determinants and Political Consequences of Prejudice," in *Cambridge Handbook of Experimental Political Science*. James N. Druckman, Donald P. Green, James H. Kuklinski, and Arthur Lupia, eds. New York, NY: Cambridge University Press.

Hutchings, Vincent L. and Spencer Piston. 2011b. "Knowledge, Sophistication, and Issue Publics," in *Oxford Handbook of American Public Opinion and the Media*. Steven Thompson and Robert Shapiro, eds. Oxford: Oxford University Press.

Hyman, Herbert H. 1960. "Reflections on Reference Groups." *Public Opinion Quarterly* 24(3): 383–396.

1968. "Reference Groups." *International Encyclopedia of the Social Sciences* 13: 353–361.

Irwin, Neil. "Winners and Losers in the Trump Tax Plan." *The Upshot*, April 26, 2017. Accessed online: www.nytimes.com/2017/04/26/upshot/winners-and -losers-in-the-trump-tax-plan.html.

Israel-Trummel, Mackenzie and Ariela Schachter. 2016. "New Poll Shows That Black Voters Really Aren't 'Feeling The Bern'." *The Monkey Cage*. www .washingtonpost.com/news/monkey-cage/wp/2016/02/18/new-poll-shows-tha t-black-voters-really-arent-feeling-the-bern/?utm_term=.9e0559a5d8d6.

Iyengar, Shanto and Sean J. Westwood. 2015. "Fear and Loathing across Party Lines: New Evidence on Group Polarization." *American Journal of Political Science* 59(3): 690–707.

Jackman, Mary R. and Robert W. Jackman. 1983. *Class Awareness in the United States*. Berkeley, Los Angeles, London: University of California Press.

Jacobs, Harrison. 2017. "One poll shows why passing Republicans' healthcare plan could be so politically toxic." *Business Insider*, June 27, 2017. Accessed online: www.businessinsider.com/bcra-ahca-medicaid-polls-cuts-healthcare -bill-2017-6.

Jacobs, Lawrence R. and Robert Y. Shapiro. 1999. *Myths and Misunderstandings About Public Opinion toward Social Security: Knowledge, Support, and Reformism*. Century Foundation Report. New York, NY: The Century Foundation.

Jacobs, Lawrence R. and Robert Y. Shapiro. 2000. *Politicians Don't Pander: Political Manipulation and the Loss of Democratic Responsiveness*. Chicago, IL: University of Chicago Press.

Jacobs, Lawrence R. and Joe Soss. 2010. "The Politics of Inequality in America: A Political Economy Framework." *Annual Review of Political Science* 13: 341– 364.

Jardina, Ashley, Sean McElwee, and Spencer Piston. 2016. "How Do Trump Supporters See Black People?" *Slate*, November 7, 2016. Accessed online: www.slate.com/articles/news_and_politics/politics/2016/11/the_majori ty_of_trump_supporters_surveyed_described_black_people_as_less.html.

Jennings, M. Kent and Gregory B. Markus. 1984. "Partisan Orientations over the Long Haul: Results from the Three-Wave Political Socialization Panel Study." *American Political Science Review* 78: 1000–1018.

Johnson, Sarah E., Jennifer A. Richeson, and Eli J. Finkel. 2011. "Middle Class and Marginal? Socioeconomic Status, Stigma, and Self-Regulation at an Elite University." *Journal of Personality and Social Psychology* 100: 838–852.

Johnston, Christopher D. and Benjamin Newman. 2015. "Economic Inequality and Policy Mood across Time and Space." Forthcoming in *American Politics Research*.

Jost, John T., Mahzarin R. Banaji, and Brian A. Nosek. 2004. "A Decade of System Justification Theory: Accumulated Evidence of Conscious and Unconscious Bolstering of the Status Quo. *Political Psychology* 25(6): 881– 919.

Kalmoe, Nathan P. 2014. "Fueling the Fire: Violent Metaphors, Trait Aggression, and Support for Political Violence." *Political Communication*, 31(4): 545– 563.

Kalmoe, Nathan P. and Spencer Piston. 2013. "Is Implicit Prejudice against Blacks Politically Consequential? Evidence from the AMP." *Public Opinion Quarterly* 77(1): 305–322.

Kantor, Jodi. 2012. "Clinton's Countless Choices Hinge on One: 2016." *The New York Times*. www.nytimes.com/2012/12/09/us/politics/hillary-clintons-cou ntless-choices-could-hinge-on-2016-election.html.

Kaplan, Thomas and Robert Pear. 2017. "G.O.P. Senators Vow to Unveil Health Bill Thursday, Despite Deep Divisions." *The New York Times*, July 11, 2017. Accessed online: www.nytimes.com/2017/07/11/us/politics/senate-republi cans-health-bill.html?hp&action=click&pgtype=Homepage&clickSourceT he =story-heading&module=first-column-region&region=top-news&WT.n av=top-news.

Karpowitz, Christopher F. 2009. "What Can a President Learn from the News Media? The Instructive Case of Richard Nixon." *British Journal of Political Science* 39: 755–780.

Katz, Michael B. 1989. *The Undeserving Poor: from the War on Poverty to the War on Welfare*. New York, NY: Random House, Inc.

Katznelson, Ira. 2005. *When Affirmative Action Was White: An Untold history of Racial Inequality in Twentieth-Century America*. New York, NY: W.W. Norton and Company, Inc.

Keizer, Garret. 2016. "What are we to make of Trump's blue-collar support?" *Los Angeles Times*, January 31, 2016. Accessed online: www.latimes.com/ opinion/op-ed/la-oe-keizer-why-blue-collar-voters-like-trump-20160131 The -story.html.

Kelly, Nathan J. 2009. *The Politics of Income Inequality in the United States*. Cambridge: Cambridge University Press.

Kelly, Nathan J. and Peter K. Enns. 2010. "Inequality and the Dynamics of Public Opinion: The Self-Reinforcing Link between Economic Inequality and Mass Preference." *American Journal of Political Science* 54(4): 855–870.

Kenski, Kate, Bruce W. Hardy, and Kathleen Hall Jamieson. 2010. "The Obama Victory: How Media, Money, and Message Shaped the 2008 Election." New York: Oxford University Press.

Kim, Eunji, Rasmus Pedersen, and Diana Mutz. 2016. "What Do Americans Talk about When They Talk about Economic Inequality?" Unpublished manuscript. Available at SSRN: https://ssrn.com/abstract=2805330or http:// dx.doi.org/10.2139/ssrn.2805330.

Kinder, Donald R. 1986. "The Continuing American Dilemma: White Resistance to Racial Change 40 Years after Myrdal." *Journal of Social Issues* 42(2): 151–171.

Kinder, Donald R. and Allison Dale-Riddle. 2012. *The End of Race? Obama, 2008, and Racial Politics in America*. New Haven: Yale University Press.

Kinder, Donald R. and Nathan P. Kalmoe. 2017. *Neither Liberal nor Conservative: Ideological Innocence in the American Public*. Chicago, IL: University of Chicago Press.

Kinder, Donald R. and Cindy D. Kam. 2009. *Us against Them: Ethnocentric Foundations of American Opinion*. Chicago, IL: University of Chicago Press.

Kinder, Donald R. and D. Roderick Kiewiet. 1979. "Economic Discontent and Political Behavior: The Role of Personal Grievances and Collective Economic

Judgments in Congressional Voting." *American Journal of Political Science* 23(3): 495–527.

1981. "Sociotropic Politics: The American Case." *British Journal of Political Science* 11(2): 129–161.

Kinder, Donald R. and Corrine M. McConnaughy. 2006. "Military Triumph, Racial Transcendence, and Colin Powell." *Public Opinion Quarterly* 70: 139–165.

Kinder, Donald R. and Thomas R. Palfrey. 1993. *Experimental Foundations of Political Science*. Ann Arbor: University of Michigan Press.

Kinder, Donald R. and Lynn M. Sanders. 1996. *Divided by Color: Racial Politics and Democratic Ideals*. Chicago, IL: University of Chicago Press.

Kinder, Donald R. and Nicholas Winter. 2001. "Exploring the Racial Divide: Blacks, Whites, and Opinion on National Policy." *American Journal of Political Science* 45: 439–456.

Kliff, Sarah. 2016. "Why Obamacare Enrollees Voted for Trump." *Vox*. Accessed online: www.vox.com/science-and-health/2016/12/13/13848794/kentucky-obamacare-trump.

Kluegel, James R. and Eliot R. Smith. 1986. *Beliefs about Inequality: Americans' Views of What Is and What Ought to Be*. Piscataway, NJ: Transaction Publishers.

Knecht, Tom and Lisa M. Martinez. 2009. "Humanizing the Homeless: Does Contact Erode Stereotypes?" *Social Science Research* 38: 521–534.

Krugman, Paul. 2012. "Notes on the Political Economy of Redistribution." *The New York Times*. Accessed online: https://krugman.blogs.nytimes.com/2012/09/21/notes-on-the-political-economy-of-redistribution/.

Krugman, Paul. 2014. "The Myth of the Deserving Rich." *The New York Times*. Accessed online: https://krugman.blogs.nytimes.com/2014/01/18/the-myth-of-the-deserving-rich/.

Krupnikov, Yanna, Adam Seth Levine, Arthur Lupia, and Markus Prior. 2006. "Public Ignorance and Estate Tax Repeal: The Effect of Partisan Differences and Survey Incentives." *National Tax Journal*: 425–437.

Krupnikov, Yanna and Spencer Piston. 2015a. "Accentuating the Negative: Candidate Race and Campaign Strategy." *Political Communication* 32(1): 152–173.

Krupnikov, Yanna and Spencer Piston. 2015b. "Racial Prejudice, Partisanship, and White Turnout in Elections with Black Candidates." *Political Behavior* 37: 397–418.

Krupnikov, Yanna, and Spencer Piston. 2016. "The Political Consequences of Latino Prejudice against Blacks." *Public Opinion Quarterly* 80: 480–509.

Krupnikov, Yanna, Spencer Piston, and Nichole Bauer. 2016. "Saving Face: Identifying Responses to Black and Female Candidates." *Political Psychology* 37: 253–273.

Kuklinski, J.H., Ellen Riggle, Victor Ottati, Norbert Schwarz, et al. 1991. "The Cognitive and Affective Bases of Political Tolerance Judgments." *American Journal of Political Science* 35: 1–27.

Lajevardi, Nazita. 2016. "The Media Matters: Muslim American Media Coverage from 1992–2015 and Effects on Mass Attitudes." Paper presented at the

Annual Meeting of the American Political Science Association, September 2016.

Lane, Robert E. 1962. *Political Ideology*. New York, NY: Free Press.

Lang, Nico. "Why America Hates Its Poor." April 11, 2015. *Salon*. Accessed online: www.salon.com/2015/04/11/why_we_hate_poor_people_partner/.

Latimer, Matt. 2017. "What If Trump Had Won as a Democrat?" *Politico Magazine*, July 8, 2017. Accessed online: www.politico.com/magazine/story/2017/07/08/what-if-trump-had-won-as-a-democrat-215351.

Leach, Colin Wayne and Russell Spears. 2008. ""A Vengefulness of the Impotent": The Pain of In-Group Inferiority and Schadenfreude toward Successful Out-Groups." *Journal of Personality and Social Psychology* 95: 1383–1396.

Lee, Barrett A., Chad R. Farrell, and Bruce G. Link. 2004. "Revising the Contact Hypothesis: The Case of Public Exposure to Homelessness." *American Sociological Review* 69: 40–63.

Leibovich, Mark. 2007. "The Socialist Senator." *The New York Times*. www.nytimes.com/2007/01/21/magazine/21Sanders.t.html.

Leonhardt, David. 2010. "Taxing the Rich, Over Time." *The New York Times*, April 13, 2010. Accessed online: https://economix.blogs.nytimes.com/2010/04/13/taxing-the-rich-over-time/.

Lerner, Melvin J. 1981. "The Justice Motive in Human Relations," in *The Justice Motive in Social Behavior*. Melvin J. Lerner and Sally C. Lerner, eds. New York, NY: Springer U.S.

Levendusky, Matthew S. and Simon D. Jackman. 2003. "Reconsidering the Measurement of Political Knowledge." Working paper, Stanford University.

Lewis-Beck, Michael S. and Charles Tien. 2016. "The Political Economy Model: 2016 US Election Forecasts." *PS: Political Science & Politics* 49(4): 661–663.

Lippmann, Walter. 1920. *Public Opinion*. New York, NY: Harcourt, Brace, and Company.

Lipset, Seymour Martin and Gary Marks. 2001. *It Didn't Happen Here: Why Socialism Failed in the United States*. New York, NY: W.W. Norton & Co.

Lipset, Seymour Martin. 1979. *The First New Nation: The United States in Historical and Comparative Perspective*. Piscataway, NJ: Transaction Publishers.

Liu, Ling. 2006. "Provincetown straights complain of intolerance among gays." *The Salem News*, July 27, 2006. Accessed online: www.salemnews.com/news/local_news/provincetown-straights-complain-of-intolerance-among-gays/article_5dbb6da7-49ec-5df3-ada6-64f349915d7d.html.

Long, Heather. 2015. "Donald Trump: Tax the Rich More." *CNN*, August 28, 2015. Accessed online: http://money.cnn.com/2015/08/27/news/economy/donald-trumpeconomy-tax-plan/index.html.

Loury, Alden. 2008. "Why Do We Hate the Poor?" *The Huffington Post*. Accessed online: www.huffingtonpost.com/alden-loury/why-do-we-hate-the-poor_b_140586.html.

Lowry, Rich. 2015. "Class, Not Race." *The National Review*. Accessed online: www.nationalreview.com/article/415480/class-not-race-rich-lowry.

Lupia, Arthur. 2015. *Uninformed: Why People Know So Little about Politics and What We Can Do about It*. New York, NY: Oxford University Press.

Lupia, Arthur, Logan S. Casey, Kristyn L. Karl, Spencer Piston, Timothy J. Ryan, and Christopher Skovron. 2015. "What Does It Take to Reduce Racial Prejudice in Individual-Level Candidate Evaluations? A Formal Theoretic Perspective." *Political Science Research and Methods* 3(1): 1–20.

Lupia, Arthur, Yanna Krupnikov, Adam Seth Levine, Spencer Piston, and Alex Von Hagen-Jamar. 2010. "Why State Constitutions Differ in Their Treatment of Same-Sex Couples." *Journal of Politics* 72(4): 1222–1235.

Luttig, Matthew. "The Structure of Inequality and Americans' Attitudes toward Redistribution." *Public Opinion Quarterly*, 77(3): 811–821.

MACPAC. 2016. *Trends in Medicaid Spending*. MACPAC Report, June 2016.

Mann, Thomas E. and Norman J. Ornstein. 2013. *It's Even Worse Than it Looks: How the American Constitutional System Collided with the New Politics of Extremism*. New York, NY: Basic Books.

Mansbridge, Jane J. 1990. *Beyond Self-Interest*. Chicago, IL: University of Chicago Press.

Marcos, Cristina. 2017. "House Democrat plans to attend town hall for GOP lawmaker." *The Hill*, May 8, 2017. Accessed online: http://thehill.com/home news/house/332415-house-democrat-plans-to-attend-town-hall-instead-of -gop-lawmaker-who-wont.

Markus, Gregory B. 2001. "American Individualism Reconsidered," in *Citizens and Politics*, James H. Kuklinski, ed. New York, NY: Cambridge University Press, 401–432.

Marlantes, Liz. 2012. "Are Republicans Really 'Incapable' of Beating Hillary Clinton in 2016?" *csmonitor.com*. www.csmonitor.com/USA/Politics/Decode r/2012/1210/Are-Republicans-really-incapable-of-beating-Hillary-Clinton-in -2016.

Marthur, Aparna and Abby McCloskey. 2016. "The Concerning Drop iWorkforce Participation and Role of Family-Friendly Policies." *Forbes*, May 25, 2016. Accessed online: www.forbes.com/sites/aparnamathur/2016/05/25/the-con cerning-drop-in-workforce-participation-and-role-of-family-friendly-policies/ %531fobf65c6c.

Mason, Lilliana. 2015. "'I Disrespectfully Agree': The Differential Effects of Partisan Sorting on Social and Issue Polarization." *American Journal of Political Science* 59(1): 128–145.

Matthews, Dylan. 2013. "America's taxes are the most progressive in the world. Its government is among the least." *Washington Post*, April 5, 2013. Accessed online: www.washingtonpost.com/news/wonk/wp/2013/04/05/americas-taxes -are-the-most-progressive-in-the-world-its-government-is-among-the-least/?utm _term=.c659cf4bc102.

Mayhew, David. 2000. "Electoral Realignments." *Annual Review of Political Science* 3: 449–474.

McCall, Leslie. 2013. *The Undeserving Rich*. New York, NY: Cambridge University Press.

McCall, Leslie and Lane Kenworthy. 2009. "Americans' Social Policy Preferences in the Era of Rising Inequality." *Perspectives on Politics* 7: 459–484.

McCarty, Nolan, Keith T. Poole, and Howard Rosenthal. 2008. *Polarized America: The Dance of Ideology and Unequal Riches.* Cambridge, MA: The Massachusetts Institute of Technology Press.

McClosky, Herbert and John Zaller. 1984. *The American Ethos: Public Attitudes toward Capitalism and Democracy.* Cambridge. MA: Harvard University Press.

Meertens, Roel W. and Thomas F. Pettigrew. 1997. "Is Subtle Prejudice Really Prejudice?" *Public Opinion Quarterly* 61(1): 54–71.

Mendelberg, Tali, Katherine T. McCabe, and Adam Thal. 2017. "College Socialization and the Economic Views of Affluent Americans." *American Journal of Political Science* 61: 606–623.

Merton, Robert King. 1968. *Social Theory and Social Structure.* New York, NY: Simon and Schuster.

Merton, Robert K. and Alice S. Rossi. 1950. "Contributions to the Theory of Reference Group Behavior," in Continuities in Social Research: Studies in the Scope and Method of "The American Soldier." Robert K. Merton and Paul Lazarsfeld, eds. New York: Free Press, 40–105.

Mettler, Suzanne. 2011. *The Submerged State.* Chicago, IL: University of Chicago Press.

Miller, Arthur H., Patricia Gurin, Gerald Gurin, and Oksana Malanchuk. 1981. "Group Consciousness and Political Participation." *American Journal of Political Science* 25(3): 494–511.

Miller, Warren E. and Donald E. Stokes. 1963. "Constituency Influence in Congress." *American Political Science Review* 57(1): 45–56.

Mishel, Lawrence, John Schmitt, and Heidi Shierholz. 2013. "Assessing the Job Polarization Explanation of Growing Wage Inequality." Presented at the Labor Economics Seminar at the University of California, Berkeley (March 7, 2013).

Moe, Terry M. 2005. "Power and Political Institutions." *Perspectives on Politics* 3(2): 215–233.

Montgomery, Lori. 2012. "Officials: Obama ready to veto a bill blocking 'fiscal cliff' without tax hike for rich." *Washington Post,* October 17, 2012. Accessed online: www.washingtonpost.com/business/economy/officials-oba ma-ready-to-veto-a-bill-blocking-fiscal-cliff-without-tax-hike-for-rich/2012/ 10/17/64400224-1870-11e2-9855-71f2b202721b_story.html.

Montgomery, Lori and Paul Kane. 2013. "Obama, Senate Republicans reach agreement on 'fiscal cliff'." *Washington Post,* January 1, 2013. Accessed online: www.washingtonpost.com/business/fiscal-cliff/biden-mcconnell-con tinue-cliff-talks-as-clock-winds-down/2012/12/31/66c044e2-534d-11e2-8b 9e-dd8773594efc_story.html.

Montopoli, Brian. 2008. "Obama Ad Attacks McCain for Owning Seven Houses." *cbsnews.com.* www.cbsnews.com/news/obama-ad-attacks-mccain-for-own ing-seven-houses/.

Moore, Suzanne. 2012. "Instead of Being Disgusted by Poverty, We Are Disgusted by Poor People Themselves." *The Guardian.* Accessed online: www.theguar dian.com/commentisfree/2012/feb/16/suzanne-moore-disgusted-by-poor.

Moore, Suzanne. 2016. "Why I was wrong about men." *New Statesman*, September 5, 2016. Accessed online: www.newstatesman.com/politics/femin ism/2016/09/suzanne-moore-why-i-was-wrong-about-men.

Morelli, Salvatore, Timothy M. Smeeding, and Jeffrey P. Thompson. 2014. "Post-1970 Trends in Within-Country Inequality and Poverty: Rich and Middle Income Countries," in *Handbook of Income Distribution*, Volume 2. A.B. Atkinson and F. Bourguignon, eds. Amsterdam: Elsevier-North Holland.

Mother Jones. 2012. "Full Transcript of Mitt Romney Secret Video." *Mother Jones*, September 19, 2012. Accessed online: www.motherjones.com/politics/2012/09/full-transcript-mitt-romney-secret-video/.

Nelson, Thomas E. and Donald R. Kinder. 1996. "Issue Frames and Group-Centrism in American Public Opinion." *Journal of Politics* 58: 1055–1078.

Neustadt, Richard E. 1991. *Presidential Power and the Modern Presidents: The Politics of Leadership from Roosevelt to Reagan*, revised edition. New York, NY: The Free Press.

New York Times. 2011. "The New Resentment of the Poor." The Editorial Board. www.nytimes.com/2011/08/31/opinion/the-new-resentment-of-th e-poor.html.

Newman, Benjamin J. 2014. "My Poor Friend: Financial Distress in One's Social Network, the Perceived Power of the Rich, and Support for Redistribution." *Journal of Politics* 76: 126–138.

Newman, Katherine S. and Elisabeth S. Jacobs. 2010. *Who Cares? Public Ambivalence and New Deal Activism from the New Deal to the Second Gilded Age*. Princeton: Princeton University Press.

Newport, Frank. 2016. "Americans Still Say Upper-Income Pay too Little in Taxes." *Gallup*, April 15, 2016. Accessed online: www.gallup.com/poll/190 775/americans-say-upper-income-pay-little-taxes.aspx.

Newport, Frank. 2017. "Majority Say Wealthy Americans, Corporations Taxed Too Little." *Gallup*, April 18, 2017. Accessed online: www.gallup.com/poll/208685/majority-say-wealthy-americans-corporations-taxed-little.aspx.

Norpoth, Helmut. 2004. "From Primary to General Election: A Forecast of the Presidential Vote." *PS: Political Science & Politics* 37(4): 737–740.

Norpoth, Helmut. 2016. "Primary Model Predicts Trump Victory." *PS: Political Science & Politics* 49(4): 655–658.

Norton, Michael I. and Dan Ariely. 2011. "Building a Better America—One Wealth Quintile at a Time." *Perspectives on Psychological Science* 6: 9–12.

Nussbaum, Martha. 2001. *Upheavals of Thought*. New York, NY: Cambridge University Press.

O'Connor, Lydia and Daniel Marans. 2017. "Here Are 16 Examples of Donald Trump Being Racist." *Huffington Post*, February 16, 2017. Accessed online: www.huffingtonpost.com/entry/president-donald-trump-ra cist-examples_us_584f2ccae4bobd9c3dfe5566.

Overby, Peter. 2016. "The Clintons Wrote the Book on How to Climb Out of Middle Class." *NPR*, August 17, 2016. Accessed online: www.npr.org/2016/08/17/490102648/the-clintons-wrote-the-book-on-how-politicians-climb-o ut-of-middle-class.

Page, Benjamin I., Larry M. Bartels, and Jason Seawright. 2013. "Democracy and the Policy Preferences of Wealthy Americans." *Perspectives on Politics* 11(1): 51–73.

Page, Benjamin I. and Lawrence R. Jacobs. 2009. *Class War?* Chicago, IL: University of Chicago Press.

Palmer, Maxwell and Benjamin Schneer. 2016. "Capitol Gains: The Returns to Elected Office from Corporate Board Directorships." *Journal of Politics* 78(1): 181–196.

Parnes, Amie. 2012. "Stumping in Ohio, Obama hits Romney with 'silver spoon'." *The Hill*, April 18, 2012. Accessed online: http://thehill.com/video/campaign/222359-obama-in-ohio-hits-romney-with-silver-spoon.

Parrott, W. G. (1991). "The Emotional Experiences of Envy and Jealousy," in *The Psychology of Envy and Jealousy*. P. Salovey, ed. New York, NY: Guilford, 3–30.

Pasek, Josh and Jon A. Krosnick. 2010. "Optimizing Survey Questionnaire Design in Political Science: Insights from Psychology," in *Oxford Handbook of American Elections and Political Behavior*. Jan E. Leighley and J.C. Edwards, eds. New York, NY: Oxford University Press.

Pasek, Josh, Tobias H. Stark, Jon A. Krosnick, Trevor Tompson, and B. Keith Payne. 2014. "Attitudes toward Blacks in the Obama Era: Changing Distributions and Impacts of Job Approval and Electoral Choice, 2008–2012." *Public Opinion Quarterly*, 78(S1): 276–302.

Pasek, Josh, Alexander Tahk, Yphtach Lelkes, Jon A. Krosnick, B. Keith Payne, Omair Akhtar, and Trevor Tompson. 2009. "Determinants of Turnout and Candidate Choice in the 2008 Presidential Election: Illuminating the Impact of Racial Prejudice and Other Considerations." *Public Opinion Quarterly*, 73(5): 943–994.

Patashnik, Eric M. 2008. *Reforms at Risk: What Happens after Major Policy Changes Are Enacted*. Princeton, NJ: Princeton University Press.

PBS NewsHour. 2013. "Taxes on Rich Rise with Fiscal Cliff Deal." *PBS NewsHour*, January 2, 2013. Accessed online: www.pbs.org/newshour/extra/2013/01/taxes-on-rich-rise-with-fiscal-cliff-deal/.

Petrocik, John R. 1996. "Issue Ownership in Presidential Elections, with a 1980 Case Study." *American Journal of Political Science*: 825–850.

Pew Center. 2013. *In Deficit Debate, Public Resists Cuts in Entitlements and Aid to Poor: Half Would Cut Military Spending to Reduce Deficit*. Report by Pew Research Center, December 19, 2013.

Pew Center. 2014. *How Americans Feel about Religious Groups*. Report by Pew Research Center, July 16, 2014.

Pew Center. 2016. "Most Americans Say Government Doesn't Do Enough to Help Middle Class." 2016. *pewsocialtrends.org*. www.pewsocialtrends.org/2016/02/04/most-americans-say-government-doesnt-do-enough-to-help-middle-class/.

Pew Center. 2017. *What Bothers Americans about the Federal Tax System?* Report by Pew Research Center, April 13, 2017.

Piketty, Thomas and Emmanuel Saez. 2007. "How Progressive is the U.S. Federal Tax System? A Historical and Institutional Perspective." *The Journal of Economic Perspectives* 21(1): 2–34.

Piston, Spencer. 2010. "How Explicit Racial Prejudice Hurt Obama in the 2008 Election." *Political Behavior* 32: 431–451.

Piston, Spencer, Yanna Krupnikov, Kerri Milita, and John Barry Ryan. "Clear as Black and White: The Effects of Ambiguous Rhetoric Depend on Candidate Race." Forthcoming at *Journal of Politics.*

Piven, Frances Fox. 2015. "Regulating Today's Poor: Reflections on Andrea Campbell's Trapped in America's Safety Net." *Perspectives on Politics* 13: 1113–1116.

Poole, Keith. 2012. "Graphic picture of a polarized Congress." *UGA Research* 41(1): 32–33.

Porter, Eduardo. 2017. "Trump Budget Proposal Reflects Working-Class Resentment of the Poor." *The New York Times.* Accessed online: www.nyti mes.com/2017/03/07/business/economy/trump-budget-entitlements-working-class.html.

Przybyla, Heidi M. 2017. "Republicans avoid town halls after health care votes." *USA Today,* April 10, 2017. Accessed online: www.usatoday.com/story/news/politics/2017/04/10/republicans-avoid-town-halls-after-health-care-votes/100286290/.

Rae, Douglas Whiting and Douglas Yates. 1981. *Equalities.* Harvard University Press.

Rahn, Wendy and Eric Oliver. 2016. "Trump voters aren't authoritarians, new research says." *The Washington Post,* March 3, 2016. Accessed online: www.washingtonpost.com/news/monkey-cage/wp/2016/03/09/trumps-voters-arent-authoritarians-new-research-says-so-what-are-they/?tid=a_inl&utm_term=.f845fcc28602.

Rampell, Catherine. 2016. "Why the White Working Class Votes against Itself." *The Washington Post.* Accessed online: www.washingtonpost.com/opinions/why-the-white-working-class-votes-against-itself/2016/12/22/3aa65c04-c88b-11e6-8bee-54e800ef2a63_story.html?utm_term=.3b77cb430d45.

Rappeport, Alan. 2015. "Bernie Sanders, Long-Serving Independent, Enters Presidential Race as a Democrat." *The New York Times.* www.nytimes.com/2015/04/30/us/politics/bernie-sanders-campaign-for-president.html.

Rappeport, Alan. 2017. "The 7 Key Elements of the White House Tax Plan." *The New York Times,* April 26, 2017. Accessed online: www.nytimes.com/2017/04/26/us/politics/white-house-tax-plan.html?action=click&contentCollection=The %20Upshot&module=RelatedCoverage&region=Marginalia&pgtype=article.

Rasmussen, Dennis C. 2016. "Adam Smith on What Is Wrong with Economic Inequality." *American Political Science Review* 110(2): 342–352.

Rawls, J. 1971. *A Theory of Justice.* Cambridge, MA: Harvard University Press.

Reeves, Richard. 2014. "Classless America, Still?" The Brookings Institution. Accessed online: www.brookings.edu/blog/social-mobility-memos/2014/08/27/classless-america-still/.

Rivers, Douglas. 2006. "Sample Matching: Representative Sampling from Internet Panels." Polimetrix White Paper Series.

Romer, Thomas and Howard Rosenthal. 1978. "Political Resource Allocation, Controlled Agendas, and the Status Quo." *Public Choice* 33(4): 27–43.

Rose, Max and Frank R. Baumgartner. 2013. "Framing the Poor: Media Coverage and U.S. Poverty Policy, 1960–2008." *Policy Studies Journal* 41(1): 22–53.

Rossiter, Clinton, ed. 1961. *The Federalist Papers*. New York, NY: Penguin Group.

Rothkopf, David. 2013. "President Hillary Clinton? If She Wants It." *CNN.Com*. www.cnn.com/2013/01/26/opinion/rothkopf-hillary-clinton/.

Roush, Carolyn E. 2016. "The Dislikability Heuristic: Out-Party Negativity and Partisan Preferences, 1988–2012." Paper presented at the Annual Meeting of the Southern Political Science Association.

Rubin, Richard. 2017. "Trump Unveils Broad Tax-Cut Plan." *Wall Street Journal*, April 26, 2017. Accessed online: www.wsj.com/articles/mnuchin -says-trump-will-offer-biggest-tax-cut-in-u-s-history-1493213275.

Saad, Lydia. 2013. "Half in U.S. Support Publicly Financed Federal Campaigns." Gallup. June 24, 2014. Accessed online: www.gallup.com/poll/163208/half -support-publicly-financed-federal-campaigns.aspx.

Saez, Emmanuel and Gabriel Zucman. 2016. "Wealth Inequality in the United States since 1913: Evidence from Capitalized Income Tax Data." *Quarterly Journal of Economics* 131: 519–578.

Sands, Melissa. 2017. "Exposure to Inequality Affects Support for Redistribution." *Proceedings of the National Academy of Sciences* 114: 663–668.

Sanger-Katz, Margot. 2017. "Who Wins and Who Loses in the Latest G.O.P. Health Care Bill." *The Upshot*, May 4, 2017. Accessed online: www.nytimes .com/2017/05/04/upshot/who-wins-and-who-loses-in-the-latest-gop-health -care-bill.html.

Savransky, Rebecca. 2017. "Poll: Majority disapprove of healthcare plan." *The Hill*, May 25, 2017. Accessed online: http://thehill.com/policy/healthcare/33 5136-poll-majority-disapproves-of-gop-healthcare-plan.

Schaffner, Brian F., Matthew MacWilliams, and Tatishe Nteta. 2017. "Explaining White Polarization in the 2016 Vote for President: The Sobering Role of Racism and Sexism." Paper presented at the Conference on the U.S. Elections of 2016: Domestic and International Aspects. January 8–9, 2017.

Schlozman, Kay Lehman, and Sidney Verba. 1979. *Injury to Insult: Unemployment, Class, and Political Response*. Cambridge: Harvard University Press.

Schlozman, Kay Lehman, Sidney Verba, and Henry E. Brady. 2012. *The Unheavenly Chorus*. Princeton, NJ: Princeton University Press.

Schneider, Anne and Helen Ingram. 1993. "Social Construction of Target Populations: Implications for Politics and Policy." *American Political Science Review* 87: 334–347.

Sears, David O. 2001. "The Role of Affect in Symbolic Politics," in Citizens and Politics: Perspectives from Political Psychology, J. H. Kuklinski, ed. New York: Cambridge University Press, 14–40.

Sears, David O. and Carolyn L. Funk. 1991. "The Role of Self-Interest in Social and Political Attitudes." *Advances in Experimental Social Psychology* 24: 1–91.

Sears, David O., Richard R. Lau, Tom R. Tyler, and Harris M. Allen. 1980. "Self-Interest vs. Symbolic Politics in Policy Attitudes and Presidential Voting." *American Political Science Review* 74(3): 670–684.

Shapiro, Ian. 2002. "Why the Poor Don't Soak the Rich." *Daedalus*, 131(1): 118–128.

Shen, Fuyuan and Heidi Hatfield Edwards. 2005. "Economic Individualism, Humanitarianism, and Welfare Reform: A Value-Based Account of Framing Effects." *Journal of Communication* 55(4): 795–809.

Shephard, Steven. 2017. "Polls show GOP health bill bleeding out." *Politico*, June 28, 2017. Accessed online: www.politico.com/story/2017/06/28/health-care-polls-republicans-240062.

Sidanius, Jim and Felicia Pratto. 1999. *Social Dominance*. New York, NY: Cambridge University Press.

Sides, John. 2010. "Stories, Science, and Public Opinion about the Estate Tax." Unpublished Manuscript.

Sides, John. 2017. "Race, Religion, and Immigration." Research Report from the Democracy Fund Voter Study Group.

Sides, John and Kimberly Gross. 2013. "Stereotypes of Muslims and Support for the War on Terror." *Journal of Politics* 75(3): 583–598.

Sides, John, Michael Tesler, and Lynn Vavreck. 2016. "The Electoral Landscape of 2016." *The Annals of the American Academy of Political and Social Science* 667(1): 50–71.

Siff, Andrew. 2016. "Millionaires March Targets NY's Richest." *nbcnewyork. com*. www.nbcnewyork.com/news/local/Millionaires-March-1-Percent-99-Percent-Occupy-Wall-Street-131528853.html.

Simon, Herbert. 1956. "Rational Choice and the Structure of the Environment." *Psychological Review* 63(2): 129–138.

Sinyangwe, Samuel. 2012. "The Significance of Mixed-Race: Perceptions of Barack Obama's Race and the Effect of Obama's Race on Favorability." Available at SSRN: http://ssrn.com/abstract=1910209 or http://dx.doi.org/10.2139/ssrn.1910209.

Sisk, Richard. 2008. "A Housing Issue: McCain Not Sure How Many They Own." *nydailynews.com*. www.nydailynews.com/news/politics/housing-issue-john-mccain-not-wife-cindy-article-1.317262.

Skocpol, Theda. 1992. *Protecting Soldiers and Mothers: The Political Origins of Social Policy in the United States*. Cambridge: Belknap Harvard.

Slemron, Joel. 2006. "The Role of Misconceptions in Support for Regressive Tax Reform." *National Tax Journal*: 57–75.

Smith, David. 2014. "The Mormon Dilemma: How Old and New Religious Divides Hurt Mormon Candidates in the United States." *Electoral Studies* 35: 283–291.

Smith, David. 2016. "Predicting Acceptance of Mormons as Christians by Religion and Party Identity." *Public Opinion Quarterly* 80: 783–795.

Smith, Matt. 2013. "Obama signs bill warding off fiscal cliff." *CNN*, January 3, 2013. Accessed online: www.cnn.com/2013/01/02/politics/fiscal-cliff/index.html.

Smith, R. H., Turner, T. J., Garonzik, R., Leach, C. W., Urch-Druskat, V., & Weston, C. M. 1996. "Envy and Schadenfreude." *Personality and Social Psychology Bulletin* 22: 158–168.

Sniderman, Paul M., Philip E. Tetlock, James M. Glaser, Donald Philip Green, and Michael Hout. 1989. "Principled Tolerance and the American Mass Public." *British Journal of Political Science* 19(1): 25–45.

Sniderman, Paul M., Richard A. Brody, and Philip Tetlock. 1991. *Reasoning and Choice: Explorations in Political Psychology*. Cambridge: Cambridge University Press.

Solman, Paul. 2016. "A Historian's Take on Trump's Economic Plan for Blue-Collar, o." *PBS NewsHour*, November 11, 2016. Accessed online: www.pbs .org/newshour/making-sense/historians-take-trumps-economic-plan-blue-co llar-manufacturing-jobs/.

Sombart, Werner. 1976. *Why is There No Socialism in the United States?* London: The Macmillan Press.

Somin, Ilya. 2015. *The Grasping Hand: Kelo v. City of New London and the Limits of Eminent Domain*. Chicago, IL: University of Chicago Press.

Soroka, Stuart N. and Christopher Wlezien. 2008. "On the Limits to Inequality in Representation." *PS: Political Science and Politics* 41(2): 2008.

2011. "Inequality in Policy Representativeness?" in *Who Gets Represented?* Peter K. Enns and Christopher Wlezien, eds. New York, NY: Russell Sage Foundation, 285–310.

Soss, Joe, Richard C. Fording, and Sanford Schram. 2011. *Disciplining the Poor: Neoliberal Paternalism and the Persistent Power of Race*. Chicago, IL: University of Chicago Press.

Starr, Paul. 2016. "What If Trump Had Run as a Democrat?" *The American Prospect*, March 17, 2016. Accessed online: http://prospect.org/article/what -if-trump-had-run-democrat.

Stoker, Laura and Jennifer Hochschild. 2004. "Measuring Values: The Case of Equality." Unpublished Manuscript.

Strother, Logan. 2016. "Beyond Kelo: An Experimental Study of Public Opposition to Eminent Domain." *Journal of Law and Courts* 4(2): 339–375.

Strother, Logan. 2017. "The National Flood Insurance Program: A Case Study in Policy Failure, Reform, and Retrenchment." *Policy Studies Journal*. Early view: doi:10.1111/psj.12189.

Strother, Logan, Spencer Piston, and Thomas Ogorzalek. "Pride or Prejudice? Racial Prejudice, Southern Heritage, and White Support for the Confederate Battle Flag." Forthcoming at *DuBois Review*.

Sullivan, John L., James E. Piereson, and George E. Marcus. 1982. *Political Tolerance and American Democracy*. Chicago, IL: University of Chicago Press.

Sumner, William G. 1906. *Folkways: A Study of the Sociological Importance of Usages, Manners, Customs, Mores, and Morals*. New York, NY: New American Library.

Swift, Art. 2016. "Support for Legal Marijuana Use Up to 60% in U.S." Gallup. October 19, 2016. Accessed online: www.gallup.com/poll/196550/support -legal-marijuana.aspx.

Taibbi, Matt. 2014. *The Divide: American Injustice in the Age of the Wealth Gap.* New York, NY: Spiegel & Grau.

Tajfel, Henri. 1981. "Social Stereotypes and Social Groups." *Intergroup Behaviour*: 144–167.

Tajfel, Henri and John C. Turner. 1979. "An Integrative Theory of Intergroup Conflict." *The Social Psychology of Intergroup Relations* 33(47): 74.

Tax Policy Center. 2017. T17-0023: Distribution of Major Tax Cut Provisions in the American Health Care Act of 2017 (AHCA) as approved by House Ways and Means Committee, Excluding Changes to Health Insurance Tax Credits, by Expanded Cash Income Percentile, 2022. Report by the Tax Policy Center, March 10, 2017.

Taylor, Jessica. 2017. "Just 17 Percent of Americans Approve of Republican Senate Health Care Bill." *NPR*, June 28, 2017. Accessed online: www.npr .org/2017/06/28/534612954/just-17-percent-of-americans-approve-of-repu blican-senate-health-care-bill.

Tesler, Michael. 2012. "The Spillover of Racialization into Health Care: How President Obama Polarized Public Opinion by Racial Attitudes and Race." *American Journal of Political Science*, 56(3): 690–704.

Tesler, Michael. 2015. "Bernie Sanders's Surge Doesn't Mean the Democratic Race is Wide Open. Here's Why." *The Monkey Cage*. www.washingtonpost .com/news/monkey-cage/wp/2015/09/17/bernie-sanderss-surge-doesnt-mea n-the-democratic-race-is-wide-open-heres-why/?utm_term=.01a2eb5a900c.

Tesler, Michael. 2016. *Post-Racial or Most-Racial? Race and Politics in the Obama Era.* Chicago, IL: University of Chicago Press.

Tesler, Michael. 2016. "Views about race mattered more in electing Trump than in electing Obama." *Washington Post*, November 22, 2016. Accessed online: www.washingtonpost.com/news/monkeycage/wp/2016/11/22/peoples-view s-about-race-mattered-more-in-electing-trump-than-inelecting-obama/? utm_term=.61db10beeaac.

Tesler, Michael and David O. Sears. 2010. *Obama's Race: The 2008 Election and the Dream of a Post-Racial America.* Chicago, IL: University of Chicago Press.

Thompson, Derek. 2016. "The Missing Men." *The Atlantic*, June 27, 2016. Accessed online: www.theatlantic.com/business/archive/2016/06/the-miss ing-men/488858/.

Toi, Miho and C. Daniel Batson. 1982. "More evidence that empathy is a source of altruistic motivation." *Journal of Personality and Social Psychology* 43: 281–292.

Ura, Joseph D. and Christopher R. Ellis. 2008. "Income, Preferences, and the Dynamics of Policy Responsiveness." *PS: Political Science and Politics* 41(4): 785–794.

Vaish, Amrisha, Malinda Carpenter, and Michael Tomasello. "Sympathy through Affective Perspective Taking and Its Relation to Prosocial Behavior in Toddlers." *Developmental Psychology* 45: 534–543.

Valentino, Nicholas A. and David O. Sears. 2005. "Old Times There Are Not Forgotten: Race and Partisan Realignment in the Contemporary South." *American Journal of Political Science* 49(3): 672–688.

Vavreck, Lynn and Douglas Rivers. 2008. "The 2006 Cooperative Congressional Election Study." *Journal of Elections, Public Opinion, and Policy* 18(4): 355–366.

Vavreck, Lynn and John Sides. 2014. *The Gamble: Choice and Chance in the 2012 Presidential Election*. Princeton, NJ: Princeton University Press.

Viscelli, Steve. 2016. "Truck Stop: How One of America's Steadiest Jobs Turned Into One of Its Most Grueling." *The Atlantic*. Accessed online: www.thea tlantic.com/business/archive/2016/05/truck-stop/481926/.

Wagner, John. 2015a. "Bernie Sanders, The Surprise Story of the Year." *Washington Post*. www.washingtonpost.com/news/post-politics/wp/2015/ 10/13/who-is-bernie-sanders/?utm_term=.c4f8c55ed637.

Wagner, John. 2015b. "Sanders Draws More than 20,000 in Boston, Building on a Strong Week." *Washington Post*. www.washingtonpost.com/news/post -politics/wp/2015/10/03/sanders-draws-20000-in-boston-building-on-a-stro ng-week/?utm_term=.668721a678ae.

Wall Street Journal. 2002. Editorial, "The Non-Taxpaying Class." *wsj.com*. www .wsj.com/articles/SB1037748678534174748.

Walters, Stephen J. K. 2017. "In the Class War, a Flanking Maneuver." *National Review*, May 5, 2017. Accessed online: www.nationalreview.com/article/44 7346/trump-tax-standard-deduction-increase.

Wayne, Carly, Nicholas Valentino, and Marzia Oceno. 2016. "How sexism drives support for Donald Trump." *Washington Post*, October 23, 2016. Accessed online: www.washingtonpost.com/news/monkey-cage/wp/2016/10/23/how -sexism-drives-support-for-donald-trump/?utm_term=.8bf5493a53c4.

Webb, S. and B. Webb. 1927. *English Local Government: English Poor Law History: Part I. The Old Poor Law*. London: Longman, Green, & Co.

Weber, Max (Talcott Parsons, trans). 1930. *The Protestant Ethic and the Spirit of Capitalism*. Crows Nest, New South Wales, Australia: G. Allen and Unwin Ltd.

Weeks, Matthew and Michael B. Lupfer. 2004. "Complicating Race: The Relationship between Prejudice, Race, and Social Class Categorizations." *Personality and Social Psychology Bulletin* 30: 972–984.

Weinberg, Jill D., Jeremy Freese, and David McElhattan. 2014. "Comparing Data Characteristics and Results of an Online Factorial Survey between a Population-Based and Crowdsource-Recruited Sample." *Sociological Science* 1: 292–310.

Weisman, Jonathan. 2001. "Linking Tax to Death May Have Brought Its Doom." *USA Today*. http://usatoday30.usatoday.com/news/washdc/2001-05-21-estate .htm.

Weissmann, Jordan. 2015. "Most Americans Think We Should Soak the Rich and Redistribute Wealth." *Slate*, May 5, 2015. Accessed online: www.slate.com/ blogs/moneybox/2015/05/05/gallup_52_percent_of_americans_think_we _should_use_heavy_taxes_on_the_rich.html.

Weldon, Kathleen. 2015. "If I Were a Rich Man: Public Attitudes about Wealth and Taxes." *Huffington Post*, February 4, 2015. Accessed online: www.huf fingtonpost.com/kathleen-weldon/wealth-taxes-public-opinion-polls _b_6613264.html.

White, Ben. 2016. "Shady accounting underpins Donald Trump's wealth." *Politico*, May 31, 2016. Accessed online: www.politico.eu/article/shady-fina nce-tax-accounting-underpins-donald-trump-wealth/.

Williams, Juan. 2017. "On health care, Senate Republicans determined to ignore warning signs of political derailment." *Fox News*, June 20, 2017. Accessed online: www.foxnews.com/opinion/2017/06/20/juan-williams-on-health-care-se nate-republicans-determined-to-ignore-warning-signs-political-derailment.html.

Williams, Linda Faye. 2010. *Constraint of Race: Legacies of White Skin Privilege in America*. University Park, PA: Penn State Press.

Williams, Matt and Rory Carroll. 2012. "Fiscal cliff deadline hangs heavy as Obama makes final plea to Congress." *The Guardian*, December 30, 2012. Accessed online: www.theguardian.com/world/2012/dec/30/fiscal-cliff-dead line-obama-congress.

Williamson, Vanessa. 2017. *Read My Lips: Why Americans Are Proud to Pay Taxes*. Princeton, NJ: Princeton University Press.

Wilson, George. 1996. "Toward a Revised Framework for Examining Beliefs about the Causes of Poverty." *The Sociological Quarterly* 37: 413–428.

Wolfgang, Ben. 2016. "Donald Trump: I Might Raise Taxes on the Rich." *The Washington Times*, May 8, 2016. Accessed online: www.washingtontim.es /com/news/2016/may/8/donald-trump-i-might-raise-taxes-on-the-rich/.

Wong, Cara J. 2010. *Boundaries of Obligation in American Politics: Geographic, National, and Racial Communities*. New York: Cambridge University Press.

Wong, Scott. 2012. "McConnell: Go Ahead and Try to Pass Obama Fiscal Cliff Plan." *Politico*, December 5, 2012. Accessed online: www.politico.com/blogs/ on-congress/2012/12/mcconnell-go-ahead-and-try-to-pass-obama-fiscal-cliff -plan-151189.

Wright, John R. 1990. "Contributions, Lobbying, and Committee Voting in the US House of Representatives." *American Political Science Review* 84(2): 417–438.

Yadon, Nicole and Spencer Piston. "Examining Whites' Anti-Black Attitudes after Obama's Presidency." Forthcoming at *Politics, Groups, and Identities*.

Index

Achen, Christopher, 124, 193
Activists, 151–153
Adler, Jerry, 173–174
Affluence and Influence (Gilens), 8
Affordable Care Act
  attempts to repeal, 130, 194
  conditional consequences of theoretical
    framework of class attitudes and, 40
  political knowledge and, 79–83
Aid for Families with Dependent Children
  (AFDC), 8, 145–146, 198
American National Election Studies (ANES)
  generally, 3, 9–10, 13–14, 178
  coefficient tables, 160, 161–162
  distinct outgroup attitudes and, 36
  downward redistribution, class attitudes
    toward and, 61, 71, 75, 187–188
  estate tax and, 84
  political knowledge, class attitudes and,
    79–81
  research into class attitudes, 17, 18, 21,
    23, 179
  resentment toward rich and, 34, 44–45,
    46–47, 48, 51–53
  surveys, 41–42, 154–156, 184
  sympathy toward poor and, 33, 44–45,
    46–47, 48, 51–53
  2008 election and, 109
  2012 election and, 113
  vote choice and, 94
The American Political Science Review, 96,
  176
The American Prospect, 115

American Taxpayer Relief Act of 2012,
  152–153
The American Voter (Campbell et al.), 135
ANES. *See* American National Election
  Studies (ANES)

Bachmann, Michelle, 96, 100, 102
Bain Capital, 112
Bartels, Larry M., 4, 30, 33, 34, 49, 82–84,
  110–111, 124, 175–176, 189, 193, 196
Biden, Joe, 115
Bindel, Julie, 197
Bobo, Lawrence, 197
Boehner, John, 152
Brady, Henry, 31
Brandolini, Andrea, 125
Broockman, David, 128, 130, 194
Brooks, Clem, 178
Bureau of Labor Statistics, 195
Bush, George W.
  mentions in surveys, 109, 110
  tax cuts, 108, 138, 151–152, 196
  unpopularity of, 108

Campaign contributions, political
  knowledge and, 79–83
Campbell, Andrea, 124, 148–149
Capital gains tax, 152–153
Carnes, Nicholas, 15
CCES. *See* Cooperative Congressional
  Election Studies (CCES)
Checks and balances, 7
Chudy, Jennifer, 144

227